the Autobiography
of Emanuel Carnevali

the Autobiography
of
Emanuel Carnevali

compiled & prefaced by
Kay Boyle

Horizon Press   New York

Contents

Illustrations

Acknowledgements

A debt of gratitude is owed to Edward Dahlberg for having brought this work to the attention of the publishers;

to Norman Holmes Pearson for supplying the typescript of the book, which the editor had made a gift of to him in 1964;

and to the publishers, Ben Raeburn and Coburn Britton, for having recognized the importance of Emanuel Carnevali as a figure in the literary history of this century.

K. B.

Preface by Kay Boyle

"They were just two kids, she a girl who happened to live across the corridor some place where he was staying," William Carlos Williams has written of Emanuel Carnevali and the young wife he so quickly set aside. "She was not literary. He was straight, slim, with a beautiful young man's head, keenly intelligent — an obviously lost soul. Before him she was in obvious adoration. She was a peasant from the high mountains of northwestern Italy, he from one of the cities of the northern plain: here they were in New York, headed out but not toward money. This was New York at its best, the highest potential which you saw there with a catch in your throat, knowing it was almost certainly doomed to destruction . . . the first time he read in public somewhere, he had made her sit on the platform beside him, scared, not knowing much what it was all about — but he insisted on it, that those who heard might know *who* the writer was, not just he, but the two of them."*

The marriage, the career as a poet, the young Italian poet's life itself, were indeed doomed to destruction. And yet Carnevali's autobiography should not be read as a tragedy. Surely no greater reward is offered to a writer than the knowledge that other men are reading the words that he has, by some miracle, retrieved from the depths of his own silence; the knowledge that other men are actually listening for the sound of his voice to call out from the page to them, and, above all, the knowledge that they believe the words they hear. This reward Carnevali was given, and if it was given for only a little while, this does not diminish the value of that high tribute he was paid.

*The Autobiography of William Carlos Williams, pp. 266-7, New Directions Paperback, New York, 1967.

I was nineteen when I first heard Carnevali's name: I had come East from the Middle West, and the editor in the New York office of *Broom* magazine (a handsome art and literary review published in Europe by Americans) took me on as typist and bookkeeper of sorts. The editor was Lola Ridge, an Australian poet of savage talent and fervent dedication to the arts. The day I began to work for her in the basement of 3 East Ninth Street, she gave me some poetry of Carnevali's to read. She had known him in Chicago and New York, and now he had gone back, young, alone, and very ill, she told me, to Italy. The way Lola spoke of him was as eloquent as the poems themselves. I did not know then that it was only with unabashed eloquence and a kind of furious heedless courage that one could hope to seize in one's bare hands the blazing meaning of his name. I was young then and I had no way of knowing that Carnevali's radiant vision, unextinguished by the misery of his defeat, was already metaphor to the poets of America for all that daily circumstances demanded they endure.

Perhaps the disinherited of every generation ask quite reasonably, quite humbly, that they be allowed to hear one living man, just one, actually shout aloud their disputed tongue, and that they may be permitted to set eye on the actual substance of their own poetic logic. However it is, it is a lucky time that has its true poet, its Rimbaud, and in the 1920's Carnevali suddenly and almost inexplicably took on this rôle. He was the rebel, the man on the run, the stranger beating his head against the stars, that the others had been writing and waiting for. As was to be true of Dylan Thomas in a later decade, the syllables of Carnevali's name had the power to ignite the minds and hearts of those who did not fear to burn in the hottest, brightest fires of man's creative hell. William Carlos Williams was one of these. As early as 1919 he wrote of Carnevali: "We older can compose, we seek the seclusion of a style, of a technique, we make replicas of the world we live in and we live in them and not in the world. It is for you we went out, old men in the dark. It is for you that the rubbish stirred and a rat crawled from the garbage, alive! . . . The reason for our having been alive is here!" But in the same breath that he celebrated Carnevali's arrival and survival, Williams grieved over the inevitable departure and defeat. "Jesus, Jesus, save Carnevali for me," he besought America, or the history of the lost, or something as blind and deaf as life itself. "He is only beginning to disintegrate . . . But he is slipping into the afternoon at twenty-one . . . Rimbaud, Laforgue, Corbière, they offer him solace. They prove to him that he is foredoomed . . . Carnevali, perhaps you will do as they did . . . We salute you."*

Every resistance fighter in the underground literary movement of the 1920's came at one time or another to the basement office that Lola kept functioning on practically no funds at all. Williams, Marianne Moore, Bodenheim, Louis Ginzberg, John Dos Passos, Kenneth Burke, Jean Toomer, Slater Brown, Waldo Frank, were among those who came down the outside steps to the basement door. In the late afternoon, you could see their legs through the window, coming in from the rain or the snow. The resistance was against the established English language, and the fight was for the recognition of a new American tongue. Carnevali, had at the age of sixteen fled the war in Europe and had acquired that new language, and in the brief eight years that he was in America he had turned it into revolutionary poetry and prose. A French critic, Regis Michaud, wrote that Carnevali was "one of the two American poets whose work attained an international standard." (The other, it is to be presumed, was William Carlos Williams who used old words with an astonishing freshness, saying for instance, "the fates of ideas living against the grain in a nondescript world have always held me breathless.") An American writer, Dorothy Dudley Harvey, to whom Carnevali dedicated his long poem describing his return to Italy, was to write of him that once he had abandoned the Tuscan tongue, our "limber, informal, changing slang became a part of him." Of his years in America, she wrote:

> He came without money, lived as he could, sometimes through jobs, sometimes through friends, but meagrely; his friends quite naturally, in the fashion of the country, saying among themselves, "He is young, he ought to be able to keep a job, we all of us manage to keep jobs." He worked first in

Others, Vol. V, No. 6, July 1919.

restaurants, in Grand Central station, in the Yale Club, among others in New York . . . And he told how once, without work for days or a real meal, he had picked up a piece of bread in Washington Square, and had thrown it down with tears . . . At length he published — first in the magazine of *Poetry,* then in other magazines, *The Little Review, Others . . . Vogue . . .* He was a hurried man, as in his tales he calls himself, until sickness overtook him. Among doctors who disagreed as to what the matter was, one called it by a Latin name which means intolerance of the spirit. In health he had that too. Sights and sounds were not enough for their color, their tone, their wave-lengths. They must be presage of amazing days, heroic vision . . . He fought the drabness of this country he had given himself to. How much longer he would have fought . . . not as some men do for a change of government, but for a change of temper, who can say? . . . He is the new modern, one of the first rebels against the ugliness of revolution. A marvelous poem of his by that name sees revolution dispassionately — its grandeur and its stupidity. And another, "Making a Fool of God," belongs to us especially for a kind of shrewdness.*

Actually, Carnevali's illness had been diagnosed, Lola told me, as *encephalitis lethargica,* a form of sleeping sickness which seizes its victims by the hair of his head and shakes and shakes him endlessly until death intervenes. Carnevali's bold black eyes and his strong white teeth were shaken like dice in his head, Lola told me, shaken night and day, day and night, without respite. At times even tears were shaken from his eyes, she said, although he had no wish to cry. He was absolute in his refusal of this illness, and adamant in his will not to go under. Among the poems written after his return to Italy there are these lines that are like a fist shaken in death's face:

I know
that for having slept much
the dead have grown strong.

*Parts of this are taken from Dorothy Dudley Harvey's foreword to *A Hurried Man,* by Emanuel Carnevali, Contact Editions, Three Mountains Press, Paris, 1925, and parts from a revised foreword, written some years later.

On days as these
they kick open their graves
and skip elegantly out.

They whisper horrible secrets
to each other and to me.
They carry their shrouds and
shake them valiantly.

O Goddess of dismay and melancholy
come to my help!
I still have withered kisses for you,
kisses I don't want to throw away for
    I'm very poor.
Cleave me from my memories!

They bother me so that sleep flirts and flees,
flirts and flees.

Carnevali had not yet had a book out when I went to work
in the office of *Broom*. That was to come later, after Robert
McAlmon had founded his publishing house, Contact Editions,
in Paris. In 1923, McAlmon published Hemingway's first book,
Three Stories and Ten Poems, and then, among other distinguished books, had come the first publication of a canto of Ezra
Pound's, illustrated, and Gertrude Stein's *The Making of Americans,* and William Carlos Williams' *The Great American Novel.*
Carnevali's collection, *A Hurried Man,* became renowned in this
literature of underground resistance. It was one of the most exceptional in the list of thirty or more exceptional volumes to appear in that decade under the imprint of McAlmon's Contact
Editions or William Bird's Three Mountains Press. ". . . one of the
best examples of — what?" Williams wrote of it. "A book, a book
that is all of a man, a young man, superbly alive. Doomed. When
I think of what gets published and what gets read and praised
and rewarded regularly with prizes, when such a book as that gets
shoved under the heap of corpses, I swear never to be successful,

I am disgusted, the old lusts revive. What else can a book do for a man?"*

Of Carnevali's work McAlmon remarked that its violence was the violence of adolescence, but violence given another dimension by his Latin irony and wit. Being purely Italian, McAlmon wrote is his own autobiography**, Carnevali had the Italian lack of cant about "morals" and "soul" and "conscience." The two men had exchanged letters over a period of a year while McAlmon was in college and Carnevali was in Chicago, on the staff of *Poetry* magazine. "I concluded that it was because he was a foreigner that he so passionately loved Whitman, and, later, Sherwood Anderson and Carl Sandburg." McAlmon wrote in true amazement. "Carnevali was to me more interesting than his American heroes." (Robert McAlmon has been called the forgotten man of the Paris literary scene of the 'twenties; but by those who knew and valued him he is not forgotten. Year by year, his work and his positive presence on that scene are being given new definitions. Neither as writer nor as publisher does he deserve oblivion). Then, in that decade, it was not a rarity when strong tentacles of faith reached out from poet to poet. It was in no way remarkable that Robert McAlmon should be publishing in Paris the book of a man lying ill in Bazzano, and that Bill Williams should write from Rutherford, N. J. that the book was one of the best possible examples of what a book should be.

When Lola first spoke to me of Carnevali, a few of my own poems had been printed in magazines, as well as small critical pieces on Remy de Gourmont and other contemporary French writers, and a few unsigned book reviews in the old *Dial*. Because of the apparent parallels in our published writing careers, and because I was poor in New York on the same streets, perhaps even in the same rooming-houses, where Carnevali had been poor, I felt an immediate commitment to him, a deep and unequivocal affinity. But it was not until 1923, when my French husband and I went to France to live, that I began writing to Carnevali in Italy. Out of my poverty into the depths of his, I sent books, magazines, and whatever bounty others sent my way;

---

*Williams, *op. cit.*, p. 267.
***Being Geniuses Together*, p. 152, Secker and Warburg, Ltd., London 1938.

and letters, endless letters. And out of his poverty and desperate illness, he sent me poems, letters, and sections of the book he was trying to write in the public ward of the hospital in Bazzano. Everything he sent was typed — even his signature — on the thinnest, shiniest paper that was truly like an onion's skin. Ten pages or more of his writing, when folded over and then folded again, could be carried in one's pocket, as bulkless and weightless as a silk handkerchief. The letters, the poems, the sections of the book are now lost, but I remember each word always had a reddish halo above it, as if the typewriter ribbon was stretched taut between black and red in its furious striving to get the sentences down.

Sometimes it would take Carnevali a day to do a sentence, a week to do a paragraph, for while he shook with the terrible ague of his illness, he would have to hold his right hand in the grip of his left in order to be able to strike the keys. And there would be long intervals when he would be too ill to set so much as a sentence down. He wanted the book to be called *The First God* or *Religious Stammering*. It was ten years later that I began to compile this story of his life for him, to piece it together from his letters to me through that decade, to trace it through the pages of *A Hurried Man,* and assemble it with the chapters of the novel, as he called it, that he was never able to finish. With every word he wrote me, Carnevali sent that simple gift which men take away from themselves to give so grudgingly, so sparingly, with such caution, to others; and that was the gift of tireless love.

In 1925, before bringing out the first number of their new quarterly, *This Quarter,* Ethel Moorhead and Ernest Walsh, ill himself with tuberculosis, journeyed from Paris to Bazzano to see Carnevali. In the first issue of *This Quarter,* and in the numbers that followed, they published Carnevali's work. After that visit to Bazzano, Ernest Walsh wrote: "His [Carnevali's] illness would kill most men. I felt he had become ill not because he was weak but because he was too strong. I never felt death in him. I tell you he had the power to entertain and buoy me although he was suffering much at the moment I had the feeling that a god or a devil had exploded within him and fought for escape. But this prisoner made me laugh with him so I knew it was a god that had exploded . . . There is no death in Carnevali. He is a live warm laughing and fighting man."*

There were others who made the long pilgrimage to see Carnevali, among them Dorothy Dudley Harvey and her sister, Caroline, the wife of Joseph Delteil; Harriet Monroe, Robert McAlmon (who had him removed to a private sanatorium, and paid for a year's treatment there); Edward Dahlberg, who has written of his visit to him; and once Ezra Pound went from Rapallo to take Carnevali a radio which my husband and I had collected the money to buy for him. Finally, in 1933, as we drove with our children through Italy on our way to Austria, where living would be cheap, we were able to get to Bazzano. On the 18th of July of that year I wrote a long letter from Cavalese to my beloved friend, Caresse Crosby. It reads in part:

> I have been to see Carnevali, and I write you the first moment I can after . . . We went on a blazing day, in the middle of the day, driving across the Italian plain which is certainly the hottest place this side of hell — and we got to the worst town of all, stopped in a dead white square with dust three inches thick on it, and went to the little café where he lives. I expected to find him downstairs, or sitting somewhere, but after a quarter of an hour the woman took us up to his room. The room faces on that blazing square, and the room is big enough just to hold a narrow iron bed, a cupboard with his piles of books, and a tin wash table on which his old typewriter sits. The gramophone Ernest Walsh gave him is on the floor . . . the thing one feels when one walks into that cell and sees the figure on the bed can never be explained. On that bed there is the most beautiful man, shaking completely, all over, like a pinned butterfly. The whole bed seems in motion with his shaking — as if waves of water were breaking over and over and over and would never stop. But such a face on the pillow — a strong, big face, with black eyes, and the skin as pure and clean as ivory, and black locks of hair. A great strong well-made man with a great chest that lies bare — and with such beauty

---

*This Quarter, Vol. II, No. II, Cannes, France, 1927.

in his face that your breath is taken away. I don't know why it is, you do not feel illness. You feel this endless agitation which *will* stop — you feel it has to stop. But he says it never stops —— neither in the night. Never, never. It never stops at all. And you don't feel weakness or sorrow — except the kind of sorrow no words can ever say. He is gay — he is the gayest person alive — the way Harry* and Ernest Walsh were gay. He has a laugh that fills your heart — he says wonderful simple things. And we sat there and laughed and talked (how can I tell you that he made me feel gayer and bolder and more courageous than I have felt in years?), and drank two bottles of sickening sweet champagne in that ghastly filthy room which is his life.

I was writing this letter so quickly to Caresse that I did not mention two things which are still as clear as sunlight in my mind: first, that Carnevali held fiercely onto the bars of the bed behind his head as he talked, trying to still his shaking, and that his bare arms had been made strong as a prizefighter's by the endless vibrations that passed through them; and secondly, that small white moths flew in and out of his poor clothing that hung, grey with dust, on a hat-tree in one corner of the room.

And in a little while [the letter goes on], but only for a second, I was crying in his arms as I never cry with anyone except you. No, there is no way to find the words to tell you. He is so tender, and he is so filled with love. It runs down his arms and out his fingertips. And he asks for nothing, nothing, for it is he himself who has everything to give.

One thing: when they brought the champagne, he made them set the glasses one on top of the other to make a tower so that the champagne brimmed over from the first, into the second, and so on, down, in a yellow torrent.

. . . the sight of him haunts me. I see him all the time waking or sleeping — quivering and quivering and quivering as if his whole soul were in revulsion from the filth and heat of the terrific place . . . the thing is so clear to me, my

*Harry Crosby, Caresse's husband, who died in 1929.

Caresse, that I should be with him always, for he is to me the last, the almost shattered remains of courage and beauty that are left. I don't know what to do — for I know that every day I live will be a rebuke to me, for I should be with him, and I have not the courage to say that everything else is a distortion except being with him. It is not as easy as explaining this as love — it is a necessity, for if the thing he is did not exist and had never existed, there would be no reason to live at all.

We are going back to see him . . . I promised to go back in three weeks, and he said: "Three weeks is twenty-one days for you, it is three hundred years for me."*

Once I had seen Carnevali, it became an obsession with me, the compiling of this book. The words of it were now the only speech left to him to exchange with the men of his time and kind, and their responses to the questions he asked would be like a wild chorale of hope soaring above the blazing heat of that small café room. I typed and re-typed the bits and pieces he sent me, wrote to Bill Williams in Rutherford to send me all the writing that Carnevali had ever sent to him. In August 1933, I wrote again to Caresse, this time from Vienna, saying: "It must be placed this book, or I will never write again."

In the end, all I had written to Caresse was little better than a lie. I did not find a publisher for Carnevali's autobiography in his lifetime, and I was never able to go back to Italy. (How weak this sounds now, so weak that the words fairly totter on the page, to say that I was never "able" to go back! I believe one is always "able" to do what one requires of oneself, and between my return to Bazzano and my own life stood obstacles that I, quite unconsciously, did not choose to set aside.) I spoke of Carnevali to every writer I met, and those who could emptied their pocketbooks for him (Caresse Crosby, Ira Morris, Eugene and Maria Jolas among those who did so generously.)

Until the fall of France in 1940, Carnevali in Bazzano, and I in Megève, in the Haute-Savoie, wrote every week to each other.

---

*From the Black Sun Press Collection, Southern Illinois University Library, Carbondale, Illinois.

I was still fitting the sentences and paragraphs of the book together when the dark curtain came down between France and Italy. Since then there has been silence, and it can only be concluded that Carnevali died during the course of the war. There is no record of his death, no trace of his name or of the few poor things he owned. "That single book published by Contact Editions is as far as I know his sole testament," Williams writes in his autobiography. But now there is this book to add to the earlier testament of a man of whom Carl Sandburg said long ago: "He is of the sun treader tribe, also a walker in dark shadows. He seemed sometimes to be throwing himself at the sun . . . He had a dream in Chicago of publishing a magazine to redeem perhaps some of the redeemables of America and Europe, even Russia and China, perhaps even Mars and Betelgeuse . . . His writings are the record of a personality that burned with twentieth century flames, and that was marvelously alive to the intensities and the contrasts of American life."*

Kay Boyle

---

*From the foreword to *A Hurried Man.*

the Autobiography
of Emanuel Carnevali

Mother

Never once did I see my mother that she wasn't sick. She was a morphino-maniac: she had got used to the terrible drug after the laborious parturition of this poor champion, Mister Me. My father, whom I was to see only when I was eleven years old, lived separately from her. (This was natural and easily understood.) When they were together he used to abuse and beat her on the smallest pretext. I was told by my aunt of the ferocious jealousy of my father. Once he gave my mother a beating simply because her hair was undone after a half a day of ironing. Another time he beat her with a walking-stick because, in the street, she had stopped to tie her shoe. He beat my poor little mother almost to death, certainly to despair. . . . Once the poor woman attempted suicide by throwing herself out of a window. He caught her in time. My father was and still is the most ignoble of men.

This book contains all of my mother, or at least it should, for I am her son. Romance is life projected into a written form, and I am in love with romance. My mother was in love with pain and sorrow, as were all the saints before her. I remember how she suffered and this memory is a sword, a hot sword scorching my mind. I remember that she was marvelous and this wonder stays with me.

She had a great heart, as great as the sea whose veins are the many rivers that flow into it. Listening to the silence that was the life of my mother, I hear the words of my poetry, the words with which I could make a wreath for her head. My mother was asleep most of the time and I should have given to that sleep a voice, given a speech to that immobility. But instead I have been broken by a tremendous disease, the most unreal and most real of diseases, called encephalitis, and I am nothing but a pot full of lilies, a noise, wind, nothing more.

The morphine kept my mother asleep or sleepy three-quarters of the days. But that was no easy sleep. Mother, mother dolorous, I should cry thinking of you, but my heart is cold and very like a stone. Mother, I would give you now all the affection your misery claimed, but I am too sick and fully engrossed with my own sickness. Your life was a long agony, the prize awarded it being death. I stare into the face of destiny and it is like a mirror rejecting my life. But the life of my mother which I shall never write is like a mirror rejecting nothing. Somewhere you must be suffering still, mother. You think of your beautiful youth wasted by living with a brute. I think of your dead mouth.

Mother, because you carried ladyness with you, they called you "the lady" in the little Piedmont town where we went to live and my aunt to work for all of us. She had to do so since you were crippled by enormous abscesses which came from having used dirty needles for your injections. You walked the streets of the village, crippled and sorrowing, and sorrowing is the crippledness of the heart. But your face still shines in my memory for you carried it like a benediction; your face was like a torch, held up on high. Mother, no prayer counts now nor does love, nor does the cleanliness of my heart against your bleached one, your destroyed one, your no-longer-existing heart. I would stand by your grave glorious with an old pain and terrible because of the homage I brought you. Your head, in the little cemetery of that little town, rests against the wall. Beyond the wall is an unkempt space of tall grass, grumbling with all kinds of small and big insects. I saw you dead, you were beautiful, with your face the color of the earth. You inspired tranquillity. A fool doctor had diagnosed your case as a mere cold while it was lockjaw instead, and you told him what the matter was.

Mother, do you remember your little boy who never left you alone, who followed you everywhere with an insistence that must often have made you sick? There is an atrocious custom in some little towns of Piedmont that when one is in agony the bells play a special music to fit the case, so that often the sick man knows that the bells ring for him, in anticipation of his death. My mother, who could no longer speak, stroked my head and gave me to her sister. Then she made a gesture to mean ringing bells, and then she struck her own breast, meaning *they ring for me*.

I do not know that I ever saw a finer mouth than my mother's. It was sinuous and full-lipped and sensuous, large but beautiful, and the great purity of the forehead I remember well. You must know that I was only nine when she died. When she was dying there came to the house a spotless black cat who made friends with her right away and she used to feed him and pet him and make him purr. They say cats, black cats, bring misfortune, and whether or not I believe it, the fact is that when the coffin lay in the courtyard, the black cat could be seen going around the coffin, purring most strangely.

What can I tell you of myself, Mother, except that I have wasted in sickness a good half of my real life and that my disease beats out a stuttering? What can I tell you to give you an idea of the misery I have suffered? Mother, oh, could I press my cheek against your cheek! Yet you beat me till the blood came out of my nostrils and mouth, my little darling, my poor sick mama, you beat me because of the poison in your veins. I have nothing to forgive you.

Mater dolorosa, you suffered enough to earn half a dozen paradises. Mother, if the earth could be squeezed like a lemon one would squeeze out sorrow and sorrow and sorrow. It is long since that the earth was so stingy with its sons and daughters. It takes to its bosom dead men only; the others are forced to walk over it carrying in a bundle all their pains and their anger and their useless lives. *Mater dolorosa*, you belong to the earth-wide club of sufferers.

The White Beginning

I remember a white room with white sunlight coming in from tall windows; in it my mother and an old lady, a very white old lady, are stooping attentively over me. It is in the city of Florence where a tremendous bronchitis and pneumonia had carried me near to the grave. I may have been from two to three years old then and they kept me going with asses' milk and asses' milk is not at all drinkable. This poor being, big-headed, narrow-shouldered, cost his mother much trouble and sorrow. All this could have been avoided had I died, and a good riddance too.

There was a ditch where the frogs sang at night their raucous songs and there was a white road where I fell one day and bled from the nose so copiously as to scare me stiff. There was a farmer's house that had holes in it instead of doors and there my old nurse lived. There was a great pleasant villa which my mother and aunt had rented. My little cousin went around the vines catching cicadas and eating them, wings, rattle, and all. In this big villa, it being a country villa, my mother and aunt kept many hens and cocks and chicks. But the farmer who lived next to us poisoned all the chickens' drinking places with a mixture we called copper-green and we were left with no chickens at all.

I was the most docile little animal ever. I let my cousin beat me for the smallest reason, without protesting.

Once my mother lost a scarf-pin and she had some suspicion that I had taken it (not stolen, of course). She asked me for it. Without knowing, I suddenly got up and by means of a spade or similar instrument started to dig in a place in our garden, and after a little labor I found the pin and give it back to my Mother. Reader, if I am not mistaken this was white also.

But strongest of all in my memory are the sex adventures I

had. I used to sleep with Maria, a big girl of fifteen, and sometimes she took my little hand and . . . Another time, running after a girl, I caught her and suddenly fell on her and had an instant of intense delight. These things I can see as if they were under my eyes today. The adventure with Maria did not end there. I was four years old and already felt some pleasure in the little game, so much so that I grew thin and my mother, who must have guessed something, at last separated us.

Another villa we had was sad and full of gloom except for the wisteria falling over our garden walls. Also some olive trees nearby contributed to make it more picturesque. Dark was our villa, as if previously inhabited by ghosts, by the ghosts of people that had lived a dark life in it. But meanwhile the money of the two sisters was nearly at an end. We went to live in Pistoia, a dead little town, and then one fine day we left Tuscany for Piedmant, to be precise, for Biella, which is called the Italian Manchester, tremendously industrious and variously industrial. During this voyage I saw the sea. I saw the sea for the first time, for the first time I tasted the salty spray. I saw the sea which is such a large part of Italy. We passed through an infinite number of tunnels and in the interval between one and the other was the sea, the pulsating sea, the sea of Ulysses and Herman Melville, a playful sea of so many little waves and of spray which it spit in our faces, all in the spectacle of the sea, in the great show of the sea, the fickle sea (since it changes dress so many times); the sea of that bourgeois, Conrad, and my own sea manufactured by my own imagination and by its presence. And by way of naive contrast, there were some fishermen on the shore pulling and fixing nets, puny tormentors of that so immense father. But it was with enormous complacence that the sea watched these puny tormentors, save that it should suddenly become serious and terrific.

We stopped overnight at Vercelli and the next day took the train for Biella.

Biella and Cossato

That I was fair-haired when a small child while now I am dark, that is a little thing. And another little thing is that when I was six or seven I thought the greatest achievement was to call a woman a whore. That word had something magic and mysterious and deep and profound and philosophic and daring in it. With it I consecrated a woman. And another little thing is that when we captured cicadas we carried a long stick and then placed one end of it against the place where the insect was sitting and started to make it miserable: it felt that the place it occupied was unsafe and took a place on the stick instead. Then we lowered the stick with great gentleness and finally seized the poor insect.

I had two cousins, Leonardo and Federigo, two devilish brigands. They always walked in the most dangerous places, they always played at games the most hazardous, they defied God and His angels. At the age of three the bigger of them was so smart as to be the superstitious despair of all the nurses to whom he was confided. Now they have turned into two profligates, for Life did the wrong time to them. She manhandled them and now they are like two shipwrecks on a rock in mid-ocean. Having no profession at all, what could they do but become journalists? So now they have the precarious one of journalists of the worst and most dangerous sort.

Leonardo, the smaller, was the cicada-eater and the other ate dirt, thus causing enormous worms to breed in his belly. My play hours were divided between one friend and another and my cousins hardly ever intervened. In front of our house were two big holes that were forever filled with water. Both my cousins fell into them. They were rescued by people who came running, called by my desperate screams. Once Leonardo, while eating a piece of bread, suddenly choked from having swallowed the wrong way. My mother, even half asleep as she always was, saw the thing and sticking her finger down the boy's throat, saved his life. That too is a little thing, pleasant to remember.

Even in our country villa in Pistoia I never enjoyed life very much, even though I was a very small child. Sorrow must be the greatest thing in my life. While at Pistoia I had made friends with our landlord's son and we used to do dirty things together; this too is a little thing I warn those American prudes who would make it a big thing. At Pistoia there was then the Congregation of the Brothers of Mercy and these fools scared me stiff every time I saw them. They wore hoods pulled over their heads with only two holes for the eyes, like the great Spanish Inquisitioners in olden days. They came out every time there was a dead man to accompany to the cemetery.

Biella is a small town, very industrial, rich with many textile works. My aunt sought work there and found it, as forelady in one of the big factories of the place. Biella is a town that runs the length of a main street, Independence Street. Not far from Biella is a famous sanctuary called Oropa where one may go and stay for fifteen days at a stretch without paying a cent for one's room. But one succeeds in spending just the same because eating is tremendously expensive. One may see from afar little houses on the outside wall of which is written "POLENTA E LATTE", (which means cornmeal mush and milk.) On the contrary, however, one eats there anything from veal to chicken and sundries.

There is Biella the high and Biella the low, and Biella boasts the oldest rope-railway in Italy. I was put in a *pensione* for young people and I cannot say I liked it much. There I had scarlet fever and my aunt who came to see me had to turn her face away lest I should see that she was quietly crying. This made a tremendous impression on me and I then knew for the first time that my aunt loved me.

At Cossato, a village of Piedmont, our life was more varied and finer, except for one lurid young man who initiated us into orgies of a sexual kind. But we were children and nothing can pollute the purity every child has. There we went around the fields destroying cherry-trees and apple-trees. Puny vandals, we used to let one of our crowd climb the trees and he threw down, instead of fruit, entire branches. The farmers knew of these things but were more scared of us than we of them. Cossato was a fine little country town. The fields and hills were not far from it. We went around the hills looking for mushrooms and we found many of them often. Ah, there is no better pleasure than finding a mushroom hidden in the grass and then nearby finding another, for they go by couples, you know. Sometimes when we had a little money we bought of the farmers small cakes of cheese that were delicious. But that happened seldom because we were almost all the time dead broke.

The walk in order to reach the hills was magnificent too, but now they have put up a rope-railway to go to Oropa and the towns have most probably already polluted the countryside. Once I saw my dear aunt walking in the fields just outside Cossato. The poor thing was almost pretty, in a skirt, white with embroidered flowers, and likewise the waist. She was picking wild flowers, but some of these were painted on her dress. I never saw my aunt as genial and fine and glad. Risking being called clumsy, I told her so — that is, I told her she was pretty. It wasn't true, for she still had the same little head and the hard-looking countenance. She told me then that she was thirty-one. Ten years after she was still thirty-one. Mother and aunt quarreled very often. That is, it was my mother who quarrelled, since my aunt only kept on weeping and holding me tight, as though she expected comfort from me. Once my mother became crazy and tried to make me drink a glass of water in which she had put a dozen needles.

Goodbye, chesnut-trees of Cossato, if you are there no longer, goodbye, mushrooms and violets and strawberries, goodbye, little cakes of cheese, goodbye, small torrential rivers, goodbye, forests by the rivers — you probably have all gone, gone as all beautiful things go, not one lasts, as says great Carl.*

---

*Editor's Note: Carl Sandburg.

My Aunt

I hope something will be done about this, my God!

Her name was Melany Piano and she was born of a very good family in Turin, Piedmont, Italy. Turin is a grey serious earnest city with long straight streets, a huddle of square blocks. If she had been born out in the mountains where Emily* lived this wouldn't have happened, but then . . .

I saw the old photographs of the family, a yellowish mist on them. Photographs of the romantic period. Period in which one still believed in the solemn face or the melancholy face or the noble face or the pale face. The face of her mother was solemn and mysterious. The face of her father was that of a man with the heart of a knight, crowned with the well-balanced smile of the successful man. Life to him was an adventure in gallantry — women and war. He was, in fact, an officer of the Italian army in the Erythrean expedition. He had brought her and her sister along with him to Africa after her mother had died. She had lived well and happily in Africa, so she used to tell us children; all beautiful tales of hyenas, pestilence, devoted negro servants and Ras Alula and Ras somebody else.

She was skinny, she had a long lean nose, no curve from the nose to the lips, small eyes, a tight bulging little forehead; she was not attractive, as they say. Her hair was very beautiful but that did not make a real difference. One had to know her well to appreciate the beauty that was in her hair. That is why she longed to be well-known, well-understood. A famous explorer — there is a monument erected to his memory in the city of Parma — fell in love with her. She was to marry him. But he was

Editor's Note: Carnevali's wife.

the scientist kind, earnest and inelegant, she did not love him. He gave her a doll once, on her nineteenth birthday, and she was very angry. He told her once: "You are not attractive, Miss, but your mind has infinite beauty and I beg you to let me take you for my wife . . ." But she was too young and a bit too happy to understand a thing like that. And he was naive and she was not; she was very well-read and eaten up from within by the ever-hungry little old moth, romance. He was a good fine man to marry and she knew so, but she wanted a man with long soft hair and kind big hands. A man who could sit for hours still and perfectly sad and who would understand when the hungry hands of a well-read woman would smooth his hair; who would not turn around and, out of embarrassment, try to fight the situation with a smile or an irrelevant phrase.

She came back to Italy. She was still gay and light but, already, she was motherly. She was motherly with every man that came to her with not unkind sorrows in his manly heart. Such a man came and she talked to him and on an evening they cried together in front of a window. Because the sunset burned yellow and purple, the woman was thinking that it is sweet and heavenly to understand the sorrows that have hardened into the flesh of a man. He was to marry her but the family did not want it. But he said: "You before, the family after, though I love them very much." But instead he went away and left her pregnant.

Who will say that he was wrong? He had never loved her. It is easy to believe that you love: he was an honest man. She should have known. Now her father was dead and she hadn't any money and the man wanted to help her out. But she was proud. She went to work, she had a little monthly allowance from the government; she got along and she loved the baby, who was lean and sickly. His eyes were the eyes of the father, very black and very cold, so black that there was no bottom to them, so cold, so black that you would have called them invisible eyes; eyes that were a darkness and not a light.

She was proud. She never forgave the man. Because she was honest and hard she wasn't a loose girl and she gave herself for love. She was magnificently aloof and the negro servants in Africa thought she was a great Queen, the great White Queen: the way she was majestic and sweetly hard with them. She spoke of books, and it was a marvel to see how everyone was intimidated in her presence, to see how strangers loved her after a few minutes with her.

Another man came along. He was shrewd and hungry for a girl the way dogs and men are hungry in the summer in a North American city where a girl is hard to get if you're not initiated. He had her too. Because she loved him. Then there was another child.

Two children, not brothers, and the mother a lady, proud, now bitterly proud, but proud still like a Queen, poor White Queen. And she was honest and she was so naive that when the eyes of men who sought a girl met hers she did not really know all that they searched and lewdly touched. For she wasn't attractive and she knew it; that is why she was maternal with men.

Then she was thirty-two. She met a man, a soldier, who was twenty-five. He was beautiful, strong, a great sport, a game guy, a spoiled child, penniless and ignorant. She had a little money, she got him out of the army, where he thought he'd have to remain, and got him a job. Taught him French and how to know good books. Made him civilized and sophisticated. He was intelligent; he never, after, wanted to admit that he owed so much to her.

This man did not like the children.

He was young, so he fell in love with several girls and she understood and suffered — and then she feared he'd go away so she was good to him, she was especially good to him when he broke her heart. Sometimes her heart would break and she would fall in a swoon.

One day he was sick. He stayed in bed two months with ulcers on his body and the fool doctor never could tell what the trouble was. He went to the hospital and he was told that it probably was the syphilis but that they couldn't be sure until they had tested his blood. Next day on the cardboard tablet beside his bed, on which doctors wrote the diagnosis, he saw some signs or words that amounted to a "yes". It meant to him that he had the syphilis; he howled like a wolf that has been caught. He came back home to her. He was forced to stay in bed two more months.

He had caught it going around in brothels. But she was a great mother to him while he stayed in bed. She knew that he did not love her. She was maternal, although she was old, although she beat her children, she was maternal with him. She nursed him as a sweet nurse nurses a sweet child; and while his hair was falling out because of the syphilis he had caught in a brothel, she'd call him "her lovely child."

But he did not like the children and he did not love her. So she saw at last, well, the great grotesque.

When she beat the children she'd scream so that the tenants of the house would all come out on the balconies to gossip about "that crazy woman." She beat them and several times she fainted, after. He cursed her to hear the noise she was making. He cursed her vulgarly and she was still a lady, a proud Queen.

She knew that he was getting to hate her. But it was too late to act kindly, to be careful for his sake of what she was doing, to put up a show of kindness and to discriminate. Because oldness and ugliness and defeat were coming; and he was going away. Sometimes she sat in the kitchen alone when the children were out and she wished that he would die. She knew that he'd go away when he was well.

When she got up every morning, she used to put powder on her face. That was all right, but now she had to put too much powder on her face. After her yelling at the children the two wrinkles around her mouth were deeper. Before, a little rouge on the cheeks sufficed, but now she had to put too much rouge on and that was ugly.

And then, one day she had to buy three false teeth — the front teeth, the front teeth!

Of course, he saw them.

So she beat the children, she swooned, she had headaches for days and nights.

He had to go to the hospital again. He came back almost well, but he was doubled up and his skin showed under his thin hair. He was bitter, too. He had the syphilis so there wasn't much chance for him in life and so he wasn't going to try to get along with her — he'd go after something easier. One day he told her he was going to quit her.

First she knelt down before him and prayed. But then she stood up and fought tremendously, fought beautifully because she fought against the big failure which was now all visible; she looked at the failure and fought and it was a beautiful thing to do.

> There comes the big failure and some bend
> their heads
> over their chests
> like birds in the cold.
> And some send their miserable bodies
> to the absurd war.
> But there are eyes in the world
> that see the dance of the absurd,
> and always someone
> who carefully listens to the great song of it.

All her miserable body. Her skinny body and the last hunger within it. She called her romantic heart and all the books she had read to help her. Hurled herself — at last! — against the monster who awaits, during all the nights of the infinite years, the hour of our awful scream. He waits for it and when he has heard he waits still, to hear other screams, he waits still, he waits forever. She hurled her miserable body and her face, now like a dismal little clenched fist, in a fight of teeth and nails . . . false teeth!

And once more the world came to its symphonic night: she cursed the stupid chairs and cursed the yellow lamp and the shadows that had become infinitely old on the grey walls. Cursed the windows, and the breeze they inhaled came over her and made her sob with an agony of self-pity.

> And now she would weep softly
> because the breeze from the window was a melody of
>   remembrances.

She wanted her limbs to break; why wouldn't this thing burst through her limbs! She offered her limbs in sacrifice if the awful thing would only burst through her! Wanted to stretch her arms so violently that they'd sever from her body — nodded her head up and down.

Her head swayed up and down and sideways, sideways and up and down and she moaned, oh, oh, oh, oh, oh. . . boat in the tempest. And the children wished that she would stop sometime because they wanted to play.

I know that things await the terrible screaming. The monster in the nights, the cavern whence the cool darkness sails towards our windows and our mouths, the purest line of the evening horizon on the lake — how many times have I gone near to them, knowing that they awaited, have gone near and stopped short, was afraid, or did not know how to scream. The sheer pink flower before fantastic eyes in the morning, the sheer pink flower is a gleaming eye looking upon a horror of putrified dreams. The sky when it is farthest from the earth, the purest sky, the sky that has flown high and high because the air was so clear, the sky feels the touch of the scream we so fearfully constrain — as the very white breasts of a woman hear the caress of the desperate lover. These things await our horrible screaming.

The woman had repudiated her children, she had betrayed them. So now she did not dare to ask for the children's love. She was too hungry. She knew that children give love to everyone, but to hungry people they don't. Children are pure and they are afraid of the awful eyes of hungry persons. Children refuse love to begging hearts because their world is a world of fair and happy exchange, and they are right. And they are right because they are beautiful.

And the man, he was just as bitter, his was another fight, so he just shook her off.

God sent her a cancer in the womb and she died a week after the big fight. I saw her dead. This lady, Melany Piano, was my mother's sister, my aunt. I wrote this about her; I am a writer and I write about persons and things:

You are dead and your mouth is stretched
and pulled down at the corners,
a curve swept downward.
Your hair is tall grass after
the flood has passed over it.
You have now become the image of the cry that in your life
you have miserably and compromisingly striven to utter.

Seriously, seriously,
with cool gentlemanliness,
I lay a word of reproach
on your grave, my aunt.
That was my crime, as I was only
a child and you were not
ashamed to soil me with the sight of your tragedy.

You did not hide your awful
crazy hands from me.
Made a clown of me when
you dressed me in black
to mourn
your dead.
Still, desperate hands of last clean wind,
wind of the fall,
bring rags of noises from
the city to the cemetery;
the evening is a lady in grey
mourning for all the dead
and she is rustling by
on the road
beside
the graveyard.

Why do I come? Were you not
my aunt?
It's pity that brings me here,
or it is
your dead face projected
in all the darkness which has driven
me here. For the soul of man is a ghost
and it haunts him and it drives him.
But
it is not
sorrow.
Aunt, a sorrow for you would shatter the world,
send fragments on the horrible snout of God!
The day I saw you dead
your eyes were terribly open —
fingers searching
the infinite for
an echo to a cry of
horrible
pain.
Also, you were resting,
my aunt.

What do you want from me? I do not try to explain, I do
not care to understand. I have not been cursed by those who
have died in misery, because I have not slain anyone with misery.
But I read the newspapers, I see rouge-and-powder faces, and
sometimes as I pass alongside your houses with my hurried heart
for a moment attentive to your noises, I hear children being
beaten, yelling; and today I have seen one of those women whose
eyes have ceased to look at the world. I tell you, it's Melany
Piano's curse that is working out. Yes, surely, her life had been
accursed by a thousand other women like her who had lived
before.

I guess it's a well-balanced retaliation.

It's you who are concerned. You who are dragging yourselves along under the shadow that Melany Piano casts upon

your world. Between the moon and you, tonight, looms the dead face of Melany Piano. And you hide under your roofs.

But I, but I, I'm as light as a rubber ball. I'm a butterfly and no tragedy has shaken the light dust from my wings, no tragedy will. It is youth that accounts for that, but overmore, it is *my* youth, the youth that will last till I die. I'm on a journey beyond you and your things, you and your colors and words. On the mountains, over this city and that, I am the bird that has no nest. I am the happy stranger, I'm sailing under the sun. The sun is very kind to me, he could not be any kinder. The friends that are with me know that also.

> The crickets are singing the tale of my journey,
> the winds all have greeted my sails.
> Listen, then,
> to the crickets and
> let the wind
> play around your houses
> as you mourn
> for Melany Piano,
> my aunt.

Father

My father is a tall man, almost
six feet tall, who carries around a dark face and hides a dark
heart. My opinion is that he is sick (one more sick man, alas!).
He could not be so incoherent, so irrational, so boresome and
disturbing, were he well.

My father took me into his house when I was eleven. The
first months he treated me very decently. He gave me one lire
every week and as I often bought books (small books, I mean)
he prophesied that I should turn into a poet or a similar beast.
For if there is a man who understands less about poetry than
my father, I do not know him. He reads so coldly that I fear
for my soul when I hear him. We used to make fun of him
when he was not there of an evening. He was pleased to call
himself a great cook and there is no denying that he understood
quite a little about it. But that is all he ever knew of the arts.

When my mother died my father felt it was his duty to take
my brother and me into his house. He was good then: perhaps
owing to his romantic disposition which made him imagine me
as a poor orphan. He made me a present of a photograph-
machine, for there is nothing more piteous to certain minds than
the contemplation of an orphan. He even called me "Mano-
lucchio," a surname of his own invention which was not
altogether unsweet.

But we found fault in secret with all his ways. We called
him "Bissolati" (a member of the Italian Parliament), and made
the *iettatura* gesture after him. But we could not love our
father. That was our great tragedy. Something had willed forever that our father and we two should never come near to one

another. As for him, he grew fat on such misery. He thrived on it.

When I first came into his house, I was surprised to find that my father enjoyed life in the arms of two little school-teachers. He had re-married, taking a little woman who saw only with his eyes, felt with his feelings, obeyed him like a little dog. She was patient and stupid. Several times she wept on my vest-pocket, showing me a list of ciphers to the effect that she had given much money to the family and now my father wanted more and she had no more.

My step-mother liked me more than she did my brother, for my brother once made her cry while I had nothing but good words for her. It was all on account of two pairs of red socks which my father had discarded. My brother abhorred them since there was no way of escaping the sarcasm which the boarding-school boys were sure to give them. So he threw the unhappy socks up in the air and misfortune willed it that they should fall on the curtain-rods. My poor little step-mother came in and saw the socks dangling and began to cry. She was still crying when my father came home and after much questioning she revealed the source of her sorrow. My brother got one of the beatings of his life.

My father used to beat my brother, the son that my mother bore him, till he bled, with awful refinement in his insults, with picturesque phrases, in a frenzy of play-acting, obeying thus his sordidly romantic nature. Once he spat in my brother's face, causing the poor boy to fall into convulsions. He called a doctor when I told him my brother had swallowed a dose of sulphuric acid. The sulphuric acid turned out to be dirty water, but he told the doctor that my father had spat in his face and I never saw a man more mortified than my father at his son's words. He felt shame — an emotion I never thought him capable of.

My father had a most vicious laugh: he showed his teeth when he laughed, which gave him the aspect of a ferocious beast. He had the Romagnli's kind of laugh. He seemed to drag that laugh from the very inside and throw it out. It was like a sneer, but a sneer is short-lived while my father's laughter continued. And when it was vented upon one of his little children it was like a snake running over a white plate. Oh, how I despised him for it, how I loathed that he should so defile such little things!

When he was absent from the house he left us under the care of an old aunt, my grandmother's sister. She was to tell him whether we had been good children or not. We were not good, and when father came home we assaulted him on the stairs, screaming: "We have been bad! We have been bad!" This affair was very ridiculous but my father did not see it so.

He scolded me if with the lire he gave me once a week I bought fruit or some other good thing. There was, and there is no green thing that throws its curls to the wind in his mind or in his heart. At dinner, never a word was exchanged amongst us unless my father quarrelled with my brother. Oh, the awful, cheerless meals, the naked bad humor! What endless boiled beef, what idiocies my father uttered! (He is so terrible that he ends in being ridiculous. He is so fierce that he no longer scares any-body.) A tale ran through Bologna that he fired one of his sub-ordinates simply because the poor devil succeeded in sending his family to the mountains during the summer months. My father would make a point out of the corner of his napkin and clean his ears with it at table; he would belch most ignominiously. His humorous tales were sordid. (I cannot imagine him ever making a speech, and yet he made one in honor of the fallen in the war and it was widely appreciated.)

The case of my grandmother was as follows: she had little wrinkles all over her face, so many of them, so many of them. And she had a cracked little voice with which she sang the same old song, always the same:

Funiculi, funicula,
Yammo, Yammo!

It was the song of the celebration of the making of a rope railway up the side of Vesuvio. It was

Yammo, Yammo in coppa va,
Funiculi, funicula.

A stupid song, the stupidest ever. Casella made it into a rhapsody, and it is bad, very bad music at that.

Egghiuta Nannine, se n'e saliuta
In coppa sta.

(Do not let the student of Italian letters be dismayed at these quotations. They are not Italian, they are Neapolitan.)

Finally, a stroke liquidated my grandmother. She was fat, very fat, but when she lay straight in the coffin she seemed a thinner woman. She was powerful, a big woman full of strength and energy, but death made her something else.

She was a nagging old lady, stupid, vulgar, with a habit of disapproval. I was so little grieved by her death that I forced myself to stare hard at something in order to make my eyes water. My brother, who witnessed these tears and who did not cry at all, could not believe his eyes. He had been the Benjamin of grandmother, and I wondered at him. But I wondered still more, and was shocked, when brother August said:

"Could you really cry for the old woman?"

My father put me almost at once into another boarding-school. Love and affection were all right but he preferred to send his sons away. I imagine a cavernous song that is his song: I imagine him walking at night in dangerous places, and he white with fear for the shadows of the road. I imagine how he loves his wife — how terribly ridiculous he must be in action. Because he does not know and never knew ecstasy. This man's entrails must be dark too. He must be dark out and in.

Pink—The Second Boarding School

This part I call "pink" because in comparison with parts to come, it is surely meek and mild. But I detested them enough, these jails where terrifically immoral things are done by the inmates. I passed three years there.

My father almost immediately entered me in a school at Bologna. I was then like a little lion unchained. This national boarding-school was an old majestic palace with very high ceilings and enormous windows. The lodges and galleries were magnificently tall too. The white dormitories were impotent in their simplicity. The town that enjoyed itself outside in spite of us poor prisoners was a pretty town.

A man who tended the convicts helped to make my first spiritual and ideal education. He gave me *The Three Musketeers,* which I read in French, understanding more than one might imagine. It was the first book that I read in French and he lent me the book because its French is extremely easy. But right after that he gave me *Eugenie Grandet,* and *La Dernière Fée,* and he himself read to me the dreary, macabre, fierce poems from *Les Fleurs du Mal.* I loved to read. At home I had devoured almost everything in the way of reading matter. I read *Nick Carter, Nat Pinkerton, Buffalo Bill,* and some terrible appendix novels given me by an old uncle of mine who had, through his own patience, made fifty or sixty of such things into the shape of books.

This teacher was the first, De Fraja, who helped make my education. The first after my aunt, who might well claim that she had been responsible for my education, the education of my soul, I mean. I feel she made of me a poet, even in those early days of my infancy and boyhood. I remember how she beat her children, but she loved them like a lioness. I remember that once the river in Cossato, the Strona, flooded the nearby country and threw down one of the arches of the bridge. They told my aunt that the last they had seen of her children was over the bridge. She became frantic and showed them her lioness-love. And finally she went insane and lost so much weight as to seem a skeleton. I remember when I went to see her from the first boarding-school she frightened me, chilled my veins, and I could not help crying. She folded me in her arms and loved me for having come, and loved me for being there, and loved me because she sensed a certain weight of experience in me which she did not find in her children, they being very small. She used to confide in me. (I do not come like a soul in pain near your grave, my aunt. I'd be afraid were I to do so that I'd rouse once again the tempest that is in you. For death for you should be a long hush. But I do not believe that you in death cannot hear me, and see me, and watch me. And this is not a Catholic notion: for I believe that only certain fine people retain their qualities even in death. A soul comes high, not every one may purchase it.) I had no better companion, no better confidante, no better loving person. How horrible it was to have seen her dead! Her eyes were tremendously open. She was terrible: she seemed an insane rebel. There was terror and fury in her face. I never saw a worse-looking dead person. Her hair seemed like grass at the bottom of the river. It was as if a stream had passed over it. Surely death had given her no repose, she must have suffered even in death, as my mother had. Ah, that death should not be satisfied to take all from us without distorting even our miserable faces.

De Fraja was a tiny man with a head pressed in at the sides, which caused him to be called "Little Valise" by the irreverent lot of scholars. As for his estate, he was a miserable man, slave of his profession, slave of his habits which his profession implied, slave even of his little education which he quickly made mine.

Our teacher of Italian language was the then famous short-story writer, Adolfo Albertazzi. He was a fat man, tormented by gout, who could hardly move in his chair, and he had two moustaches that looked like two slices of hard cold cornmeal mush. He was the sweetest, most naive man in the world, and we took advantage of his goodness. We were a group of three: Mario, Marcello, and I. When one of us was inclined to take the straight path, the other two were there to cajole the third back.

Of my companions, I recollect Purrini, who had two left feet; Gazzoni, who boasted of the things he would do when out of jail. (I repeat it, it was a jail.) Fontana, the son of poor farming people, who had a limpid, clear intelligence and whom I admired rather than loved; Roboozi, another inmate, who had a voice like Whispering Sullivan. (He was unhappy because every time he spoke it sounded as though he were shouting.) Matteuzzi, he sang horribly and out of tune and he would not have anyone say so or even think so; Zorzi, with two Zs in his name, he still succeeded in turning many consonants into Zs. As for the others, my chief enemy was one of them. He had the face of a small monkey and he pestered me continually . . . The name of that individual was, ironically enough, Preziosi (Precious).

There was, too, Morten, a boy of German origin, a little humpback boy, a dreary sort. But it is true that the boarding-school air makes people dull, and so do the obscene practices which blossom and blow in that atmosphere of filth, in those places of enormous walls and long dormitories, of large study-rooms and crazy superiors and crazier waiters and cooks. There was also the director, a just if stern man, who came to love me when he heard all that De Fraja said in my favor.

Oh, the glorious walks on the Bolognese hills! The great hikes along the green country roads, perfumed by jasmines, by honeysuckle, gloriously clad they were in flower dresses! The dust, which our feet raised, in our eyes. Certainly these hikes were altogether more useful to us than sitting in a nasty room filled with the breath of students. All we learned in the school-room we were doomed to forget utterly, for school is a place in which one forgets all one ought to remember and remembers all one ought to forget.

I remember the long walks that got us home tired and hungry, but I have forgotten how to do long division. I damn the old boarding-school and the years spent studying the absurdities teachers asked us to swallow. (Teachers wear like a double belly the pride of the matter they teach.) Damn the old hungry gang of professors set after us, at our heels, after us all the time, insisting that we be religious (oh, that religion of theirs!), that we be quiet and still. But, poor devils, that was their bread and butter, and often bread without the butter at all. Damn the dirty things all the *collegio* boys did, for I was one of the few that did not, reeking, filthy with a sterile, awful love.

I have never had much of an inclination for sports and I did not join the kind of football club. I never found any pleasure in watching a boxing-match, nor a cyclist race, not to speak of golf or baseball. There is always something brutal in one man seeking to win at the expense of another. There is violence in every race, always something awful in a match. The only sport I love is swimming: I was not a professional swimmer but I could swim a mile and a half.

Peloni was the leader of our gymnastic games. He was a fine piece of a man, tall and awfully strong. He played the trombone in our band. He was one of the most genial boys in the whole school, ready to laugh, ready to play, slow to take offense, slow to be angry with anyone. Once I went to his study-room, the study-room of the bigger boys, and inside his desk, scratched there with a pen-knife, was written: *This year is the last and then I shall go home whether God wills or God doesn't will.*

At that time he was ill, and it developed into meningitis, and the poor boy died of it.

I won five years of board and room at one of the best national boarding-schools, but my brother had won nearly nothing so my father gave us the same clothes and scolded us both bitterly. My brother died of wounds received in the war and when my father sent me this news to America he added that he forgave the unfortunate boy for all the sorrow he had caused him. This forgiveness repelled me so that I never answered the letter. I hold my own rancour against my brother, even though he is dead. I was very small, very little, and he liked to elaborate his ways of beating me. A favorite way was to catch me by the feet and hold me up thus, and then suddenly drop me to the floor. Upon the heap of memories concerning him is the memory of the beatings I got.

But there are other things I remember of him: I remember

that my brother, a tall lanky contraption, was once in love with a school-teacher who taught in a village near Bologna. It was towards this village we rode, a party of us, to make our serenade. Serenading is never done in solitude, and I remember there was a muddle of bicycles: four bicycles should have been produced and there were only three. We were unfamiliar with the road and we woke up a peasant to ask him the way. He was angry and cursed us all, but finally he put us onto the right road. The night was cold and very foggy and we rode along in silence, following the infinite roadway to her window, feeling we were always just there, but yet never quite arriving. There was just enough of a path beside the ditch, and we kept to this, for the rest of the road was unspeakably muddy.

When we at last arrived, my brother took the violin from its case which seemed so like a coffin. As soon as he began to play a string snapped with a *tuck*. But he went on with his: *O, Lola che di latti hai la camise* . . . singing courageously, for courage was all he had left. No window ever lit or opened. The lady was probably asleep, fast asleep. The rest of us were hidden near the hedge, but my brother stood out conspicuously, and so I can see him now, playing his broken violin to the absolute silence of the night.

Myself

The time has come at last when I must discourse on my outward appearance. Here goes:

First of all, my face: keen, stubborn, sometimes very hard but more often soft. Women tell me I have beautiful eyes but I could never believe them. I have a very high forehead (Oscar Wilde once said that a high forehead was a sign of stupidity; of course, he had a very low forehead.) My lips are fine, sensuous with quaint sinuosities. Once I fell in love with my hair: so smooth, unwavy, straight in a not unpleasant way, almost black. (A different tale could now be told about my hair that was.)

I am a shabby, untidy, lazy fellow. I do not know how to tie a necktie and my pants can never keep the crease nor the jacket the original shape. (I'm speaking now of the time when I was comparatively healthy.) My shoes are never shined, for a shine costs ten cents and ten cents is money even for a millionaire, nay, more so for a millionaire.

I improve now every time I shave, but only while the shave lasts. I like the curve that is in the articulation of the jaw. This curve is sweet but it would have been better had it been square and strong. I look a little like a poet, by way of wistfulness and dreaminess, but my face is often fierce, especially when I get up in the morning. It mellows as the day grows. . . .

My face means explosion, and that will happen soon. It means stagnation, and I am in no hurry to make it different. In my face there is the whole struggle of stale ideas, impressions, sensations. Who said the face mirrors the soul? What deluge would this thing be if often repeated!

To call a man romantic now is the lowest form of abuse, but

what can I do? My face is hopelessly romantic. Surely, I am fat-headed in this sense: if we were to detach Kay Boyle's head from the body it would drop down and then bounce back to its owner. It is elastic. But if mine fell from my body it would drop down and stay wistfully there. The old christian saying: "Love thy neighbor as thyself" does not work with me since I detest myself. I have noticed that my eyes have a Chinese slant which is not pretty. I always had a funny way of walking which was accentuated as the years went by and my sickness grew more and more serious. That is, I bend my right leg at the knee and swing my feet as though I wanted to throw them away.

Speaking of my inner appearance, I must acknowledge that I possess the quality of forgiveness to others, which is very dangerous; and also that of being eager to admit anything to my cost and peril. Yes, I believe no woman is able to admit her faults. (Because she is afraid of her own weakness: she believes that if she cedes she loses — perhaps because she has little to lose.) To admit is eminently Christian and women are very seldom good Christians.

I become angry when I think of women's will to get the vote. For years men have been making a mess of the damn thing, and who would tell me that women could make a lesser mess of the damn thing? I should like to throw the whole thing in the lap of women, give them full power, and see. Women could not do much worse than men but there is no reason why she should do much better. The Vote, oh, thank you! You can have it, whole and untrammelled. You can sleep sweet sleep, resting your head upon this terrible octopus, the Vote.

Yes, this is my inner appearance, so called with a reason. Some of the rays emitted by my outer appearance filter through and stain my inner self. My mind cannot be beautiful because it is bovine and obese. I have a great reserve of goodness that rots in the long run. My goodness is a real power. It means that I often flatter others.

Since I fell sick my reservoir of tears dried up and I cried no more. That is a terrible thing. . . .

First Love

The lawn was as clean and cool as a lake. We had evening conversations there. We made love there. We were so many girls and boys together, as many boys. Pre-ten-year-olds' love. She would take me by the hand and whisper to me. We made love, or thought we did, love being such a delicate thing that making love or thinking you are making it is about the same thing.

Everyone of the crowd had his sweetheart. There was the daughter of a famous industrial man. She would take me by the hand and confess in a whisper:

"I love you and I love Dick and I love Joe."

I enjoyed the precedence, but only to a certain extent, for a doubt, subtle as a flea in the ear, murmured to me that when she talked with another of her lovers she probably gave him the precedence.

One evening, a friend of mine — a boy — moved by some impulse I cannot remember, kissed me soundly, and she who had been a spectator said:

"I bet you wouldn't kiss any of us girls so nicely."

With a thread of a voice I answered that I could kiss with equal expansion . . . So she put a tiny hand to my mouth and I kissed it; but, oh, so bashfully, oh, so gently, and I thought I might become an all-day sucker and almost fainted.

How dear was that magical hand from that day on, it is difficult to say. I was submerged in a flood of passion, ten-year-old passion. For one is often passionately in love at an early age.

Platonic love is nearer to the essence of love than sexual love. I deduce this from the fact that it is the usual thing to have

somebody say of his sweetheart that he never thinks of love for
her except platonically. For a young man, a woman who gives
herself is generally despised and often called a whore, and a *fille
mère* has the same name.

Isolda was a poem of gracefulness and beauty — (how is it
then that she appears to my mind now as very unbeautiful with
too large a nose and too thin a face?) She was thin, delicate. She
was also so ingenuous that she believed calves came into the
world through their mother's mouths.

She opened my heart and threw into it with her beautiful
hands a handful of love. So sweet was the sensation that I could
not help considering this a great love. I never dared formulate a
wish or prayer about this love. Everything that was very human
spoiled it: it feared extraneous intervention terribly.

*All the spring songs were you, the birds sang for you —
and my heart, light and slight, sang too. You deserve remembrance and I give it to you with full hands. There is a tiny place
in my heart where you live and suffer and talk and weep. You
are there completely, tremendously, and fatally.*

She walked about like a peacock but there was pity for
poor men in her sweet babble. Her small face was all aflame as
she talked of things she necessarily knew nothing about.

There was another little lawn girl who had a deal more
common-sense than Isolda. She was very pretty: she was a
modern beauty, romantic, while Isolda had an ancient sort of
beauty, classic. With this girl all the boys spoke of forbidden
things. But she would not let herself be touched. So many women
are like that: free in their talk but pure in their ways.

*Oh, how many dreams I threw after you and you never knew
them! How many dreams, lonely and melancholy dreams, my
up-to-date, my barren heart conceived! They were pushed along
the road of dreams by your small white hand. So small was your
heart, a little fist merely, and yet how big was the love you hid
there!*

A few years after the days of the lawn, they told me she had
given herself to a nasty way of living. She was fire — until she
burned out. Because there is the youth of the city (but I am
ashamed to give such a name as "youth" to those sinister individ-

uals) who lie in wait for such burning girls. The city is on watch for just such victims: victims of their own strong passion, victims of their own dark lust.

But Isolda was the queen of the lawn and when she went away the lawn became (from green) yellow and squalid and desolate. I knew her city address so I passed and re-passed before her house, hoping at least for a sight of her. But that never happened. I carried my sorrow about.

All the splendor of the new-cut grass lost its intensity for me. Sleep was the most difficult thing; eating came next. Love gathers together every mood, every new mood, every need and every lust. Keats said once that not every man may love. Only the best people or the poets may love. Our love was aristocratic, aloof, austere.

The Third Boarding School

My father put me in prison again. This time it was in one of the first *collegio* of Italy, perhaps the best of all. He would never have been able to support me there had I not won the prize which meant room and board free to the end of my schooling.

The most beautiful place in the most beautiful town, for that *collegio* was one of the splendors of Venice. For me Venice is the loveliest city in all the world. Is there anywhere such a great thing as the *Canal Grande* or the *Palazzo Vendramin* (it has now been half destroyed by Austrian aeroplanes), and the lace in stone which adorns the famous Gold House, *Ca' d'Oro?* And the small *rios* of Venice, poor and wonderfully silent. *Venezia* is like a lotus flower on a thread of water. Nothing in Venice is unbeautiful. All is resplendent, all speaks of ancient artists who have given their living hearts to the creation of this naive little girl.

Some prefer the noise of other cities to the silence of Venice. But the silence of Venice has something magical in it. She is the only silent city in the world. She has a warm soft mysterious silence. Queen of the lagoon; she huddles in a corner of it, but she is still a Queen. Her palaces are her laces. She is always ready to get married, therefore the laces.

How much dreaming was necessary to think you out, Venice? It seems impossible that human hands made you. I would give away all modernity for one look at Venice. I would give away all the unlovely new things for a single look at you.

The Lido did not have my enthusiasm, for the Lido is essentially bourgeois. Although she is at times dishevelled, she is still a prude. The Lido is your new thing: think of it in connection with Venice and it disappears in shame. Venice slides over the lagoon, ever so light, ethereal almost. That is the secret of Venice, her lightness upon shallow waters. The only filthy thing in Venice is when they shut off a canal in order to clean it. The mud is almost blue, so black it is! And the smell is pestilential. But if the Grand Canal is not altogether clean, neither were the hands of Michel Angelo.

No, Dante even could not shut her in hell for she is all Paradise. She is all holy and majestic. She is all of lace. She seems to float upon the waters and from afar the buildings seem to emerge from water. The gondola belongs to no one but a poet. Perhaps there is something swifter, but there is nothing lovelier, nothing so light, so elegant, gliding with such ease, with such peace, and with such majesty. They say a gondola costs more than an automobile and I am the first to believe it.

In this beautiful town there is a national boarding-school and there my father put me.

At the boarding-school I fell in love with a boy a year younger than I. A real, fervid, passionate, beautiful love. I loved this little boy and I besieged him with letter upon letter. Although we lived in the same place, I tormented him with my letters. He was a very good-looking little fellow and he returned my love, but weakly and without enthusiasm.

I was in love: all the world took on a different aspect. I was in a sort of fog, in a daze, in a trance. Love of the purest kind was mine. I loved him deeply, with all the love a poor heart can afford. My letters were passionate, and with the environment of beautiful Venice, my love grew very strong. He, being a Venetian, seemed not to feel the beauty of the Grand Canal.

The *Collegio Marco Foscarini di Venezia* was a kind of militaristic institution. On review day, the first Sunday in June, we were mustered to the *Piazza San Marco* like the rest of the army. Moreover, we were the best marching men. But although I hated the place, I mixed my love for the Grand Canal with my love for Giovanni Genovali. He and Venice were the two splendors of my life. When I had his hand in mine, I was happy. When I was walking by his side in the hour we spent promenading, I was in the seventh heaven. When I was free to talk with him, I was embarrassed, shy, shameful. In short, ours was the ordinary love affair.

I wasn't much of a beauty when I was in this last boarding-school, but afterwards, of course, I became very handsome. (Except for now, a period in which there is no beauty for me. Yet, I am handsome still, even though I am almost bald-headed, because some female judged me so.) I had a great deal of straight hair which I insisted on calling "abject". I thought I was a repulsive little human being. I bathed my yellow face in great profusions of lavender water. During these days I thought I was fearfully ugly. The mirrors sold me so, or I thought they did. Yet, judging from later years, I could not have been so very ugly and Giovanni assured me that I was not quite ugly.

When I left Venice to go to Milan, I spent a day loafing through the city, and he with me. I don't know how many kisses I gave him on the pretext that I was leaving Venice forever. He hardly returned them, those unfortunate kisses.

I know from *Jean Christophe* that such love-affairs between boys are frequent, and often are the most innocent and pure things ever. I think they became pure by the force of their greatness and power. But at last the superiors noticed something between me and Giovanni Genovali and we were separated. They put him in one *escaude* and me in the next. It was the superiors at the school who profaned our love and covered us with abuse for a thing they could not understand. We two, we knew of the orgies, the ribaldry and scoundrelism about us, and we two who were innocent must pay for the sins of the others.

But in the new place, Giovanni had to do with a man whom they considered even more dangerous than myself, and in the end they put him back with me. But then came the tragedy.

We had gone for many miles into the country on a so-called strategic walk. All the time I noticed that Giovanni paid more attention to the above-mentioned profligate than to me and jealousy rose in waves over my brain. I walked in a yellow fog, speaking to no one, and how at such moments one resents the thoughtless joy and noise the others make! I was shut within myself, twice as miserable because I was not able to cry. I was like the shrunken rag of a man. I desired to die, to die on the spot.

But what I really desired was that he come to me and beg forgiveness, or that he come to me and make a glorious and lasting peace.

Giovanni did come to me, then, but with some foolish remarks. I merely greeted him. I had fallen into the bad habit of calling him *Nino* and he fiercely resented this name. So after a word or two spoken aloud, terrifically loud, we parted in anger. That evening he had a letter brought to me in which he said that he wished to have nothing more to do with me. I wrote to him, once, twice, several times, seeking to put in my letters all the sorrow he had given me. But these he never answered.

So my first symptoms of hysteria came on me: once I fancied that I heard a keen thread-like noise, a far-off whistle. I jumped up from my study table and the silence was broken by my loud fierce sobs. Another time I had a wild attack of nerves because of the humiliation of being put with my face to the wall.

It all ended by my being expelled from school, very delicately expulsed, but thrown out just the same. Some letters were sent to my father in one of which was the justification. The day I left the boarding-school was the last day Giovanni and I saw each other. We were together all day and went bathing at the Lido. There I noticed for the first time how strong my sweet boy had grown during those years of gymnastics at school. Now he was as strong as a bullock, with a great chest and strong arms. Such a type of man, I knew, was not made for my affection.

At first, my father refused bitterly to take me back, but the Prefect, my father's immediate superior, was written to and my father at last agreed. No one can describe how fiercely, how wildly, how horribly he welcomed me. All the vicious expressions that had rankled in his heart for years were vomited on me. My whole being was revolted. Certainly I had never seen a man as angry as he was that day. I never heard anyone so vilely rebuking.

And now, for a time, my nerves were such that I broke almost everything I touched. I broke the English water-closet by stepping on it to see how the thing functioned; thus I broke a set of oil and vinegar bottles, and many other things. My father's sharp and only comment was: *"I scienta Tott."* There was great bitterness in that utterance and it gave me pain.

One day the servant attacked me by saying: "The President of the school has telephoned your father . . ." I immediately left the house. It turned out later that the man who had telephoned was the president of my brother's school, but that remark to me filled the cup to the brim. I went to Mario's and there, sobbing like a damn fool, I wrote a letter to my father in which I said that I was sick of his house, terribly sick of it, that I had quit school forever and that I wanted to go to America as soon as possible. When I saw my father he told me he agreed to my going to America since, and these were his words: "For the enemy in flight we build a golden bridge." I understood. I was then the enemy of that big beast.

He gave me two lire to spend on food and lodging, these lire which would come to me every day. Instead, things were arranged like this: Mario's mother and father wanted me to stay with them . . . but I anticipate.

Last Days in Italy

I had conceived a great love for the family Pacini in which Mario, one of the best friends I ever had, played the part of son. I loved the little mother and also the little father: the latter was so strong that when he shut the water faucet or similar things the rest of the family had to unite all their efforts in order to open it again, or they had to use wrenches. He was the dearest man.

They fixed up a sort of cot and I slept by them. And I ate with them also. So the two lire were intact and every evening we went to the theatre, in the top gallery, to see things which pleased me, the reader of *Nick Carter,* very much. The Grand Guignol, fierce sort of one-act plays in which there were often more dead men than personages. The actor was one of the worst Italy ever had. To give you an idea, I shall mention a few of his plays:

À La Morgue. A man is suspected of having killed a red-breeches. They bring him to the morgue and place a bottle of presumed absinthe near him. He finishes the bottle and then, turning around, sees for the first time the body of the gendarme, all dressed up as when he had killed him, stretched out on a case. Not only is he horrified by this sight but he thinks he sees the cadaver move. He jumps up, screaming that he is ready to eat his own tongue as he had eaten his heart, and the Commissaire, hearing these hysterical words, jumps into the room, and screaming too, accuses the man of murder and puts him under arrest. That ends it.

The Terrible Experiment. A doctor believes he has discovered a way to bring dead men back to life. He tries this experiment on his own daughter who has died. But as she comes back to life she grasps her father by the throat and will not let him go. Thus the old man dies a horrible death.

And so on, many more in that style, which may seem boring to you but which made my delight.

Meanwhile, my friendship with Mario was growing and assuming a special form. The thing I admired most in him was his muscles, his strength. In that sense, he was quite like his father. He was also a kind of poet. He wrote such exotic drivel, so utterly obscure and incomprehensible that it was a marvel and a wonder. But he laughed full-heartedly at his own efforts and was the first to recognize how clumsy they were.

I was almost in love with Mario's sister, but that was so long ago that I have even forgotten her name. She studied medicine and was a good student. But then I was ready to fall in love with all and any girls: if a girl turned around to look at me I was sure right away that the girl in question was madly in love with me. But I never dared approach any girl: indeed, I feared them all and every one. (I remember a girl schoolfellow whose sympathy I won by defending d'Annunzio against Manzoni. Of all the queer discussions this was surely the queerest! None of us knew much about the two authors, none of us had any particularly definite reason for defending or accusing either of the two writers, and why did we choose two such different human beings as Manzoni and d'Annunzio? These were two opposites, no comparison was possible.)

These last days of Italy were the very best of my life. Mrs. Pacini's food was excellent, and her hands on my face when she wanted to wake me up in the morning were very dear. There was a mystery in Mr. Pacini's life and he did not like being reminded of it. He had made a great invention concerning the telephone and he kept all the drafts of this hidden in a drawer, and woe to him who opened this *Barbe Bleue's* forbidden room.

I lived with them and we went to the theatre every night and my father and his two little school-teachers could go to hell: that was my wish for them. But if he'd ever come to know how I spent the money he gave me, the sky would have opened up and showered all the cataracts of heaven! He would not have beaten me (he never beat me, he hated me too much to beat me), but he would have spared no words. He would have called me all sorts of dirty names.

I have never regretted one day that I was not at school. I had the spirit of rebellion and these days marked my awakening to many things. For instance, I discovered *"Futurismo"*. I wore a flowing necktie and was believed to be either an anarchist or a futurist, the two things being strangely linked together. We would go up to the Santa Luca, a kind of sanctuary, and on the platform beside the porches we built, with snow, an enormous phallus. Old Paderno heard our riotous voices, our singing, our screaming, and the priests that passed by cursed us and threatened to have us put in jail.

Bologna had become so dear to me that when I left her I wept for her. I did not weep for the friends who had come to the station to say goodbye, but the last bits of Bologna I saluted with great respect, almost religiously.

At Milano I stopped to see my two cousins and we went to the theatre to see an old *pochade* by Hennequin and Weber. I spent the rest of the night, from the theatre until four in the morning, on a bench in the station waiting-room, trying hard and uselessly to sleep. The next day I was in Genoa, with the prospect of spending two whole days in that city. I saw but little of it but that little did not please me at all. There is something awfully tawdry about this city which people insist on calling "The Superb."

There is a kind of alley in Genoa where one can buy all sorts of tarts made of vegetables cooked in great pans. I bought and ate a lot of these things, with the result that I was barely aboard ship when I had a violent attack of sea-sickness. That sickness clung to me the length of the Mediterranean while the sea was as smooth as oil.

So I said goodbye to Italy, she to whom I gave so little and from whom I received less. (Oh, yes, she gave me something, too. While I was still at school I was made a member of a Society for the Redemption of Trent and Trieste. I collected some money making new members and spent a happy Christmas with the appropriated funds. That was almost all she gave me. Not even a sweetheart. Also, although now I can taste nothing, there was a time when I and my brother stole bottles of "Lambrusco" which we drank at our ease during the night in boarding-school. And, of course, we always stole the best bottles from my father's cellar.)

To Italy I owed my spoiled childhood. No thanks go to Italy and no thanks shall I give her. (But I must at least be dutifully thankful to her for being beautiful and that chance sent me to school in the most beautiful of all her cities.) Beautiful, sea-embraced Italy, beautifully girt by Florence, crowned by the Alps, not a bit of your shore is less than marvelous. How I loved the beautiful sea of Italy, even when it is as ugly as the Lido is (like Coney Island, put to shame by the crowds of bathers.) Here is a parable of the sea: Oh, sea, you stretch out calm and serene, an open page on which the word "Peace" is written in enormous letters; or you pound the beach with the closed fists of your waves. You are forever beautiful, oh, sea; sea of my beloved Italy, when you are calm your little waves run in and out on the beach like a smile and a sigh. When you fling your great horses onto the shore, this is your tremendous laughter; it is your incomparable beauty which erodes the rocks and denudes and laves them. All the oldest songs are yours; in you it would be easy to die, for one would need only to let oneself go, without struggling, and death would come.

Nor is it difficult to live in you, for shipwrecks are rare now that man has got the best of you, you the unconquerable, beautiful wild beast. You thunder on through the night, trampling under foot the sleep of those who are not accustomed to your voice. Or you whisper your love to the beach which listens reverently to you. You are our common possession and at the same time the most beautiful of all the gods. From the ship I saw that the sea near Genoa is dark blue and the sky the same.

Goodbye to ravioli of Milano, zampone from Modena, agnolotti of Turin, spaghetti à la Napolitaine, goodbye! And yet is was not food I was nostalgic for, leaving Italy. It was the essence, the choice part of Italy I was leaving forever perhaps. I remember that in America when I happened to sing an Italian song in the streets, I started to weep like a fool. One song does sometimes mean a whole nation. Besides, it is possible to long even more for a country in which one has suffered much. The longing becomes in time a kind of compensation for the suffering.

There is an intimacy with a country one has suffered in and it is this intimacy one misses most when away.

Yet at first I must confess that I felt no great sorrow or nostalgia, for Italy meant my father to me; it meant the beatings my brother gave me, and it meant my terrible grandmother, and the loss (why "loss" then?) of her who had been a familiar thing.

Arthur Rimbaud

His life is an adventure of the gods; anybody who has not dropped his useless bundle and gone on a great adventure will not understand him. I have gone on a great adventure and I may sometime personify a god I have seen for a moment. I would, as much as I could, personify him. If you do not believe in Youth do not utter vague blasphemies. Rimbaud is the advent of Youth. Almost everything else in the world is unbelief in Youth; diplomats, statesmen, chiefs of all works, generals, they're all old because they say, queerly, old age is ripeness — as if an apple is ripe when it has wrinkles on its face! Almost everything else in the world, besides the poets, who have all believed in Youth, is a consecration of the error that life is from Youth up. It is from Youth down.

Critics are dead leaves lying still while the hurricane sweeps by high above. To utter something while enraptured in the hurricane, that is the only way to compensate to me my not being the hurricane; and the only way to criticize a poet. Rimbaud said gloriously that the attainment of poetry is the attainment of life. To know myself and to possess it — the perfect image is the perfect sensation and the perfect life.

To have myself in the days of youth, with every inch of my body tense, looking and listening and interpreting, the dualism of body and soul and the dualism of life and immortality being then risible questions which are the appropriate doubt of people who have lost IT (both things, both times, forever: old people). To mould myself, then, through a "long, immense and reasoned upheaval of all the senses." Certainties of the age of seventeen and eighteen, certainties born of a perfect harmony of youth's life and being, certainties of God.

The old words woke from their death-sleep and sang again with the power that was theirs before cowards drugged them: "I want liberty in salvation," "I want to possess truth in a body and a soul." And for liberty, expression, poetry — the world found, the beautiful Genesis known. Who but God himself might have done this — "The fraternal awakening of all the choral and orchestral energies and their instantaneous application — the only occasion to disengage our senses." This is the consecration of the trinity, ethic-aesthetic-logic, which is godhead. To achieve liberty, to write perfect poetry, to sense perfectly, to love perfectly, to live — these are vague phrases, meaning to the great but one thing. And that thing, to me, to a man who has no sign from God otherwise than from books, is godhead itself.

The querulous, fearful, fretful and rash god of Moses is not a more beautiful vision than the god of *La Saison en Enfer* and *Les Illuminations*. Rimbaud's judgment is saner. He sought to achieve, sometimes did achieve, beauty that would enable him to smite the world with absolute judgments. And some of his poems are absolute. If the eyes that see are clear, damned be the ugly and only the ugly. If the heart that beats knows its throbs, cursed be the dead and only the dead. *Les Assis,* the sitting men, is an apocalyptic vision: the irrevocable, ultimate, terrible judgment of beauty, judgment ethical, practical and utilitarian, also absolute. Use any of your standards and tests and tell me what is the end of any ugliness.

But here come the reporters, the doctors, the caretakers, the undertakers, the beauty makers (barbers), the pimps of the concubinage between God and the dwarfs of rotten flesh, the purveyors of death, "the hearts of filth, the mouths of stench." Each one carries a pall and each one came to cover Rimbaud's infinite body with his or her own rag and no other rag. On the palls, these inscriptions:

HATER OF THE BOURGEOISIE

FREE VERSE INVENTOR

WHO DEVISED SYMBOLISM

WHO MENDED TECHNIQUE

EMANUEL CARNEVALI

ANARCHIST, INSANE DEGENERATE
WE DON'T GIVE A DAMN
MESSIAH OF SEVENTEEN? pooh-pooh
COLORIST OF LES VOYELLES

And there are as many of these as there are squinting or bloodshot or swollen-eyed in the world. Let me say it, there are as many of these as there are cowards in the world. Indeed, I advise you, let an easy term of compromise make you forget him who is the Youth you couldn't remember. Not even as worshippers could you do this. It is in a vase more beautiful than your soul that this fragrance of his may be held in the ineffable hand of a flower: the flower being the only reason for the vase. Which of you would give up the life every one of you hates, which of you would die in order to understand him — or any god, anyway? Because you must die; not dwindle into a state of neutrality, as aesthetic critics say, but die with long sorrow, through the genetic emotions. . . . Oh, Jesus Christ, most beautiful, you have forever spoken the words of the miracle interpretation!

"Ah, ha," you laugh. "This fellow is one more of the religion-of-art!" You laugh, and it would appear that you have placed me, for indeed I feel ridiculous, because of this pen and this ink and the need of writing readable English. . . . And because all your cowardly sophistication is in me and your laugh is a wound talking to a wound inside of me, all these things shame me. If I were sure no one were listening I would indeed cry out: I am a worshipper who has died many times for Dostoievsky, for Nietszche, for Christ, for Rimbaud.

In '71 he was a rebel of *La Commune*. He had written a project for a constitution. I know from Carlyle that revolution is sometimes the people producing poetry *en masse*. Clear as the fire of even the things most rotten is revolution in the pure vision of the seer, the inspired man who wants revolution for the beauty of his eyes, for the beauty of his limbs, for the beauty of his heart — who wants and has long wanted the world to be his own body speaking.

Arthur Rimbaud was religious, as all great men are. For himself, for the beautiful god he built out of his soul, he sought apostles. He found Verlaine, a splendidly sensitive soul, who could not understand him. . . .

Men do not wait for a saviour. Each man seeks drunkenness and forgetfulness and a hiding place. And the disease inherited from the centuries is perhaps one at last with a man's soul. As for me, I know Youth in love, I know Youth encountering the first men: I know Youth believing in the vision that arises, like the First Dawn, over the encounters. I know the first, valid, absolute axioms of godhead: "I love you, you beautiful. I will bring all the world to your feet." "I shall become beautiful for you." And the realization of possible godhead: "I am not worthy of you." For this I believe in Arthur Rimbaud and even in all the distorted and queer and desperate signs of godhead that Youths give the world as they pass.

As they pass. . . . He too went away, having found no worshipper. Having heard no echo to his song, he doubted it. And if a god be no more than a conceivable being, then the way he abandons literature, the way he kisses the dream of godhead goodbye makes me think that it is still divine to know why one is not a god. The simple gesture, humble like a peasant of Tolstoy's: "I have been idle like a toad, doing nothing, I managed to live everywhere. I will beg pardon for having fed on lies, *allons!*"

The sense of loss proved only in abysses and woods by him who knows the language of abysses and woods; the gesture under a tremendously still sky: "Oh, I'm so forsaken that I offer to any divine image my efforts at perfection!" "Oh, witches, oh, misery, oh, hatred, it is you that I trusted with my treasure." Or the doubt, infinite as the mystery of creation, the doubt of the god-contemplator, the certainty of a great Buddha sitting in a sunset with all the earth like a cataract of opals and emeralds and rubies; the doubt that is like the certainty that would exist in beautiful trees and rivers if they were conscious:

"The friend not eager, nor weak. The friend.
The beloved not tormenting nor tormented. The beloved.
The air and the world not sought after. Life.
Was it this, then?"

Then? — in the beginning. Doubt of all life seeking, like almighty eyes, the beginning.

Rimbaud is, in me, a prayer to things more beautiful than I, the perfectly soul-less things, the unconscious, beautiful things. Which are, as they were in the beginning, the witnesses of man's original greatness, the eternal (soul-less, therefore unchangeable) mirrors. The things which are not God and which are the only ones to pray to. They which sustain a poet:

Bathe me in the vision of my youth, communicate me forever.

Do not let me go back with the rest to fornicate and forget.

Let me accept the vision utterly, even to insanity.

Do not murder me with the drunkenness of you, do not choke me with the words of the beauty of you when I'm alone.

Let me accept "the atrocious death of the faithful and the lovers."

The Great Jump—Italy, U.S.A.

With a quiet majestic sea, I was sick to Gibraltar. As soon as we entered the Atlantic a fierce sea arose to greet us. Then, as if by enchantment, my sea-sickness disappeared. I ate like a hog out of dishes kept from falling from the table by little devices in wood.

Most lugubrious of all were the fog-whistles. At night they were terrific, with something somehow human in their voices. There was an old man, scared by the storm and the whistles, who kept on saying:

"Eternal Father, Eternal Father darling, Eternal Father, do me the favor of letting me live through tonight and then take me or leave me, darling Eternal Father."

In the morning we were able to admire the tremendously enraged sea. The waves were what one calls in Italian *"Cavalloni,"* equal to "Great Horses," so solid they were, large, majestic waves, grey-green. They seemed so solid and then they broke into a million diamonds and the ship proceeded through them, a-slant, one side almost out of the water. The wind blew so strongly that it did not seem safe to walk on the other side of the ship. The propellers were most of the time free of the water, and the noise they made was ominous, lugubrious.

The ship was an old, decayed hulk, having but two classes, third and second, and the waves seemed to be always oncoming, driving upon us, none running away. (Yet you are servile, waves, because you merely reflect the color of the sky.) But there is no playing with words concerning the sea. Humans only get a glimpse of what it may mean. There was no vestige left of the former blue; but there is no abusing the sea. It refuses even to call people names, it is the most powerful of powers.

On the ship there were two Genoese, elderly persons, man and wife, who ate so much, so very much, that they made one think they had never eaten enough before. Also there were three girls, laughing girls, full-breasted, red and full-faced, damnably silly. There was the old man who prayed to his damn god during the storm and there was a man that seemed to be a real friend. Morea was an anarchist. He was a handsome man, a fairly good singer and a very fine *bombardino* player. He had a grimace to his mouth which, however, seemed goodnatured and not an augury of evil things.

There was also my improvised tutor who was all that is fatuous, stupid and cowardly: a braggart, a typical bank or shop employee who dressed elegantly, talked with a drawl, spoke continually of the women he had conquered, showed me the marks of a shot in the legs or the belly, and told me of women who were crazy in love with him. Such was my tutor, bourgeois to the core, an imbecilic story-teller, a desperate liar when he found himself in shallow water, always intruding, always self-important. He was more afraid of a stain on his necktie than a slap in the face from Carnera.* No one could say, and he wouldn't have anyone say, that he wasn't spotlessly elegant. But enough of this damn fool. We left him behind forever as soon as we reached shore.

I made a dear good friend on the ship. His name was Missio and he was a philosopher. (At times his slowness used to infuriate me.) He liked Schopenhauer above all others and he was reading on ship-board, with great relish, *The World as Will and Idea.* (Life on board a boat forms itself into separate little families, small, human families united only by their humanity and by their common destination.) He had held a civil post in the Belgian Congo and he taught me a few words of the language of those people — *"soka," "malam," "menemene."* All of them have an obscene meaning. (The first words one learns of any language are always the obscenities and the blasphemies. Because obscenities are half the vocabulary of the people and the thing which

---

Editor's Note: Primo Carnera, World Heavyweight Boxing Champion in the 1930's.

interests them the deepest. Organized beastiality is infinitely more comprehensible than organized beauty.) He had splendid photographs of the African life and people, of the cretin zone he had taken charge of there. He had been called "Fist in the Mouth" by the negro porters, that being the punishment he inflicted on them.

Missio was wonderful. He was never still in that almost too great bulk of his. He was epigrammatic. He was encyclopedic. He was pantheistic, he was a philosopher all over. He was religious, and then he wasn't. He did not like great gestures. He liked to be one with the humble, the lowly, the meek, for he himself was meek. And yet he looked just like a fat merchant, somehow like a butcher too. He liked the girls a lot and was continually showing off to them with tricks and jokes. He had an abrupt way of bowing when he passed near a woman, with a gesture of the hand to one side as if he were about to lift her skirt. This made everyone laugh, and this pleased Missio too. His laughter was our passport which allowed us full freedom wherever we went. He was the most conciliatory and generous and jovial man that I ever met. (Even the complete stupidity of the three girls on board did not prevent Missio from making love to them.)

I must admit that my tutor bothered me very little since Missio kept him in his place. I was beginning to read an American novel in English. Missio was puzzled by *Huckleberry Finn,* saying it was not English, that no one could possibly understand it. Missio also told me that my friend Morea spoke an awful English, but then I did not know. Sometimes I shouted at Missio, exasperated by the fearful slowness of all his motions and his speech. But he went along, slowly, slowly, just like any old philosopher. (He was to go to Canada to find work on the strength of a letter he had to a superintendent of the Canadian Pacific Railroad. But he did not like the Canadians and he did not find work and after many tribulations he ended up as a street-cleaner. When I left Italy my father told me that I looked like a German out of work, so clumsy I was wearing an old suit of his; he said that all I could ever do in America was to be a street-cleaner — and indeed his prophecy was not far from wrong. From Canada, Missio was to send me his last dollar, writing that he would have preferred to come to New York where we could have lived or starved together. But that was a thing that never came true.)

The air had become terribly cold and one morning we awoke and saw for the first time the beginning of America.

Black—New York

One fine morning, Missio and I were awakened by a great to-do upstairs. We dressed quickly. Upstairs was New York. First to appear were the Jersey shores, spread about on the hills with little houses much like Japanese toys. On the other side, one could admire the Statue of Liberty, if one had the stomach to.

The pilot and several officials came on the ship but not even the officials could keep me from looking at the strange panorama. (One of them thought it very fine to ask every immigrant whether he had been in jail.) This was New York. This was the city we had dreamed so much about, and these were the fabulous skyscrapers. It was one of the great disillusions of my entire unhappy life. These famous skyscrapers were nothing more than great boxes standing upright or on one side, terrifically futile, frightfully irrelevant, so commonplace that one felt he had seen the same thing somewhere before.

This was the long-dreamed of New York, this awful network of fire-escapes. This was not the New York we had dreamed of, so dear to the imagination, so cherished among all the hopes a man may hope: this dream of the dreamless, this shelter of all the homeless, this impossible city. This miserable panorama before us was one of the greatest cities in the world.

Of course, I was wrong to condemn New York before I had quite seen it and before I knew its miles and miles of streets. But this depressing impression lasted even as I was walking through the city. We had been invited while aboard ship to visit the shop of one of our companions. He lived in Mott Street, one of the streets sacred to filth and misery. The whole Italian colony of Mott and Mulberry Streets, Oronxo Marginati said, was not worth the price of the small amount of dynamite required to blow it up.

The first thing that struck our eyes in this land of easy mystery (easy because readily solved) was a boot-black's box. Feeling that we needed a shine, we entered the box and suddenly heard the boss speaking to the little boy in the purest Neapolitan dialect. Then there was the elevated railroad station, an unpretentious, unassuming little box, that too.

Surely the Thirty-fourth Street dock is not a thing to give one an idea of what New York is, I thought. But after Mott Street, as we walked it dawned on me that this was no great city but a great village. It lacked the air, the smell, the noise, the atmosphere, of a metropolis. Even the Flatiron Building failed to impress us. We walked and walked, and Missio lurched along dreadfully slowly, self-satisfied and frightfully, frightfully slow. He, my new friend, was as dear to me as if he had been an old friend, and a good old friend at that, but I lost patience with him. I bawled him out, but all to no avail.

We went on foot to 128th Street, where Morea's house was. The smell on the stairs did not bespeak wealth. He and his brothers welcomed us, but his greetings were a bit too cordial. He was a false friend as will be shown later in this history.

It was the fifth of April when we entered Manhattan and the weather proved itself to be as crazy as the city. Up to ten o'clock it snowed, at twelve o'clock the sun shone, and at five in the evening the rain fell. Missio and I found me a room with board on Thirteenth Street. After settling me in he left with a smug and easy feeling for Canada, for he was bound for Ottawa. Thus I began my life in the rooming-house, the furnished-rooms of America. The landlady of this one was deaf as a bell, but she was Italian and she was the cook. There was a servant-girl who inevitably asked me if I wanted "Awful Pie." I tried to write down for her whatever I wanted, but to my surprise and indignation she never understood.

Looking for a job, I learned to know New York, every nook and cranny, every side and corner, from the Battery up to 110th Street. I walked the streets often in a frenzy of hatred and sang an Italian song sometimes and stopped to cry. I walked so much that I know still every street from Third Street to Columbus Circle, and in every street I have planted a remembrance. I learned to know Fifth Avenue, the majestic lady, elegant, proud, and beautiful. It always seemed to me that the crowds on it must have scraped their feet clean on the neighboring streets before daring to enter here. I knew every inch of Broadway, with her gaudy reckless nights; and Delancey Street, the triumph of Judaism; and Fourth Avenue, all drab, all useless; Sixth Avenue, rich with color and congested by the complex movement of the Greek quarter, where at Bryant Park one could always find a pederast in search of an adventure. The Greeks are usually very beautiful men and their wives extremely ugly — perhaps this explains why so many are perverted. I knew Forty-second Street with its Times Building breaking the sky's limpid blue, and the great canyons of high buildings around Nassau Street and Broad; Park Row flaunting its second-hand clothes, its second-hand bookshops, its shameful and horrible misery; Broadway, squalid in the downtown district, gradually takes on elegance as it advances — (I remember that number one thousand was the office of the Universal Motion Pictures Company where I went to try and sell my laboriously achieved scenarios — one thousand or six thousand, I can't remember which.) I thought the Bowery the most desolate street of all New York, so empty and hopeless and vacant it was; lacking even the fake character of so many side-streets which supported it. Here there is no more compromise for the sake of appearance: here poverty is brazen, giving not a damn for anyone or anything, for having lost everything it has now nothing left to lose. A dim haze always hung over the Bowery — a name surely recalling happier, more leisurely days when Bowery meant "shady."

Your free lunch counters saved my life, oh, New York! I would go pinching a bit of meat here and there without so much as buying a beer. The most beautiful institution of the new world was the free lunch, and now it exists no longer. And the most terrible song of New York was the bawling-out the bartenders reserved for men like me who carried rage and hunger through the streets of New York, walking, walking, until human strength was practically extinguished and something super-human or un-human had taken its place. The great contradiction of New York, that queen of the air with her fancy skyscrapers, was that she was as well a wretched whore with her little-windowed houses. Some of her streets were like the highways of Paradise, and others were like the alleyways of Hell. Prohibition served no purpose there; it was a futile thing because New York was parched unto feverishness. It needed to drink. New York, the hungry, the poverty-stricken, the youngest of all cities, it is the real advent of youth.

The JOB, that damnable affair, THE JOB. Nightmare of the hunted, THE JOB, this misery, this anxiety, this kind of neurasthenia, this ungrateful, this blood-sucking thing. THE JOB, this piecemeal death, this fear that grips you in the stomach, this sovereign lady who leaks terror, who eats the very heart out of man.

Presently I moved from Thirteenth to Twelfth Street and there I had a hall bedroom, stifling hot, without a window, where I lay on the bed half-naked or all naked. Sometimes the landlady came in with a prospective roomer and I then got up and hid behind the door until my destiny was decided on. There I would have starved if it had not been for the one meal a day my land-lady gave me. But the landlord soon grew tired of helping me and one fine evening he told me that I must suspend that one meal a day. I cried, lying in bed naked in the stifling room.

I had fifty-five cents and an employment agency required one dollar to get me a job at four dollars a week. I called on Morea, walking to 128th Street where I spent the five cents on a glass of beer. Morea was sleeping the sleep of the unjust and when I begged him for the dollar he refused me. . . . I left and descended the steps of the first subway station and there a surprise was waiting me. The subway employee threw back my fifty cent piece at me saying it was no good, and in a threatening voice, too. So in despair I walked back to my filthy room. It had begun to rain.

At last a kind man found me a job in an Italian restaurant, as waiter-helper. This was the first job of my life. It was in a table d'hôte in Eighth Street and there I worked seventeen hours a day and came back to my room at night to dream of plates, plates, plates. I worked there with all the ardor of the neophyte — I was full of joy and pride, working for the first time. I ran about like a madman from one floor to another. I was busboy to the waiters and my work consisted of setting tables and clearing the dishes away. There were six or seven waiters and I had to help them all.

My job was love and terror to me; thoughts of it kept me awake at night. For four days I had almost starved in that room in Twelfth Street and to think of losing my job was disaster and despair. I gave myself enthusiastically to it, working like a horse, and at night dreaming of the piles and stacks of dishes, dishes, dishes. At this time I made my first acquaintance with bedbugs. Although Italy is dirty, very dirty, I never saw a bedbug while there. Now whole battalions of bedbugs tormented my nights. New York is pitiless with the pitiful.

My job was my delirium, my loveless love. My companions were a bunch of unmitigated idiots, a lousy bunch of strike-breakers. They were lousy with the dirt a job is sure to produce. People have the nerve to say that work doesn't soil the hands! Nothing soils the hands so terribly as work and kills the conscience that cannot stand dirt. These idiots sometimes boasted to me of having kept a job for five, ten, twenty or more years! I shivered as I heard them: how beastly, how awful! They had even forbidden the Italian girl-workers to sing while at work. They had tried to stupefy that fine fire that was in the songs of the Italian girls. My job was my *via crucia,* my misery, my hatred, and yet I lived in continuous fear of losing the bloody thing. So there we are . . . .

How long ago was it
The dawn pleased Homer?
And Petrarca — was it among flowers
Dewfull, fearful for the love of the dawn
That he sang his best song
For Laura?
Did the eyes of joy of Prince Paul Fort
See it well once,
And was it then that he
"Took pleasure in being a Frenchman?"

In New York
These summer days
It's a swollen-faced hour,
Sick with a monstrous cold,
Gasping with the death of an expectancy.
Houses there
In a thick row
Militarily shut out the sky;
Another fence in the east;
Over this one a shameful blush
Strives upward.

> Nevertheless I go to perform the ceremony
> Of purification — to wash myself . . . .
> Oh, dear water . . . . dear, dear, soap . . . .

Because I am poor
No ceremony will clean me;
In this crowded room
All the things touch me,
Soil me.
To start a day
Feeling dirty
Is to go to war
Unbelieving.

A little happy pause here
For me to think of what I shall be doing in the day.

Now has the deep hot belly of the night
Given birth to noises.
The noises pass
Over me,
I lie
Insensible,
Under.
Work, milk, bread, clothes, potatoes, potatoes . . . .

This is
The big
Beauty rumbling on.
Is this
The world's
Music for evermore?
This and the irrevocable peddlars
Who will come in an hour
To hurl loose:
"Pota-a-a-a-a-tous, yeh-p-l-s, waa-ry meh-l-n."
Little apocalyptic faces,
Faces of the end of all faces —
Are these the chief musicians?
Please, listen, I have a small, dear soul, and all I want
is a noiseless beauty, any little things, I was born for a
sylvan century, may I claim to be left alone? . .
I will not even expect you to understand — only. . . . .
Under this, like a cold hating prostitute,
I lie
Insensible . . . .
And my face is sad because
Once
There was . . . .
Ah, there was a time . . . .

Now go look for the mail —
Go glean the thoughts they drop before your door,
You eternal gleaner.
Love thoughts, too?

    Out in the hall
    The gas jet
    Doesn't give a damn that it is day already.
    Stench of drenched clothes
    And snore
    Of married men.
    Who shall ask the furnished-room poets to write
    A song for the dawn?
Oh, MAIL!

Ah, beggars:

"I - am - though - I - refrain - from - saying - it - better -
than - you - in - the - end. I - am - perfectly - honest -
evidently - nothing - up - my - sleeves . . . . . . It - is - out -
of - my - bounteous - goodness - that - I - like - you - a -
little - in - spite - of . . . . . ."

These scanty rights to live —
A clear day, an articulate moment, may take them
    from us;
So we advance
At every chance
Our suffering claim and reference.

Dragging my soul along
I go to the window.
The sun-fingers reach slowly
Over the face of the house in front.
This is the hour they go to their work
Eastward and Westward —
Two processions,
Silent.

Shapeless the hats,
Too large the jackets and shoes —
Grotesques walking,
Grotesques for no one to laugh at.
Are they happy perhaps? —
For, of course . . . . but do they
Really know where they're going?
Has the first of them
Found
Down there
Something for his happiness?
And has he telephoned or telegraphed to the others
That they are going,
Without looking around,
Without knowing one another,
ALL
TOGETHER
Eastward and Westward?
The world has decreed:
These men go
Acknowledged
Eastward and Westward.

     Sit down and take the rest of your life,
     O, poets!

All my days
Are in this room
Pressing close against me.
I know what I have done, misdone, mistaken, misunder-
     stood, forgotten, overlooked.
And I have lost my youth.
Everybody knows me,
No one wonders at me;
They have placed me in their minds, made me small and
     tied me up
To throw me in a little dusty corner of their minds.
All my days are huddled

Close against me;
My youth is but a regret and a madness —
A madness . . . . Jesus Christ! I am not old yet, never mind
    what I have told you, what I have been!
I have not irremediably committed myself, I am not lost —
For pity's sake
Let me go,
Let me go free!
For pity's sake
Let me go
With my youth!

    Ah, the old days are huddled
    So close against my chest
    That no great freeing gesture
    Is possible.

After the tears,
Cool, new, sensitive,
Under my body hushed and stiff,
I open the door
Quietly,
I close the door behind me
Carefully.

The street's greeting:
I'm out of work —

Damn work — to work and come home in the evening
    hungry for all the things that could have been done
    instead!

    But to go
    Unemployed
    Without hunger
    At all!

Oh, listen, O Street,
Let your word to me be a delicate whisper:

I am young,
Nice day,
I look
Straight ahead,
Staccato steps,
Stiff and cool,
I walk
(Sweet morning, *soeur de charité!*)
It is the light mood in the streets of the morning,
Bouncing on the roofs, kicked
By the rosy foot of the wind.
Ah, we — ah, we are chained to the sidewalk but we hold
    our eyes upward,
Lightly, lightly.
Do blow away the dust of our dead,
And save us all from them who are smouldering inside our
    houses!
See the fine dust from those windows, see the dust angry
    at the sun!
Who threw these kids here among us, them and their fun
    and war, "GIMME! — GIMME!"
King of the triumphing mood, the iceman cracks easy puns
    with a landlady of the dust!
Kaiser of the lightness of the morning, the policeman,
    swinging his stick, writes sacred hieroglyphs.

    Furtively I steal,
    From what and whom
    I know,
    A little youth
    For myself.
    I know nothing,
    I forget nothing,
    I'm glad enough to live
    In the morning.

So my first job was in an Italian table d'hôte, the idea of it
being a mild kind of purgative for intellectual bourgeois. I was
fired within a month.

My Brother

My second job was that of an all-round boy in a grocery store. I earned two dollars and fifty cents a week and I may well say I earned it. I was fired by the owner, a Sicilian, because I dared tell him that I had had more schooling than he. My third job was in the Hotel Seville. I was fired from there after I upset a bottle of ink on a most costly tablecloth. My fourth job was at the Hotel Bossert in Brooklyn. I was fired for dropping a big trayful of dishes in front of the manager. My fifth job was in a nondescript lunch-room and lasted two weeks.

Another job I had was in the Thompson Restaurant in the Grand Central Station. I worked there one night — from seven in the evening until seven in the morning. It was my job to wash the floor, and I had to wash it three times — an immense floor. But they gave me something to eat and that was all that mattered. Another place I worked they fined me a dollar when they caught me eating a lobster. The days I was not employed by work I was employed by hunger. I dragged this wretched body from restaurant to restaurant, not as consumer but as server; I took it in misery from hotel to hotel. At times poems consumed my thoughts, moving like an army of ants in my brain, or devoured me like maggots. But more often I was desolate and forlorn. Why this preoccupation with words, I thought, if there is no one to listen to them.

America, great workhouse of the strong, you almost crushed me, but now and then I was able to rise to the surface and fight back. I was never strong enough to wound you. All these jobs were like old sagging broken-down chairs in which I sat for a little while before going on. It might have seemed there was nothing but hunger and poverty and misery to urge me on, for I was coupled with misery, like two dogs on a street-corner. But there was something else. There was always a little light shining that guided me through this country of America, this black country: I knew I was a poet and I had in my soul the desire to write. There were millions like me, of course, millions; and if these millions had a voice it would be the voice of God, like the voice of that poor Italian who wept desperately in the streets of New York remembering Neapolitan songs.

One morning I received a card from Europe advising me that my brother was in New York too and giving me his address. I rushed to that address and found him, and oh, what a day and a night we had of it! We, with this new city as background, were like two castaways on a raft in mid-ocean. We told each other all the tales of our new life and exhibited all the cash we had between us, which amounted altogether to less than fifty cents. My brother was no longer the brute who had beaten me mercilessly, he was no longer my own brother even, but my good old friend, my only comrade in this entire city, in this strange city that we no longer acknowledged, so full were we of Italy, our speech and our laughter so full of Italy, the happy eyes of each meeting the other's eyes.

My big brother and the big things he had to tell were a *fête* to me. The ghost into which my brother had turned put on a suit of flesh again and stood alive and lovely before me. I could have kissed him, but for some reason I did not.

How sweetly we laughed, laughed about nothing (it is always better to laugh over nothing at all). Although my brother had never been very intelligent, he now surpassed himself. He was witty, humorous, garrulous. All the insult and injury he had ever heaped on me slipped away down a valley of laughter. He was six feet tall and I thought how handsome he was, though before his face had always seemed to me unattractive, sometimes even repulsive. We walked together down Delancey Street, that multi-colored Jewish bazaar. At the end of this street, where one comes to bargain and to spend as little as one possibly can, stands Williamsburg Bridge, the most marvelous bridge in the world. I showed him everything — the side streets off from Delancey whose shops are full of Russian goods, copper samovars, copper fire-dogs, all giving a russet tinge to the street. Here were quilted covers in the old-fashioned style, and here you could buy cheap those Russian cigarettes with the empty cardboard ends. (One should come with weary legs to these little streets so as to feel them become light under one, as if by miracle.) We bought dill pickles from the Jews who sold these as well as other food, all of which passed through their unwashed hands, and perhaps even through their long, louse-infested beards. There is a lot of movement in these streets — a human writhing, a seething; and in their movie-houses one can always find a momentary girl simply by letting one's hands explore a little through the dark. (I have done this ignoble thing a thousand times. To be a man of honor means to tell everything, even the queerest, smallest happenings, even the most unprintable obscenities. For the truth of one single human being would be enough to horrify the most ferocious Krafft-Ebing imaginable — like the deleted chapter of Dostoievsky's *The Possessed,* in which he calmly waits for a child to hang herself in the next room. I have worse things to say, and certainly Dostoievsky had worse, but there are some words like canaries which you throttle in your fingers, and these are the words you can never say.)

And then the jobs continued: there was the C & L Restaurant where I worked three months, and this is the only job I ever regretted. I was fired because I was arrogant and all-in-all a good-for-nothing. Then the National Biscuit Company, which lasted one day. Then the Hotel Woodward, then the Yale Club, a snobbish hang-out from the twentieth floor of which I could see the East River meandering slowly, like a languid serpent, on its way. Then my father, that ignoble man, made a great effort and sent us eighteen dollars — a hundred lire! I abandoned my hole and my brother and I moved from room to room together. We fed on milk and buns and smoked cigarettes and tried to look from one room we had into the bathroom where a girl was bathing. In one rooming-house there was a negress, a real negress with enormous lips, white or yellow eyes, and pink palms to her hands which seemed to me very strange. At

last I found still another job, at Shanley's. At that time my
brother had to stay in the room while I went out to look for
work, for between us we had one pair of shoes.

One evening as I came out of Shanley's I found my brother
waiting for me. I naively told him I had my pay envelope and
he took the money, almost extorted it from my hands. So we
quarrelled fiercely, and then in a grand, majestic way my
brother flung the money to the ground. I grabbed it up and beat
it as fast as I could, then jumped on a street-car to escape him.
That night, it being too late to get a room, I slept in the park.
A few days later, he appeared in Shanley's bar-room and
threatened to break my head if I didn't give him money. I was
only saved by telling him the truth, that I had no money left.

When this job was done with I went four days without
eating and the sight of food in restaurants I passed began to
nauseate me. But when I found a crust of bread on the ground I
washed it carefully in a fountain and ate it. Picking up cigarette-
butts in the street was not the lowest thing I was reduced to
then, but still I never begged (at least not from strangers); later
on when I had friends I pestered them freely for pennies which
would permit me to eat. It was a wretched life in this land of
millionaires, and still they say that richness is nothing but a
state of mind and to the poor the lowest vice. But this wealth,
which I had no wish to acquire, and this poverty, from which
I never fled, were the great causes of my life's confusion. Hunted
by hunger, the bottom worn out of my threadbare pants, I came
to know every street of New York. Such is the competition of
life with death. (I was not afraid of death but I was afraid of
seeing so many die of hunger, as if at war.)

The Hotel of Spain was my next job and Twenty-ninth
Street my next room. (How much of myself have I left in furnished rooms, such as my falling hair which I left on every pillow?
How much of my life has been torn and lacerated and abused
and enslaved by the furnished rooms of America? If all the
hours I spent in furnished rooms could be strung as beads are
strung they would form the notes of one eternal howl that might
perhaps at last reach the ears of God. Everything that took place
passed in an enormous night through which I carried that tiny

lamp which is now about to go out.) Mr. Lehman, a German
Jew, was my landlord. I could never make out whether he was
a thorough idiot or a smart fellow playing the fool. His love
affair was a small bottle of gin, judiciously sipped. He had a
mystery, by God, but only inasmuch as we each have the mystery
of our own souls. His voice was all in his nose and he talked too
much. There I passed for a Frenchman, because I had come to
the conclusion that Italians were not well seen out of Italy. The
enormous landlady used to call me "Frenchsciugno," and when
I was behind in paying the rent she could mutter:

"You vill never pay me, nun, Frenchy, you devilish
Frenchy . . . ."

There were several bad women in this furnished-room
house, and I had many adventures with each of them. There was
Marcelle, the little Parisian prostitute, and we became good
friends when her *souteneur* was not around. We used to sit talking until three in the morning and she never thought that I
might want to possess her. She had narrow shoulders and large
hips. Thousands of years of prostitution had had this spiritual
offspring. Her laughter was good and innocent and it was with
much gracefulness that she threw her arms around my neck and
called me: "Brotha!" When either of us had money, we both ate,
but otherwise we went hungry most mirthfully together. She had
replaced Missio in my hungry heart.

One night her *souteneur* came after her and then there
was hell to pay. He called me a son of a bitch and threatened to
kill me. But he was not a bad chap and soon we made friends.
She did not love her pimp but she feared him, which is a feeling
akin to love. She told me that her task was to *"soulager le genre
humain,"* but her sin was surely never so exalted. She was merely
after her bread and butter. But the short spasm which everyone
knows was not all she gave even the foolest man who crossed her
way and her bed.

She was the daughter of a wine merchant who had educated
her by beating her black and blue. She had rebelled and run
away from home. She believed in nothing and that made her all
the more vicious and evil. For believing in God beautifies, somehow. Her flesh was accursed, and yet I craved it. Perhaps a

prostitute means disease, she means shamelessness, she means destruction to all the notions of cleanliness that infest the world. Yet she was a very clean little woman, for I assisted more than once at her ablutions. She was as good as any little girl, with a pleasant smile and a pleasing little face.

Once, as I was on the stairs talking to the landlady, a big cushion suddenly fell on me from above. I ran upstairs and knocked at the door of the guilty party and hearing "come in," I opened the door. There on the bed I saw a woman lying, naked as a newborn; she wasn't a pretty sight, either. She was an ugly bit of a woman. She was a grotesque. She had a pint of beer beside her bedstead and she was smoking a fearful cigarette, not even dreaming, just bumming her time away. An enormous scar defiled her belly, and her skin itself reminded one of beer, so covered was it with short blond hair.

This was my second love, born in contempt, born in ugliness and helplessness, born to die, having nothing better to do than die.

My brother came to this house, too: except for sleeping, he was always there. One day he asked me for a dollar and I gave it to him, my last one. I told him he had caused me to lose my job at Shanley's by walking up and down with awful intensity in front of the restaurant while I was working. Of our first meeting in New York, nothing was left. Now he disappeared and I saw him again only after two months.

And the jobs went on: Moffat's, a French table d'hôte. We busboys worked in dinner-jackets, and this absurd uniform cost me five bucks. It was a greenish-black — most ridiculous. And then a job at Gangiullo's, where I upset an order of roastbeef on the silk lining of a nondescript lady's cloak. She demanded that I pay her two dollars and a half to have it cleaned, so I lost both two dollars and a half and the job. Interminable and incessant talker that I am, I could pour out a deluge of words on every place that I have worked. America, you were a tremendous weight on my frail shoulders. It seemed to me at times that I bore you, all entire, on my back. I was never able to take you lightly, to joke with you. . . .

Waiters are enormous *coleoptera* with their wings folded. Waiters go chasing for a good customer. They wait in ambush for him. They sniff him, smell him, measure him. Outside, pure, the snow and the icy blue sky. Outside men sip the blue ice-cream of air. Outside there is salvation yet.

La, la, set it loose, shake your legs, run about like a fool, bring in the bloody roastbeef, spill the juice in the back and get the sack for it. Drop a piece of ice down a lady's bosom and go fishing for it. Oh, la, choke them with mayonnaise, stifle them under a wave of potage, yell "One soup, two soup and a bottle of champagne!" and to hell and damnation. Corks struggle in vain to attain joy.

Now a religious hour has come: one or two Jesus Christs jump on tables, spill a pitcher of ice-water on their hands, make a speech. A German, with all the awkwardness of his race, makes a whole show all by himself, a speech reeking with drunken despair. Poor Jesuses, poor makers of religion.

Shout as high as the habitation of your God, shout down the steps of running waiters, shout down the food and wine. Shout down dismay and a stubborn kind of melancholy. They are sad, these crazy people, the sadness shows in one or two faces. Pleasure, a withered rose on the breast of life. Pleasure, you are a cup of cold coffee, a plate of bad soup, a slice of roastbeef whose juice the waiters spill on their pants. Oh, poor knight-errants of pleasure, waiters are domesticated wolves carrying plates of meat they do not dare to touch.

There is nothing nice in the whole racket except for a little boy who pisses in a woman's lap and weeps, hollering: "I want to go home!" The snow outside is a virginal breast, waiting. These people are afraid of the deep hush that follows laughter.

The morning after, waiters seek for lost money in the dirt.

My Brother Returns

When my brother came back to me, which he did not fail to do when he had no more money, we took Marcelle to a fine little Italian place to eat and be merry. She was extremely grateful, which is strange enough amongst women of her trade.

Meanwhile, I had found a job in a Fifth Avenue restaurant, and my partial prosperity bred ingratitude in my breast. My brother had convinced me that we would do better to move out of Lehman's and added to that Mr. Lehman called me a man who had the education of a wood-chopper. He was aroused to this pitch of indignation because I addressed his spouse as "mistress." I explained that in Italy women are always addressed as Signora which I believed meant "mistress," and no one would ever dream of calling a lady by her actual name. Moreover, it was very hard to be grateful to such an ungainly-looking man as Mr. Lehman. So we moved away.

The new room was on Third Avenue and the elevated rushed by past our windows and was a terrible nuisance. I lost one job and found another, but in between these two jobs we knew what slow and steadfast starvation was. We ate once every two days in one of those filthy restaurants of the Bowery where they let you eat all the bread you want — that is, they do not let you but trust to your sense of decency not to eat too much bread. Pork and beans, beans and pork, pork and beans, this was our usual meal.

Then I lost the second job mentioned above, and when I announced this loss to my brother, he answered in these very words:

"Well, now you must think of earning your living by your-self."

The dirty cur — I had supported him all the while. So the next morning I beat it and left him in the lurch. I never saw him again. I did not hear of him again until they wrote me he had been killed in the war, peace to his soul.

Seventeenth Street was my next boarding-place. Here I would have starved to death if it hadn't been for the saloons where I stole food from the free lunch counter. I could not pay my rent. And here already a certain dreaminess and a certain vagueness while talking to anyone marked my days. I began reading good books, dived fearlessly into George Bernard Shaw. I remember I fell in love with one word of which I did not get the real significance: *disparagingly*.

I knew I could love to fierceness. I could squeeze a woman until her dregs came out. I had loved women but they were for the most part unbeautiful. But a beautiful woman cannot change except for the worse, any change must be towards ugliness, whereas an ugly woman can change only for the better, and they are both bound to change features every now and then. I had in my soul the image of a hen that was hatching eggs: something sweetly familiar and quiet and fecund and fertile, but something dirty, too, because all that is familiar and quiet and fecund is, in the end, dirty. Think of the awful sloppiness and dirt that flourishes in most families. And the more they love one another the more they stick to one another and everything that sticks to something must do so because it is dirty. I knew I was the most unsuccessful man in my ways of loving and playing cards and in the smaller things that took the place of my family which I had never had.

(A propos, I once slept with a young, a very young boy of the Ponente Riviera, and he did nothing but hug me all night and call me endearing names. There was not a shadow of pederasty in it, you may be sure, reader. And all the while I was being beaten, devoured by an *esquade* of fleas and worse. That was love with contour, like roasted meat and potatoes.)

I knew there were flowers in my inner self: violets in the deep grass for deep thought, roses in the open air for blood, cherry-blossoms for light joy, peonies in the sun for fierce love, daises for modesty, dandelions for fearlessness, buttercups for all that the name implies, for skipping happiness; crocuses for old men, hard to pick and when picked becoming nothing soon, and forget-me-nots, which one soon forgets because they are so small and irrelevant.

But above all I was, and I am, an envious man, madly jealous of all the writers who have got out more than one book. I was jealous (guess what I am jealous of!) — jealous even of Shakespeare. I was frantically in need of praise, crazy about my being considered a major poet. The fact that there may be other poets better than I makes my heart sick. Yet I knew I was futile, the triumph of futility.

I was comfortable without any notion of God (though I may be wicked and ugly in this connection). To be with God and not to be with God — this is a dramatic phrase that works both ways. Christ never ceased being immense to me, and I think the Evangel is the most beautiful book that was ever written. The paraphernalia of divinity has done nothing but hurt that evershining man which is Christ. Religion is always wrong, Christ is always right, even when he speaks in a minor key of the Kingdom of Heaven. He has never had my prayers but he can easily do without them. Jesus Christ was the proudest man of any and all the centuries; if he is divine, it is due simply to this pride. (Lover of poetic quarrels, he was also, this great blond poet, very beautiful according to some, and very ugly according to others.)

I have never believed in God, not even as a child, and when I utter the word "God" it is only as a sentimental symbol. Somehow God found no place in my spirit. I had always before me the things that religion had accomplished in me and other mortals. God meant often the Spanish Inquisition. . . . It seems to me that to take care of the whole universe, the stars and planets and everything, God would have to shake a mean leg. (But this is just an attempt to make God ridiculous on my part.)

At times I believed myself to be black clouds ready to burst into a blossoming of thunder and lightning, impending, always impending, never ready for big things. If you knew how brave I was when there was no need to be brave. . . .! If you knew how greatly I loved literature and yet how contemptuously I rejected it!

I was friendly now with a Dutchman who had got hold of the idea of writing scenarios for the movies. One play of ours was entitled *The Bagpipe's Call*. It was a drastic muddle of love, death, crime, and malefactors. We also wrote together *The Seven Black Men,* an absurd and interminable detective story which was naturally rejected by everyone. Another of my plays was *The Moral Law,* and it was about a priest who ended up praying for his depraved mother who had tried to have him killed by a most improbable lover. I spent five dollars to have this play typed, my first real literary work. All nonsense, but somehow the memory of it is not unpleasant. My Dutch friend, who was after all an idiot, never did much on his own account in the writing of these scenarios. In fact, he did nothing at all. He was my typist on an invisible typewriter and I saw the last of him when I abandoned him in a furnished room one early morning. It was necessary for me to beat it without being seen.

I took my waiter's jacket and escaped from this room in Seventeenth Street where I owed three or four dollars, and I set out for Coney Island. After four or five hours of walking, during which I spent my last nickel on a glass of beer, I reached that buffoon's paradise. I had some cigarettes on me and, as happens on an empty stomach, the smoke descended like living fire into my guts. Along the way I looked in the ditches for any edible roots and devoured what I found with appetite. But once in Coney Island I could find no work at once, although I tried in all the restaurants for a job as a waiter. I spent the night in an unfinished house. It was raining and I remember that lightning struck a few yards from my shelter and as I fell asleep I heard the fire-engine bell when they came to put out the fire.

The next day I got a job as dishwasher in Percoraro's Inn, a dirty shop near the sea where one could eat doubtfully-clean boiled corn on the cob. There was no beauty in the whole show of Coney Island. Insanity here reigned supreme. And the job itself was an awful proposition. At night I went to bed all wet, drenched, sick, tired, sick of being sick, a miserable boy lost in the filth and misery of a filthy job. I slept too little and too badly, and yet every morning I was able to go bathing in the sea. This was my great marriage with misery, and the offspring of this match was hunger. A wretched puny struggle to keep alive this body which wasn't worth the trouble. I was the captain of the ship of American Misery. To continue this parable of the sea: the sea offers a big glass of bitters to the sky and the sky drinks slowly and then gives it back in rain, rain falling like the tears of the sky. (Have you ever seen during a great calm the terrible lion that roars all night and will not let you sleep?) The little bathing-huts are like a dirty comment on this great poem which is the sea. Puny men try to plough it with their ships, but their ships pass and leave no trace behind them. Mother of heroes and father of fishermen, the sea hides its treasures and the shameless man seeks them so as to sell them ignominiously. In this place I heard the great bugle of the wind sound its tally-ho and the wild horses of the sea sprang up and chased each other, aroused from lethargy and champing for battle. Man spreads everywhere, like a contagious disease, and it is God Almighty, who sifts and renews the stock of the sea (as d'Annunzio has said, taking excessive liberties with this nameless God). It is our human conceit which makes us believe that we can communicate with God. (The unique, intrinsic God is certainly not good, but evil.)

I have spoken already of the sense of silent exaltation I felt sometimes while working: a faint dreaminess, a vagueness of emotion, a feeling — I say *feeling* — like a messiah, like a sweet Christ. (That has cost me many a job, I guess, for a dreamful man doesn't work right. . . .) And all of a sudden I began to write: rhymed poems at first, absurd, rhymed poetry which I sent to more than twenty magazines, getting nothing but rejection slips in return. They were variously colored slips, and from them I took stereotyped encouragement to continue. It is difficult to say how rotten the poems were and how impossible the stories. I even poetized that old drab mask, Pierrot. And then the springtime, and several other standard subjects; among them my conspicuously bad poem about the East River which oozed outside the windows of the Yale Club. I wrote desperate appeals to the magazine editors, among them William Rose Benét. He wrote me that my poems were "turgid." I was compelled to lose some precious time going to my dictionary to find out what turgid meant.

Finally an editor accepted two of my poems: it was A. R. Orage of the *Seven Arts Magazine*!

My Wife

Now let me talk about my little wife: I met her when she was on a vacation. Her room was next to mine and when either door opened one felt his own door was being opened. We fell in love right away.

(This is the way of furnished rooms. There was a young girl once who had the room next to mine. One day she showed me her naked breasts, but I was so much in need of a woman that I could do nothing about it. I gave her a box of candy but that didn't help any. She left me there, alone with a fistful of flies; which is always the case with me in life. I have always been too late, always the belated gleaner after the other gleaners have passed.)

I lived in a rooming-house kept by Vincenzo Bevilacqua, a fat moron who had a recently-imported little sister who slept in the passageway which led to my room. (Once as she was undressing and had nothing but her shirt on, I came along and seeing her had a terrible desire to attack her. But she started screaming so I let her alone.) It was thanks to Bevilacqua that I got a job at the Yale Club, and my wife came to see me there, and there we went through the whole repertoire of tricks, but still I didn't possess her. That came later in my room, where I took her half-drunk one night and where she spent a whole night with me. The result was she got pregnant and I had to have her operated — or rather she had to be operated, as she, of course, paid the bill.

(Looking from my window into the houses opposite I could see half-naked or completely naked women who did not mind showing themselves like this to my or anybody else's eyes. All living in squalid, miserable rooms, all alike, bug-ridden, hope-

lessly filthy; little ripples, these women were, on the enormous
sea of my despondency. Once in a little furnished room in Brooklyn I considered corrupting a boy of eight. This is horrible, unspeakable, and even Joseph Delteil, complete sensualist that he is,
flees aghast from his Don Juan when he entices two children to
make love together. Delteil, so sensual that he loves even the smell
of feet, has only words of censure for this precocious act. But a
clown of sensuality such as I, I know I am capable of the worst
crimes there are.)

She was a blessed little woman, my wife; blessed for the
song that was in her face, blessed for all her misfortune. Blessed
because she loved unloved, because she was a very little thing
and her love was big, her love was despair, her love depended
solely on me. Her voice was the sweetest ever, sensual in a small
way, pretty as a bird's song. Her voice was a synthesis of many
splendors. We were like fools, kissing in full Broadway.

I remember her ecstatic face, the ecstasy lasting but a few
moments. She expressed a frenzied love, with something of a
wrathful expression. It was as if her soul showed in her face.
Sweet she was, sweeter than I ever knew her to be before or after.
She cried profusely; indeed, there was not a day that passed
when she came to me that she did not cry. At first this crying of
hers sent me into an agony of pity, then gradually I got used to it,
and then finally I could not stand it any more. (Once she made
me cry by criticizing my shoes which were down at the heels.)
Everything seemed to her a good reason for crying, damn her.
She had a great receptacle of tears ready to be spilled, and this
became ludicrous.

But she could tell stories of her past in the Italian mountains
very effectively, picturesquely, and vividly. That's all she knew
how to do. She was so entirely ignorant that she wondered who
Shakespeare was, and I told her that I had just met him in the
street. The same was true of Dante. I took her to the French
theatre (she really took me, for I was always broke) to see *The
Brothers Karamazov*. She wept through the entire play. There was
a certain power in her, this little woman. She was stubborn, ob-
stinate, and sullen; but her flesh was sweet: brown, brown as the
Madonna's. She had black hair and black eyes. We went to

Coney Island together, and we went to the Italian restaurant in Sullivan Street. She was very pretty sometimes. She had a way of pushing back with her lips the veil that got entangled there.

I began to live in a glorious mist. My work on earth was different now. A heavy fog was mine, even in those days. I felt vaguely but passionately that I could be a king over kings, no Jesus Christ about it now. Maybe I could save the whole bloody world. I thought about that too. Save it from what? For save the world is easier said than done. Save the world from vain desires, from dissimulated hunger, from considering love a secondary affair, from eating too much. Save the world from all kinds of sentimentality (though I am quite sentimental myself, inasmuch as sentimentality is often sweet). Save the world from all kinds of bigotry, clerical or otherwise. Save the world from being too tired and worn-out. Save the world from being too difficult to understand, too hard to die in and too hard to live in. Save the world from being flowerless, from being too pitiful.

Keats has said that to make love is a thing very few people can do, and that no menial should boast of his ability. But I am not boasting when I speak of love here. To love is a privilege of the great, Keats said as well, and a privilege of the beautiful; but I must add that it is also given to the lowly to love, and to the ugly. Perhaps it is truer to say, as Leonardo did, that all are beautiful and great while they love, so that for a little while this woman who was my wife was both beautiful and great. (Butterflies of life, such are the days of love, and from the depths of my hospital bed I now send you my ultimate and desperate farewell!)

Have you never felt the heart of your beloved throb so close to yours at night that her heart-beats were mingled and lost in yours? Have you ever lain awake, dreaming, with your four eyes watching life slip through your fingers as light as sand? Or have you ever, like a young and marvelous God, given life lavishly away with both open hands? Have you tried to halt forever an hour which was passing too quickly? Have you felt your strength tripled, your intellect finer than the greatest genius', all because one woman was near you? All this is love. Have you ever waited, counting the hours until your love came to you, thinking how many more seconds were interposed between you and her? Have you ever been very rich with only a few pennies in your pocket? Or very poor when she was absent although you had enough money to eat for the whole day? In the little village of your love there is a little steeple of a little church which summons you to pray to God. But your entire being, even though convulsed by the storm of love, has never asked for help and never prayed for it to cease, never cried out enough, enough, I cannot bear it any more!

Have you ever seen the sky at sunset, a bloody rose shedding its petals, and realized that you were the sole spectator of a display perhaps staged only for you? Have you ever felt underfoot the running of the smooth street which made you bounce with joy like a rubber ball? Have you ever felt the blood flowing through your veins and believed that all the bliss of life was yours entirely? This, all this is love.

She had black hair, I have said. (Here is the parable of women's hair, their major beauty. Some are black as deepest night, and she was one of these; some are blond as a sunny day; some are red as the beneficent sunset or the malevolent dawn; some are grey as an overcast day, or white as clouds passing in the heavens. Rain is only the grey hair of that enormous pate, the sky; and snow is nothing but the sky's white hair, while hail is only the uncombed curly hair of heaven, and here ends the parable of women's hair.) She had just enough intelligence to deceive one and because she gave herself to me when she was half-drunk, that bound us together a little more. That's about the best of my remembrances of her and her ways.

And, speaking of love, here I must mention the dearest friend of my life: Louis Grudin. He was not a good-looking boy: his features were roughly hewn and his nose shapeless, his mouth too thick-lipped, his eyes vague but not unbeautiful, his stride too much for him, his voice quite booming, his hat out-of-mode and ugly, his pants without any creases, bagging at the knees, his jacket ill-fitting, his ways rough but not indelicate, his heart good and big, his sense of irony strong, his sense of humor keen and always alert, his love affairs always unfortunate, his sweetheart a ridiculously fat girl in whom he believed as in an oracle, his appearance in military clothes ponderous but not startling, his love for noises and his own noisiness there all the time, his disgust for sex and his love for coffee (red hot coffee which he swallowed valiantly), his utter purity concerning sexual matters, his revolutionary ideas concerning love, his country, his government, his being a Litvak Jew — all these things made him himself. (I find myself curiously satisfied with the friendship of Jews. There is nothing equivalent to their intelligence, their hospitality; utterly misunderstood, despised, treated with a solemn presumption, these fine and beautiful people! Only the aesthetic of a barber could maintain they are unbeautiful.)

Big boy, Lou, you were bursting through your soldier-uniform, big fat boy, you! We sent the universe to smithereens, we conquered the world, nay, the worlds! We were lords of the road, walking all night. We sang *"Winter Sturme Weichen den Wonne Mond,"* not caring whether we were grammatically correct. We walked sometimes the whole night through, shouting our ideas to the stars and the moon, awfully glad we were intelligent, terribly proud of our intelligence, that saviour of our bodies, that which saved and proclaimed this manner of living.

Every time we passed under the Woolworth Building, Louis Grudin would take off his hat in homage. I liked him so well because I thought he was a better edition of myself. But instead, we were as different as bread and butter are, although both things are food. His verse was more beautiful than he ever imagined. In it were large, majestic rhythms, and a certain prettiness, a certain humor. He called me "master" and "teacher," but if I brought him my knowledge of Rimbaud and Laforgue, he gave me the knowledge of American letters. I told him he resembled Romain Rolland's Jean-Christophe, and he told me I was being sentimental.

You are a whole sky for my memory, dear Lou. I ate and drank of you, I admired you, however incoherently, tremendously. Though you called me "master," it was I who learned from you, all the time. Your strength, your manliness, your energy were things you gave away. Very humbly I acknowledge all you did for me. Yes, my dear, your friendship was a great thing for me. I know that I was inferior to you, and once you wrote in a little book:

"He was afraid of me and his bed was filthy."

"Va, garde ta pitié
comme ton ironie—" Rimbaud

She brought a dove to the house. She had caught it in the street as she was coming home from work:

"It couldn't fly and I just caught it!"

I had just come home from work, too, and the dried sweat covered me like a second skin. With nostalgia for my heart, my nose was sipping the evening Spring.

So the dove came through the door in her hand into my life.

I took it and touched the soft grey wing of it with my dirty face. The two dots of its eyes said nothing. The grip of its red claws was gentle, and in my fingers it rested as lightly as a cloudlet of fog. If I put it on the floor, it just ran away. It ran away all the time. Every time I attempted to go near it, it just began to stagger along, faster and faster, away from my impending fingers. We had to feed it: open its beak and force in chunks of soaked bread and hard-boiled egg. It did not like to eat and it would shake its head in quick disgust.

But, above all, it would make dirty things all over the house. In every corner, everywhere, in the morning, I found green and white little things. Rosaries and constellations of them, sometimes like an ornament, sometimes like a disease. It made us sick, the way that creature indulged in that! Even on my jacket it did it once when I lay down to read and put it on my chest for aesthetic accompaniment to my reading.

If the window was open it would attempt a clumsily desperate flight toward it. The real light, not borrowed or stolen lights of the houses, was there, I suppose; the air, and whatever a dove eats with pleasure; mother and sister and brother and real home — I suppose. But we did not want to let it go. We thought we'd fatten it and eat it afterwards. We could not let it go.

And we couldn't seriously think of fattening it with the view of eating it afterwards. Because we both hovered over the dove for long stretches of time, talking about it, making vague suppositions. Because we were happy looking at it, seeing how the room awoke to the tingle of its clean grey. Perhaps it was rather the room sinking into the most dismal realization of its own squalid slovenliness, as the little grey note rang unconcernedly before the hardened and self-important face of the immobile furniture.

I was often angry to think of my emotion as I had touched the dove for the first time. Not a response to my affection had it given. Not a noise.

It would only run away and twist its head extraordinarily and shudder with its neck and beak when I forced bits of hard-boiled egg down its clean brown throat. If I left it alone it would puff up and burrow into its ruffled plumes and remain still for hours.

She did not like it because it made of the whole house a filthy place. But she never really thought of killing it. And neither did I, though I hated it, often, when it tried to run away. Once it tried to make for the door as I was going out and I kicked it inside. I kicked it up in the air. It flapped badly down and struck the ground with one wing spread. But it didn't complain. It did not twist its head around to see who had done it; it just ran away.

To try to explain, so as to make the sadness bearable. Which means, to rebel against sadness, which would lead us to a splendid and terrible death. The dove would not acknowledge us. We were two sad persons longing for a sweetness that had forever flown out of the reach of our heavy fingertips.

"Damn strangers," it must have thought of us. Desperately so, rather, little dove, desperately and hopelessly strangers.

One may not touch sweetness with hands that are sweet but not sweet enough — only coarse hands or divine hands may

touch you, stubborn little grey dream. But I can imprison you
here and you won't go away, you must stay — yon can't deny
that I am keeping you, that you are somewhat with me. That's
where I have one on you, as they say, those horrible persons.

Ah, you are a little darling cloud descended . . .
descended to prove to them that clouds may be held
in our hands and caressed, as though
they were things of our own, of a tissue alike to our flesh.

No, you don't want to be caressed. A long time ago there
was a covenant of silence between the clouds and men. The first
human word broke the covenant and now all the human words
in all the books are not sufficient to piece together the covenant
again.

Dove,
with your red claws like
a frozen lean red flower.
Your breast is so soft
that human fingers
might die there,
Dove.

I am not yet beautiful because no one has come to ask of
my flesh all the love that is in my flesh. So I am anchored to
their streets and to the floors of their houses by the weight of
sunken desires. But I know that children will come to me, my
own children, and I know that I will not caress my child with
hands that are less than beautiful. And children answer us,
whereas you, dove, are silent.

But children . . . .
do children answer us?

As we expected, it died. She, who had gone in my room
where the dove's sleeping-place was, got its box from under the
table and saw it — half-spread wings pushed against the corner
of the box, still warm.

It stayed unwillingly and it was too proud to formulate a protest. So it objected by dying, a haughty objection, perhaps an infinite objection, certainly an irrevocable and an irrefutable one.

"Ooooh," cried she. She ran to me. "It died, you know. Come and see it."

I bewailed its death for a few minutes. I was in dismay. We were silent for a long time after, both of us, knowing that if we should speak we'd have to mention the dove. I could have told her things and things. I could have told her: "Let's cry now, not because we really loved it, not because it is a loss, but because . . ." I could have told her things and things, but they were things I could not tell *her*. She was not anything like a dove, ah!

Instead, instead — I write here a sort of lying tale. And I imagine, here, that I spoke to the dove after its death, thus: You died.

I'm so tired, the weather is close and I wanted to whip this damned silence away from me with some awful words, and you — you wanted to do a sinister deed so that I shouldn't get up and whip this damned silence away from me. You wanted to do something sinister and you did it and death has knocked the curves off your body, sucked the flowing liquor in your wings and left them dry and half-spread, shrunken; pushed you crudely down into the corner of that box.

I am glad, dove, that you died in my room. Some disease was due, overdue, and you come and die, right here. I'm glad. Your breast is tepid and your eyelids are extraordinarily broad and loose, the eyelids of an old woman with wrinkles of lead. Your eyelids cover only half the two still small moons of your eyes, as though the weird mystery were not ended. (Ah, get a zoologist and ask him why a dove's eyes do not shut when a dove has died. . . .) Your claws are an old little twig. Your beak has tight curves and ridges. It looks like the nose of an old man which debauchery has smoothed and polished so that it is smooth and lean and shiny. My hands that hold you are horrible! It is sweetness that is dead. Sweetness came into my house and its death has been sinister. Do you wonder?

"Oooh, cried she. "It died, you know."

I asked: "What'll you do with it? We can't eat it, can we?"

"Of course not. It died of itself."

"I'll throw it — out of the window."

"Do," she whispered.

"Where?"

"Oh, in the yard," she whispered.

"Yes," I whispered.

I took it gently. I remember how gently I took it. I was afraid to squeeze it, afraid to hurt it. I did not look at it. I held my arm stiff, held it down, as if it stank — but of course it was still warm. I opened the window with one hand and I threw it down — no, I didn't. I dropped it. I just opened my hand, quickly. And I did not look at it fall. It was absolutely black, and a passing train that moment whistled. I shivered for that whistle. Damned little corpse!

I only remember it at times, on these occasions: when I try to light a match and can't, whenever, washing my hands, I get wet all over, whenever I drop a fork or a spoon and pick it up and it falls again — then I remember the dove: how I wouldn't let it be anywhere, how it would stagger away, faster and faster, annoyed.

Home, Sweet Home!

The way to my house begins half a mile away from it. It begins at the corner where the grey-purple sweating Hartford Lunch is. From Broadway into the street, the air becomes denser, the facades are more resolutely drab, a sagging of the Broadway mood makes my heart faint in an indefinite sorrow. This little tragedy happens every day, each time I am on the way to my house.

I walk on, westward. Amsterdam Avenue is low and broad; its face is sullen and without a forehead. Food stores, like men that are too fat, cigar stores like little bigoted spinsters dressed in clothes not dirty but brittle with oldness. Broken and old is the Avenue's bed and adorned only by the car-line. Then, further westward, I march into open misery: usual red facades or sick-yellow ones, riddled full of black windows. Rags, like flags of poverty, dangle from windows; grey panes where misery writes with dust and rain things that the tenants are too dismal to want to cancel. Opposite the tower the obese gas tanks, dolorous wih rust, sick with blotches of grey paint, grotesquely solemn. Along this block human beings prefer the street to the home; so they are all outside, the children playing, the women gossiping, the men loafing. Burnt-out coal and ashes spilled from the overflowing ash-cans are strewn over the bulging and rippled and cracked sidewalk.

I turn at the corner where the necessary wooden-faced saloon is. And there is West End Avenue. Whitish and greenish the houses, the colors of the wives of the poor wops. Here is a valley formed by two smooth asphalt hillsides. And here is my house. The door of it is as dirty and drivelling as the mouth of a very old man who chews tobacco. Way upstairs are my rooms.

I enter, I open the windows. . . . . "Damn it, why does she close them?" She says that they might get in from the fire-escape. I would like to meet the desperado who'd be so desperate as to come around these quarters to steal! A wave of dank smell has lapped me around. I have taken a chair and sat down. Now I'm in my own home!

The rooms face north. Till ten o'clock in the morning we have the sun. The rest of the day it's on the house opposite. In front of my window there is a straight, windowless, white wall, jagged along its edge with chimney stacks. These crazy stacks are poised gently against the sky which today is very blue. Craning my neck out I can see the river, and the freight railroad station with its asthmatic locomotives.

There was a stretch of bare ground between the railroad and my house. It was a meeting place for cats and dogs without a home, and at night a fine big hall for their orchestra. That's where they came to die, too, and where their corpses were thrown. They went there to fumble in the rubbish for food. A single shoe here, and a pair of shoes down there, half a dish, a saucepan camouflaged by rust, a smashed box, the brim of a derby, and rags hardened with dirt; a battlefield after the battle, with the lonely corpse of a cat and the lonely corpse of a dog, one left by the fence, the other in a big crater in the middle. There came children to reconstruct, with their fiery imaginations, the battle of the cats and dogs. But they didn't stay long because it smelled bad. Sometimes after a rain, as a great big puddle collected there, you could see them running all around what they called its shore, romancing with little paper boats and seeking the ever-new sensation of throwing a stone into the water.

Now, in that space, they are building another house. A house like this, I suppose. It will be so near the railroad and the asthma of the locomotives is so nasty, so sore, especially at night, that the tenants of the future house won't be able to sleep — not until they've all become deaf! Another poor house, and there are thousands and thousands. It's preparedness, to build a house to shelter the poor. Like making guns and gasmasks for the next war, the war that isn't here yet. And the city is totally grey . . . . and they're making another grey house! Houses that are born poor and old, or ugly, as in the middle-class or rich quarters. In Italy I saw houses born white and beautiful; and when they were old and miserable, they wore their misery like a soldier his uniform that bullets have tattered. Add grey on grey, brown on brown, masons of the New World, makers of the New World, grey on grey, brown on brown, work for the great blindness to come!

But, as I write, the dredge is wheezing and crackling and whistling, and its three-toothed jaws are eating the ground, then vomiting it into a motorcar which staggers, tired and drunk, up the slope out of the big hole where the dredge is sitting.

But let's begin with the roof; it's nearer the sky. Let's begin from the roof. I breathe better up here than in my room or in the street. It is sunset time. The burning clouds breathe the rosy air that caresses me. They give me this air the way my wife gives me perfume out of her clothes. This air throws itself, elastic, upon the dusty body of that block of houses, lover of an old man, young lover. And the dust clings still on the houses. It passes through my fingers in ribbons, and its silver fingernails open my skull and pluck the stale misery out. Of a sudden, a great pool of melted thin gold is dropped over the roof. I am in it, burning crisp like a piece of paper. It is the gold of the sunset mixed with the black dust of the night to come. Under me, the great space of bare ground I have mentioned fills slowly with darkness; it is an enormous vase rimmed with a blue band of river water. If I were good, my mind too would fill slowly with darkness and there would be a play of silent shadows in my mind. But I stretch my arms, and my lungs and my crooked fingers would grasp something more than air. If I were old, I would be satisfied being alone, and I would sit still and let the darkness swaddle me. Night, and the friends who think or do not think of me, frighten me. The friends are afraid to dabble in me, as though they saw me as a pond of treacherous green water. My face is often green, that's why.

I don't want to go down to my rooms any more. I don't want to see her any more. I want the Earth to stop running around like a damn fool, and I want him to listen to a thing I have to say. I want the Earth to stop going, and I want him to watch me die. I could touch this intangible air if I sent my body whirling through it, in a spider's dance, to break over the flagstones. I would give a hundred persons at least the thrill of their lives. I want the setting sun to steal my eyes and carry them along with him under the earth.

But I reckon I shall walk down again to my apartment. And every day that cranes its grey face toward me will have my offering of a few words. I reckon I shall walk down to my apartment and open the door with a Yale key, just like everybody. And they will not say that I have gone away from them to find the truth. They will not say I did not love them, and they will admit that I am the most American of Americans. . . . Always my great sadness looms beyond my world and theirs, just as the sun lies beyond all weathers. Words do not make me glad, and I am not an artist. Frightful words uttered by a thousand in a thousand ways are all comprehensible to me, because my own word is more frightful than any. That is the word that was first and which shall be the last when they join my eyelashes in their last kiss and my two hands shall touch in their last caress; a word that you might mistake for the word Death.

I am an emigrant and I have left my home. I am homeless and I want a home. You look at me with evil eyes, with squinting eyes; you don't look at me, you sneer at me. I am an emigrant waiting. I know millions that are like me.

Come, friends! We shall find one another again with the words of my confession! Don't insult me by calling me "writer" and I won't call you "butcher," "grocer," "waiter," "doctor," "businessman," "thief," and "murderer." Listen a while, if you please. Beside a few scandalous items, such as: the wife works oftener than I (in fact, she works all the time, and I only now and then), I am all right. And, don't worry, I have them all on my conscience, the days of loafing and writing! (But, God! still heavier on my conscience are the days lost working in a restaurant or in a factory.)

Let God congratulate himself on the simple things He

turns out of the ground which go, dressed in humility's colors, to bring a modest happiness into every house: potatoes, rhubarb, beans, lettuce, and radishes. (The wife is working and I am not, so I do the things around the house.) You peel the rhubarb, and slowly a soft heap of pink and green and silver-green ribbons accumulates under your fingers. And the potatoes spit a whiff of country sturdiness to your nose. Perfumed reality of the dirt — ladies say you smell bad, ladies who smell bad with bad perfume, which is nothing but the perfume of flowers turned stale, turned bad. Then, when you boil the potatoes, they become white as purity and they break if you touch them with a fork. There is a miniature storm in the pot — the potatoes thunder under the swelling cloud of the steam.

As for spaghetti and ravioli, let me tell you once and for all that parsley chopped fine, and one small onion, and. . . . Yes, people do think I am interesting! Characteristically an Italian, don't you know! And it's just what they want: the local color, that attractive and light way of talking, and those very extraordinary neckties . . . oh, perfectly charming! And anyway Dante died quite a long time ago, and there was a dash of Teuton blood in him, I bet! Cagliostro is more the Latin, and today fierce men à la Cagliostro are out of fashion. "The good-mannered man is the man of the future," a certain gentleman told me. The harmless charming little man — oh, the ladies all patronize him! — and if he writes some tiny verses now and then, well, what of it? That's one quality more, it only adds to the charm; and let him be fiery too, on certain occasions — that adds to.

Alone with my wife, I have meals that are feasts. Anti-puritan meals. To the eternal glory of the magnificent eaters of my old land, Lorenzo de' Medici, Alessandro Borgia, Leone X, and Carnaro before he had got tired. Crunching a plant of dandelion under my teeth I devour with my eyes the small space of my wife's breasts that she lets me see — eating a bleeding beefsteak. . . . . God! We are in a cage, but we are lions and monkeys yet! And if, in ten years, people will chew food-stuff instead of eating, what the hell! We eat and laugh now, we eat and weep together, eh, girl? And no one knows we have a real home, by Jesus Christ, so they'll leave us alone.

I go into the kitchen, nibble at a piece of cheese and a loaf of bread, walk up and down, wash my face to chill the headache, walk all through the house, stop in front of each mirror to see whether my face has assumed at last a less vague aspect, whether there is yet on it the beginning of something that these weary hands and legs may follow.

The wind falters and gasps like a furnished-room-house landlady coming up the stairs. The wind comes, breast forward, into the space between that high wall and my window and puffs up my curtains. I sit by the window and the curtains touch my face again and again, doting lovelessly. The wife has gone to work and left everything upside down and even her room today affords no coolness of things put in their right place, nor the gleam of clean brushes and mirrors and panes. Like me, the bed is stretched in its own disorder and no invitation is in it. Sex is tormenting me, that kind of unhappy lust of a weary mind. The decay of a room is in its things and all the wind brings is some more dust and the thick stench of boiling laundry from the floor below. I went to look at the letter-box downstairs about ten times today. All they send is words, anyway, and I know all about words. I am a writer.

I have heard old men, half-blind and half-deaf, blabber of home, sweet home, and an immense lady-teacher (weighing more than two hundred and fifty pounds), a long time ago in my childhood taught me the song:

> *Casa mia, casa mia,*
> *benche piccola tu sia . . .*

(House of mine, house of mine, however small thou art . . . .) I have read all the big books, *Jean-Christophe* size books, books which contain the bulk of a house, THE HOUSE. But my house is one of today and she is like a modern girl with whom you have to be careful if you want to keep her; and the moment she jilts you, or you see a better one, everything is ended and nothing remains in the heart of you or anywhere

else; maybe a twisted smile remains. We have now become used
to tragedy.

Mornings of blue veils and rose veils fluttering in and out
of the windows. Air for butterflies in the spring. Ah, any face
in the frame of any window, how sweet and well-known! But
your face best of all, woman, when you sleep yet in the morning
and I, who got up early and am cool and smell of cleanliness
and toothpaste, come to kiss you. You awake the way a little
ripple breaks against the shore. Your drowsy arms move like
the smoke of a cigarette. Your kiss is warm with sleep. It is not
love, dear, because there is no pain. It is the home. Witness the
kids that have started making a noise that we both know so
well, witness the tranquility of my feet as they step upon the
carpet, witness the farina boiling, blabbering, blowing, sputter-
ing, puffing and spitting, on the gas range. Witness the underwear dancing on the fire-escape — and you washed it last night
while I was fooling around and bothering you. The river is only
a light surface — a blue veil, too. We shall take a walk along
the Drive. . . .

How good the home is to those who come back from a
walk! These things that know me too. Lunchtime, lunchtime!
Oh, the dear little tree of parsley in the glass by the sink! Last
night all the carpets were swollen with dust. Now they are clean,
naked. The bed is so well made — it is like a new book, yet
unopened. Black-stained bananas, what perfume your skin holds!
Peel them and delight! The smell of cooking food is incense for
the gods that will never die, and the color of the salad you are
making is the flag of mine own soul!

The eyes of the wife are two little black cats, washed and
smooth-haired. If we weren't here together I should never have
the time to see her so well. And there is the river — if you take
the trouble to crane your neck out the window. When you are
quiet, when the hungers are hushed, then you will get a lot of
fun out of hearing a wop sing, while downstairs the neighbors
fight over their horrible old troubles. The light wind winnows
your hungers, sifts them — and sometimes leaves only a gentle

sadness, crisp and clean, like yellow leaves by the roadside. Every locomotive that passes is a new image in the brain, every fierce puff a different part of the same not unpleasant sonata.

At night, the lights alongside the river kindle many diamonds everywhere — glints of ripples, rails, and window-panes. The fires of the city in the night are the fireplaces beside which the tragic old gods sit in order to forget how intricate is the world they made. In the moonlit night, the frayed profile of the Palisades is deep black. Spring air, which you had forgotten, which you never thought would come again, is here, aloofly holding in her kind hands our weary hearts.

The wife moves about, working, and from her childish hands come cleanliness, order, and good smell to the home — and caresses for me. If I have done my work well, I have kept sadness away. Despair always comes from outside. The trouble is, one can't keep the place shut well enough. In the night, the gaslight is a sun of a diseased world, and the table, the chairs, the bookshelf, are sapless and silent, like lepers. The bookshelf. The books. Any book. The first line of the first book pulls along all the lines of all the books. I have them all in my blood, these little black microbes — once you read one you're infected and chronic. And they shout too loud! It's a shame to let people print such things! Aren't you afraid? We, the readers, pass before the gaping graves of these books, before these bodies torn asunder, we watch a man stretch an arm out of his grave and shake his bloody heart at us, and we say, "I like . . . I like . . . I don't like . . ."

I burn with restlessness, I smoulder without fire, and my bed sheets smell with my yesterdays. I can't sleep. There are many persons here, bothering me. All uninvited guests crowding around my bed, shamelessly curious — I can't dismiss them. I can't touch them. I can't grasp a hand and feel it like a realization in my fingers — these are real ghosts! They ask all sorts of impossible questions, and each of them has a naked soul to show me that nauseates me. You come into my home, at night, to exhibit your shames, damn little beggars, you! Those eyes I saw today that seemed to acknowledge me so naively, now they want to know so much. To them all I can't be anything else but a man who is in bed and can't sleep. And these people are the same whom I said I loved, whom I caressed, whom I even kissed, during this same day. The daylight is a liar! I must run away from those people who do not love me enough.

I go into the other room where she sleeps. I go there to get from her all the strength my heart needs to beat its next beat. If she knew how many things I want she'd be so desperate, she'd scream and die. But as it is she gives back the kiss and a drowsy arm comes out and binds me to her warm face. Thus I take much, very much, and I steal back into my room afraid that even the silence might know of my theft. . . .

Now you can see the dust on everything, there's no sun and no wind. Outside, the rain is drilling holes into the aching skull of the dirty earth. The room throws its yellow breath on the tall white wall. Everything is resting. Everything weighs upon something else and if a metaphor were miraculous, this whole room would dash down to the ground. Everything is still but nothing sleeps at night except the men and women who snore, who whistle and wheeze and grunt and roar in a regular, rhythmical, continuous rage.

I get up and go into the kitchen. To survey the pans and dishes a little. An aluminum pan shines like a bald head in a darkened theatre and some sauce-pans are holes of deeper darkness in the darkness. A chair is sitting quietly in the shadow. A sinister shadow binds the legs of the table. The fire-escape is a skeleton peeping in.

In my room, the typewriter hides under its cover, the white-glaring bed shrieks. The scars and blotches on the wall make strange faces at me. Outside, the trains puff and blow fiercely. They want to rip the universe! They are throbbings of the physical pain of the Earth. The locomotive driver, the damn fool who makes that noise, who thinks it's good for him or for anybody to make that noise, who thinks it is good for him not to consider me, not to consider that I can't stand that noise . . . . that I can't stand it . . . . I can't, I can't!

Beginning a Literary Career

I lived in Willoughby Street in Brooklyn for a few months — perhaps the darkest months of my life. I shovelled snow — a terrible ordeal for a weakling like myself. (It was in this room that I possessed my wife for the first time, when she was only my fiancée.) As yet I wasn't a poet, I was only a reader, but there I wrote one line. I wrote: Love is a mine hidden in the mountain of our old age.

Then I lived in Thirty-seventh Street near Eighth Avenue, in that house with green walls where I met a Polack who wanted to throw his dictionary at me when I woke him up with my singing. (It was here I won the first prize in *Poetry,* which I drank up almost entirely in gin fizzes.) I was like a fisherman adrift on the sea, floating helpless on a raft, kept afloat by God knows what promise or strength or hope. This I always was. And what did I fish in the sea of friendship, or what did I try to fish? Here came Louis Grudin, and he and I set out together to call on the best writers of New York.

We went to see Max Eastman who gave us each a copy of his *Understanding Poetry*. He had very becoming grey hair, becoming because the rest of his face was very young. There was youthfulness in the appearance of Max Eastman but there was no youth in the sermons of this man. We went to see Louis Untermeyer who also gave us autographed copies of one of his books and almost shame-facedly showed us a book of smutty pictures. We went to see Babette Deutsch who showed us her leg covered by a stocking full of indecent holes. But her mother was quite aristocratic. We went to see Alfred Kreymborg, and he was our first real acquaintance in a literary way. I think about the worst sort of autobiography is Kreymborg's *Troubadour* and Harry Kemp's *Tramping On Life*. The former is so bland that it permits of no criticism. In it Kreymborg mentions about half a hundred writers without giving us any idea of what these men are. The latter is thoroughly stupid, cold, silly, rather prepossessing, ponderous without strength — the work of a jackass of literature. He was the idol of those who look for poetry in the tail-piece of any magazine. Surely if I can't do better than those two men I am a goner, I am done for.

All is death in those two books. I read Kreymborg's first book, *Mushrooms*. It was full of nostalgia, full of little poems, sometimes irrelevant, sometimes pleasing, sometimes amusing, sometimes startling. (But the poison of his later work has got me to the bone. What he says of his wife isn't sufficient. What he repeats and repeats is not worth repeating.) Yet Kreymborg was, and still is I hope, a good friend of mine. But friendship must not interfere. As for Harry Kemp, I always despised the man and the writer. There isn't a page that can be called even lovely. He trampled on life with too careless a foot.

Alfred Kreymborg took us to the house of that ultra-modern saint, Lola Ridge. Emily Dickinson meant poetical solitude; she meant thinking solitude of a poetic kind, Chinese daintiness at times. Adelaide Crapsey meant sadness, sometimes rebellion, too, but a sweet sad rebellion. Amy Lowell meant voluminous and disorderly culture, wordiness, exaggeration; all of which may go under the heading that would comprehend the case of most women artists — Weakness. But as for Lola Ridge, to fit her case no diminutive adjective could serve. It is not a case of sweetness nor any of those qualities which, up to date, have belonged to women writers. She is a poet, that's all.

Talk of propaganda here, was what I wrote of her poems. I wish every poet had something as strong and virile to uphold! It is not a matter of politics, it's a matter of such damning hatred and love as would turn a modern city to ashes. Virile? — it may be an insult to use that adjective since Lola Ridge has begun an era in which for a woman to be virile, i.e., masculine, might mean to be weaker. I think she is one of the most beautiful signs we have of woman's emancipation and independence. Let her be a socialist; this rebellion of hers is pure beauty, it is sanctified, it is nothing less than burning human blood. It is no longer that particular fact of the revolt against actual social conditions, which is, unfortunately, what affects today's socialists and anarchists. It is an eternal thing, the thing that caused Prometheus to be bound. It's the fire of heaven burning in this wonderful woman's blood.

The words of her poems are so intensely vivid, they are so palpable, so physically tangible that they whip or stab — they hurt. There is a ghastliness here caused by an excess of pain and sorrow. And it is her integrity of impulse and emotion that makes her shun more elaborate rhythm forms for a perfectly simple and equal one; although her rhythmical sense is richer than that of certain poets who discover forms as one finds mushrooms after a rain. She is a woman suffering — with the snarl of a lioness, rather. It is a lioness flinging herself madly against the walls of the ugly city.

In this room I discovered Ezra Pound. I read his *Pavannes and Divisions,* and I wrote these words about him: there is a word which one associates with Dostoievsky's works — Sorrow; as we think of Walt Whitman the word may be Joy; for Mr. Pound the word is Irritation. Irritation inspires him and he inspires irritation in his readers. Here he had made a translation of Laforgue in which Mr. Pound achieved a thing worthy of observation: he was true to the letter (almost) of the original and at the same time had betrayed and desecrated it. Laforgue's satires are veiled by a delicate and almost haughty modesty, and they have a sorrowful humble way; this becomes boisterous in the translation, reminding one of what Billy Sunday did to Christ.

This book, taken as a whole, is Mr. Pound's profession of faith in art. A faith in art which consists of a few "DON'TS" shouted at some imaginary and improbable followers; of repetitions of phrases by old and ancient masters, duly stripped of their original glamor, as all repetitions are. (One finds in this book a formula almost directly translated from a famous passage of Rimbaud's *Les Illuminations:* "It is the presentation of such a 'complex' instantaneously which gives that sense of sudden liberation.") It is a faith in art that becomes militant in a fierce little contempt for America. Look, he's throwing pebbles at our sky-scrapers, O People! And a provincial and bourgeois quarrel with the provincial and bourgeois in art. A faith in art that has no love, no ecstasy, not even drunkenness. Here a sulking, aggressive, self-conscious man scowls at you from behind every sentence. He tells us that he takes "no pleasure in writing this. . . . ." Boosting James Joyce, he cannot find a more enthusiastic or enlightening phrase than, "He gives us Dublin as it *presumably* is"; or "He gives the thing as it is." Giving *the thing* as it is he calls realism.

I might praise the book and say that there is in it a sort of dignified love for art and art concepts. But how can I? — this love is so cold and so awkward that it inspires no sympathy. It is probably an affair between Mr. Pound and some Grecian wraiths, and we are unable to say just how immoral or lively it is. And is it love? If so, it is an ugly love. Rather the crudity and the bombast of an earnest beginner, rather all the pathetic attitudes of self-glorification and self-abnegation with which incomplete artists daily pester the world than this sophisticated love towards Her; for She is a tough-handed and strong-smelling Woman. Rather the uncouth *gaffes* of an adolescent than this philandering with fawns and nymphs and mouldy reminiscences of Pan — a nasty way of snubbing this great Woman who slings, in passing, streetfuls of dust of today's cities; whose favorite perfume is the loam — the loam that soils the hands of dudes and snobs. Rather morbid and talkative love than this ungainly abstinence from raptures for fear of clumsiness; rather coarseness that is tender-hearted and foolishly weeps and foolishly laughs than this delicacy and aloofness achieved and striven for without drama.

I would praise the book and be pleased at Mr. Pound's sincere love for James Joyce, Ford Madox Ford, T. S. Eliot, and Laforgue; exult in the fact that he was one of the first who spoke at all of Laforgue to the English-speaking-and-not-reading-public. But how can I? — I like these men well enough myself and his enthusiasm is so slack that it disconcerts mine. And as for Laforgue, I love him so that I am ashamed for Laforgue of

Mr. Pound's indecent flirting. As for the elucidations which might pass instead of enthusiasm — "If the nineteenth century had built itself on Crabbe? Ah, if! But no, they wanted confections." Naughty child, that little nineteenth century! Mr. Pound talks of the experts, of such men as may die of a harsh sound inadvertently caught by their ears. We know them, *ces delicats*. It's Oscar Wilde who wrings new postures and new words out of poor Salomé (she was an adolescent and she had a human tendency to be obvious); who writes of men flinging themselves languorously on sofas — and refuses to sit down in Whitman's room for fear of soiling his clothes. It is Remy de Gourmont, with his perfectly charming receptiveness, who cowers at the sight of such a forsaken, accursed and violent genius as Rimbaud and gossips about the tragedy of the splendid youth. It's Gustave Kahn who quibbles as to whether Laforgue is a symbolist or not, while Laforgue's aloofness and sorrow and death are among those mistakes or crimes of the world for which the world never gives an account or an apology.

Attitudes and opinions are such things as may be bought, sold, and exchanged, like clothes; they are never contributors to the welfare of the world. Men are forces within the world and when they become conscious one hears an exaltation or a complaint; and these are signs of life. Ezra Pound has estranged himself, and this is our resolution: he cannot talk to us. By us, I mean readers, artists, and shoemakers. We — and I stand together with all the fools he so hopelessly curses — acknowledge that there are many things the matter with us; but we realize that he is not really interested and we consider his talk an intrusion. He irritates us.

As it happened, the *Seven Arts* never published my work. It died before it had a chance to do so. But A. R. Orage, the editor, who was not like a storm at all, was indeed the typical great man. That is, he listened with great patience to my bellyaching and gave me a luxurious cigar. He also gave me a little grey magazine and told me to write for it, which I did. The little magazine was edited by Harriet Monroe and its name was *Poetry*. I sent her stuff and it was accepted. Later on, for these poems, I won the famous fifty-dollar prize.

I went to unstorm-like Orage once more, attracted very much by the hope of another good cigar, and he gave me twenty-five dollars for my poems. That night Mitterlechner and I got gloriously drunk. But here I must say a word concerning Mitterlechner. He was, as the name says, a German. Hard-boiled, tough, loose-tongued, boisterous, German, German, German. He was a German all right, and overmore a Rhinelander. He called his landlady "a camel." He called me "a sucker." He called his doctor "a fraud." He called his sweetheart "a whore." He called his work "slaving." He called all Italians and Greeks rotten people. He called his *vaterland* the highest most civilized land on earth. He sang "Die Wacht am Rhein" with gusto.

At intervals, he gave me much money and I was duly thankful and grateful. (By the way, as I have perhaps said before and will surely say again, being grateful is the most difficult thing on earth to accomplish. One is almost always bound to overdo it.) His love for his *vaterland* was most ugly. It consisted of shouts and guffaws and boisterousness and obstinacy. All his love was altogether as I have described it above and like his character. He befriended me and bought me lots of beer. His moustaches were refined, a little pert, a little aggressive, but they gave him an air of distinction. This was soon belied by his awful manners. He was my good friend, but in a bad way. I never liked him very much.

I was then a tenant in one of those red, furnished-room houses on the West side. I lived on the second floor and upstairs there was a sink. That's where I went to wash myself. Each step of the stairs had lost its horizontality and threatened to fall to the floor below. Through a skylight window bulging from the ceiling an ever-grey day oozed. And I often asked God-knows-whom what diabolic extremes or what extraordinary device of economic paucity had made the landlord paint the walls green. Dark shining green. Shining in winter, sweating in the summer like a degenerate's face. Upstairs there was the sink, and by the sink the toilet . . . . ah, only censurable words can say what weighed down upon the furnished-room house, dry and cracked with old red paint on its face and choked by the tenants' breath and the multitudinous dust of the carpets that were fulsome with unswept years.

I went to wash myself. The girl was straightening the rooms. It was two. Two p.m. The girl dropped the broom and its stick fell with a "tock" upon one of the closed hall-room doors. The girl went into another room. The tenant of the insulted door came out: a great white nose that stuck out of two hollow grey cheeks and a moustache like a threat.

"Listen!" he cried at me.

"Yes."

He slammed the door open, took a book in his hands, shook it before my eyes.

"I gotta fon da dichonary book, see!"

"Yes .... well .... what .... do you?"

"See?"

"Do you want to sell it? I don't want to buy it."

His big teeth appeared and disappeared, monstrously.

"I gotta fon da dichonary book. Mabbe you good .... I no say you no good .... mabbe. You make noise bump me .... I kick .... no can shleep. I gib you fon da kick .... you no stand? I good, you no good, you no see, mabbe, I no say ...." And then with a last great push, with long-bursting expansion: "I gib you fon da dichonary book."

I understood at last that he wanted to throw it at me. I explained: "I didn't do anything wrong to you. I can't understand."

It was the damn broomstick had awakened the man and all his night with him, his night darker for his ignorance of English. Then I went downstairs and laughed. I didn't know he was a night worker. Perhaps I didn't care how many night workers were in the house. I sang all the time. That is, I used to scream uproariously old songs, and Brahms' "Wiegenlied," and "Katie, K-K-K-Katie, beau-tiful Kaa-tie"! One day as he passed my door, the Pole — for he was a Pole — shouted:

"No can shleep. Some people make noise. I fix."

He shouted it so fearfully and loudly that it came upon me and shook me like thunder shakes a window.

(You pass in the street and look sideways, and down, and sideways. Hardly you lift your eyes from the broken sidewalk before you. As far as to see the sky your head never twisted. And a mother points you out to her child — ssh, look at the bogey man! They are against you, all they who know English. They enjoy knocking at your door, they who won't see how much you need your sleep, and you must get angry at yourself because you know these creatures who go to vaudevilles, and put on queer neckties on Sunday morning, you know they're awake, making a noise they have a right to make, being more beautiful than you, knowing English. What was it came to you and revealed itself? What were the new things? The wife you married in Poland is dead one year now, two months after the wedding, and that new thing for you was the shape of eternal misery. All are against you. When you open your eyes you see a broken sidewalk, broken with its own tragedy and not your own. If you would sometimes lift your eyes you would see a sky that can't possibly have anything to do with you. As for me, I wasn't the one to throw the broom against your door, but I don't care how much the broom awoke you. You think the world is a garden of happy children and you're a bugbear, don't you? Well, no one knows better than you do. You have seen one face of truth, and it's the whole truth to you who couldn't see any other, and you are snarling at it. Poor dog, snarl, and bite if you can, but it's a big city, it's many people, it's too many things are your foe.

I love you because you scream. . . . I beg you, don't stop screaming, snarling, and feeling like a mad dog must feel when he walks with his tail drawn under his belly. . . . Look in the face of these houses, look straight in the face of these houses, look straight in the face of the lunch-room cashier girl who takes with pretty fingers the coin you hand her with trembling ones. Bogey man, look straight in the warm eyes of any child out of your own frozen deep eyes. I promise you, something there in your hands will be set trembling forever, if you will but look and touch. Something will go following you, having irrevocably heard your uncompromising voice. And somebody will stop calling you insane, somebody will stop calling you insane, and he won't say one more word about it for the rest of his life.)

A Little Club in New York

What distinguished this club from any other I knew of was that its members were all very young. There was Lilly Steigman, the hefty girl who was gradually driving Louis Grudin insane; then there was Goldie Steigman, and Rebecca and Sophie. Sophie had the great honor of knowing personally the great Hebrew artist, Sholem Asch. Izzie Schneider was also a member of this club, and here he reigned supreme. (Izzie, your great nose is a nice thing to remember.) He was such a suave writer, such a charming personality, such a big Izzie, such a terse mind, such a will to fight one and everybody. His humor was sharp and cutting, and he was not what one would call handsome but his face changed expressions swiftly and without notice beforehand. (You said you'd get ahead of both of us, both Louis Grudin and me, and perhaps you were right. Now behold your friend, dear Izzie, caught by a modern sickness which makes him ridiculous, shattered and broken to smithereens. . . . .)

I liked the splendid delicacy for me in *Dr. Transit.* You said: "Emanuel Carnevali, who helped to make the man who made this book." Do you remember when we walked at night in Staten Island? We ate very green grapes which you named "gripes." There we stole green apples.

This little club used to meet once a week in the house of one of the members. A talk was given on a subject chosen the week before. Youth was the finest thing about this club and also the worst thing about it. There was freshness and there was ineptitude. Youth, sheer youth, reigned in this club and was the reason for its existence. It was a little vein of gold running through the

124

black mine of New York. Because of it, and because Harriet Monroe had printed my poetry, this became the golden period of my life. (I knew Harriet Monroe was the finest editor in the country. She was always hungry for new unpublished work, and is was for that reason that I was so easily accepted.) It was the club of the disbanded, the morally homeless, the heretics of the artistic world. Once they met to eat at my house — the Kreymborgs came too — and my wife served us such salty baccala that no one could eat a mouthful.

Once we had a talk on sexual relationships, and once I was asked to read an article on contemporary Italian literature. This was a great success and received great applause. It went: Carducci and Pascoli are dead and d'Annunzio has reached the appreciation of fat American reviews. This is about a few young poets who were acknowledged in, and contributed to, the magazine *La Voce* and the Futurists' organ *Lacerba*. As for the rest, they are many in Italy — imitators of d'Annunzio or Carducci, over-visioned, over-inspired, overwhelming saviours-of-the-world or sons-of-the-Muses. And the most popular of them is Sam Benelli, known to the French and American public for his dramatic poems.

Now I should speak of characteristics, schools, and tendencies, but I am thinking of Verlaine, Laforgue, Browning, Verhaeren, and of how they stood out and above all schools, and of how puzzled a critic would be who should want to pigeonhole them. The first good poem that was ever written started the school of Homer, Dante, and Shakespeare, and insofar as a poet succeeds in writing poetry he belongs to that school and to no other. Here then are a few names:

Palazzeschi: Simplicity and naiveté of a modern St. Francis of Assisi. Wonder-eyed playboy, swift and light artist.

Papini: "At twenty, each idea is to be suspected, each man is the enemy;" having suffered in our own great way, we have our own great remedies to suggest. But after, most of us shrink, become humbler — out of some defeat, perhaps. Papini has fulfilled the desire of his heart of twenty — he has not shrunk. More than a warrior or a martyr has Papini given his life to his country, his people; in tempestuous autobiographical complaints, articles

— criticism and pragmatism.

Slataper: Died, very young, in the war. Wrote of the Carso mountains, the sheer, hard landscapes where he lived — a big, hard and clean boy.

Govoni: The writer of the most musical, most humane free verse I have ever read. Delicate as a girl, if at times he sings the luridest, obscenest facts in the life of an old Italian city, he does so with the same delicate voice. Something of Frost in him — or, I should rather say, something of Govoni in Frost.

Di Giacomo: Writes in Neapolitan dialect short stories and poems of the irremediable sadness and the irrational tragedy of the old Naples. With a tenderness that is real in Italy because of the climate, etc., and would be sentimentality in America. He has been acknowledged by Croce and is considered to be the national poet.

Jahier: "Man of many scruples," believing that a poet is any man bothered by a great conscience. Works in an office for a living. No language and no grammar fits Jahier, and they must widen and become more hospitable in order to accept him. Jahier knows that it is the poet who shapes languages and grammars, and accomplishes many other things.

Soffici: Most advanced of them all, fights his way through French influences to a broken, jagged sort of poetry (words at liberty and lyric simultaneities) which is as haphazard as life itself.

And then Clemente Rebora, very earnest and very rich, who overflows into an imagism that is an orgy of cold senses, and dwindles into an unanimism that is emotional vagueness. Also Umberto Saba, Luciano Folgore and Camillo Sbarbaro, poets with too indefinite an attitude — sometimes borrowed.

When a heavy mood of mine crushes the appreciative attitude that I like to maintain, I see the flaws of Italian poetry as all being liable to definition under one name — Futurism. Futurism we built upon the mistakes, exaggerations and aberrations of some of the poets I have mentioned. It was born of the need for fellowship among those poets, and, with Marinetti, of the need for notoriety; and was fostered by the hustling of many vacant souls who made out of these exaggerations, etc., (which were all they could reach), a theory and a way of art. The movement, being largely a furious reaction, was largely a merely negative manifestation. The attitude was: since the *Passatisti* were obvious, we will be obscure; since they were grandiloquent with faith, we will struggle from irony to despair and backward, since with them sexual matters were more or less fig-leafed, we will trace the minutes and the seconds of our sexual sophistication; since they were too definite, soared too high astride voluminous Pegasuses blown by the wind of universal moods, we will herald the unimportance of art; we will trace the formation of the mood, but be careful to evade the mood itself; write elements of protopsychology (and Mallarmé started it). Above all, let's hate the bourgeois.

The trouble with them was, as Prezzolini put it, that they were bourgeois themselves. Vicious circles of weariness and sensualism, disease and cynicism — aren't these very bourgeois? Squalor of unemployed senses, where literature becomes an obsession; wantlessness — as with Ezra Pound who spends too many pages of his "Lustra" worrying whither and wherefore and when and how his songs go — (do they go?). Well, snobs and freaks and businessmen are always occupied with disoccupations of the sort. All the vicious circles, all the insanities, all the decadences are of the world that the artist hates. But he hates it because he suffers at seeing it thus; he does not resolve upon hating it while still he is in it and lives no better than anybody else — this the bourgeois does and the Futurist also. And as to obscurity: faces turn sour, stale, lurid, twisted, and are eaten up from inside. To whoever would preach obscurity, I say out, out in the open to be simplified by the clean weather! Out in the open and less in the rooms, for the sake of health!

And then, of course, their theories being absurd, these writers betray their theories. Marinetti is more grandiloquent, more obvious, and writes noisier classical bombast than any cheap *Passatisti*. That's why they hear him around the world. But Prezzozini, lovable critic, full of strength and cleanness, has fixed him and his gang in the only intelligent articles on Futurism that have appeared in Italian magazines where pig-headed professors wage war against and nasty ignorant youths defend it.

After all this, I see in Italian poetry now something that I want to call modern. And if participation in Futurism of the best poets of Italy has any good significance at all, it means that it had the effect of giving them a consciousness of modernity. Whether there is or is not anything new under the sun, things which must, if you will, be repeated are said in a line whereas in olden times they required a whole strophe. Modern man, grown to a consciousness that science and the experience of dead artists have given him, sees a more intricate and nearer, even if apparently smaller, world than the large one of the old artists. I think it is Yeats who said that no traditional pose is adequate to express it, this modern consciousness. (Here a friend suggests that a kind of sophistication recurs more than once through the ages, with the suavity of old civilizations. Though I advance my view humbly and would defend it from attack by saying that it is mainly pragmatic, I am thinking that my friend's observation is confirmed rather than confuted by history. Let this be food for speculation for those whose opinion that there is nothing new under the sun is also pragmatic.)

I want, finally, to point out the simple way of expression of Palazzeschi, Govoni, and Jahier, which suggests to me that the only school is that of simplicity. It has been said that making poetry is the progress wherewith one frees the thing seen of all that is not artistic — the unnecessary, the commonplace, the grandiloquent, the poetical. And I should dare to say that simplicity is then also the quality of being true, which means human, which means beautiful.

And I realize here that I owe an apology to Ezra Pound.

Emanuel Carnevali, from This Quarter

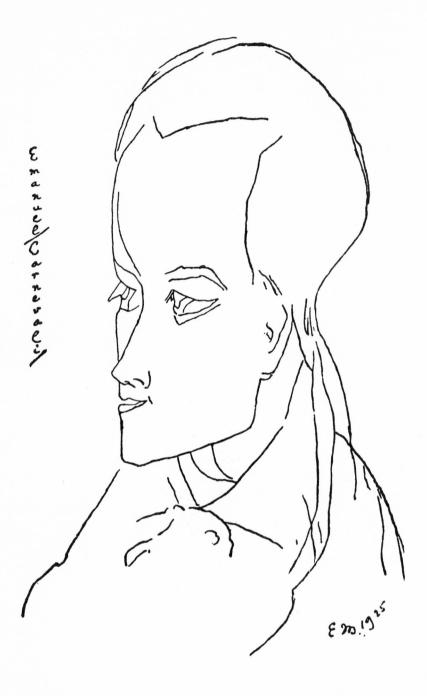

Emanuel Carnevali, drawing by Ethel Moorhead   130

Kay Boyle, photograph by Man Ray

Edward Dahlberg, photograph by Berenice Abbott

Robert McAlmon, photograph by Berenice Abbott

Harriet Monroe, courtesy of Poetry Magazine

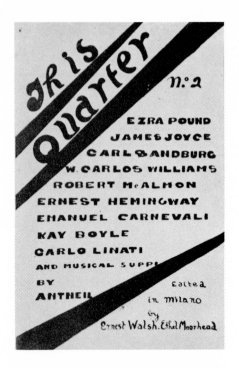

An Issue of This Quarter

Ernest Walsh,

from Americans Abroad

Ernest Walsh and Ethel Moorhead, from This Quarter

William Carlos Williams, photograph by Charles Sheeler

Spring

These flowers that are on the window-sill, I got them from the Park this afternoon. The air in the park was a luke-warm punch sipped with half-open lips at a party of perfect delicacy, where a word said a little louder would be an obscene thing

Almost everyone has flowers on the window-sill. They haven't bought them so they are there "against the law." These flowers are the result of a broken law. A perambulating battle-ship of fat has put an empty tomato can beside the lilacs on her window-sill. It yawns into the face of the lilacs, which is bent away a little.

My flowers are on the window-sill in a milk-bottle. I have looked at them again and again like a man who knows that something terrible will happen if he does not talk. They are the colors of the world: lilacs, azaleas, violets and buttercups. The azaleas were closed, furled up and lean, with long wrinkles, crude little hands. The violets I picked in the tall grass; in the shadow I found darker ones, seeming dark with thought, in the oblivion of the tangle of the deep grass. The lilacs — it was the only cluster left on the tree. Gently, though I forced it down, came the branch over me, fluttering with great impudence its skirts of leaves in my face.

And the buttercups — the gleaming buttercups — cups held high by a tiny arm. Offering a miniature of Father Sun from Mother Earth, on the dusty and black window-sill, in the grey frame of the window. They are the dance of my hands along the perfect curves, the caress of my eyes along their perfect nuances. These hands of a young man, which I hold in my pockets, want to start out, want to stop, and ask, and doubt, and begin, and falter, then twist in sorrow, twitch in sorrow back again into their forced stride of everyday. These are the hands of a destroyer and these are the hands which hold anathemas as Jupiter's hands held lightnings.

Flowers, flowers are there because of the thousand nuances I have gathered into my eyes, the thousand nuances I have gleaned, while looking from over the heads of everybody and from under everybody's heels, from the fog and across the swing of the rain. I want a home that will not insult flowers. I want a home that will not be insulted by the homes under and above it. I want a home that will not be insulted by a city. I want a city that the other cities may not insult. I want another home, but not one like any of yours. Some day, when I know more and when I shall have gained a little return, then I shall cast in a book the frame of a house, with the help of the artists of America and of the world. I shall let the frame of the house break through the heavy tangle of my bones, arise from the heap of my flesh. And it will loom over the city, against your house, frightfully, for it will be a ghost, the ghost of the man who was let die, the ghost of the song forever forgotten and forever coming again and again to shake the four walls of the sky.

Once Louis Grudin read me the beginning of a novel in which he confessed that I meant very much to him. He let escape such phrases as this:

"This is the beginning of American culture." "We shall be politicians since the attainment of metaphysics is politics." "To be in love is perfect living; it is the most rational way of being."

Once Louis Grudin's girl danced for us: she lifted her aggressively green skirt and showed her legs. We quarreled often and bloodily. (When I went to Chicago, we quarreled further when I found he had sent to the office of *Poetry,* of which I was then associate-editor, some poems written by his fat girl. The quarrel expanded and grew red hot. I wrote him such a lot of insults and abused him so awfully that he wrote me, without loss of time, threatening me. "Your nimble pen will be good and useful when I come and show you my fists," he wrote.)

At the *Seven Arts,* I met Waldo Frank, and I must say that

the first meeting was not pleasant at all. And at Lola Ridge's I met William Carlos Williams, and I have had no happier encounter (save the encounters with Kay Boyle and Dorothy Dudley). He was a most lovely man, strange, with a deprecatory voice, especially when he read poems of his own. At Lola's I made my first long speech, and this speech won Carlos Williams' friendship for me, or at least he offered it without any difficulty. I went and spent a few days at his home.

A big boy, he was, naive to a great point, more boyish than his lovely, earnest, almost-grave children. He went around in his Ford over the hills to pick wild flowers with a quantity of earth attached to them, and he transplanted them into his back-yard with a hope that they would grow and thrive there. Thoroughly modest, he was almost ashamed to read his poetry (which was full of surprises and white and powerful and true and beautiful) in public. Therefore the deprecatory twang in his voice. Sometimes his face was ghastly, fierce and unbeautiful from some inner struggle. His face was a mixture of arrogance and the good-natured slinger of all sorts of things. I never saw him composing, but I imagine him laughing while he does.

In spite of voices to the contrary, he was chaste as a virgin, delicately chaste, elusively so, in fact. In the evening, I coaxed him to lie down on a sofa and listen to my latest parturition — but he went to sleep and had the nerve to snore at me. He had the courage to dedicate the last number of the magazine *Others** to me. (That cost me a scolding from Waldo Frank.) Williams wrote:

"Emanuel Carnevali, the black poet, the empty man, the New York which does not exist . . . I celebrate your arrival. It is for you we went out, old men in the dark. It is for you that the rubbish stirred and a rat crawled from the garbage, alive! . . . What do I care if Carnevali has not written three poems I can thoroughly admire? Who can write a poem complete in every part, surrounded by this mess we live in? . . . His poems will not be constructed, they cannot be. He is wide open! He is black, speckled with flashes, but he is wide, Wide, WIDE open! He is out-of-doors. He does not look through a window.

Editor's Note: A magazine founded by Alfred Kreymborg in 1915.

"We older can compose, we seek the seclusion of a style, of a technique, we make replicas of the world we live in and we live in them and not in the world . . . Jesus, Jesus save Carnevali for me. He is only beginning to disintegrate . . . he is slipping into the afternoon at twenty-one . . . I believe he will go crazy or quit rather than write in a small way . . . We salute you."

I wrote to him once when he seemed to repent making this fine gesture, this greatest gesture of all.

My Speech at Lola's

This is an article — or whatever you will want to call it to suit your traditional gentleness, O gentle reader — obese with bombast, clamorous with objections, obstreperous and violent in an obsolete way, like ultimatums and wars. It is indeed an ultimatum and an attack. The greatest difficulty will be to answer why and how I stuck all these different names in a line to make out of them a title for this thing — Maxwell Bodenheim, Alfred Kreymborg, Lola Ridge, William Carlos Williams, William Saphier. Did not the infernal dissonance shatter my brain? Did not the wrangle of so different lights make me dizzy? The suggestive violentism and the heavy scented drunkening whirlwind that is Williams; the sweet simplicism and the capering bitterness that is Kreymborg; the voracious hunger of Lola Ridge — flashlights searching a battlefield, slicing a thick foul night, breaking one another to be drawn together into pools of swarming gold over corpses; the delicate strength of Saphier, like a hand of a laborer who has subdued work, big and perfectly wrought; Bodenheim's evanescent precision and perfectly contained and constrained demeanor of a lady that is such in every gesture and posture — how could I put them together?

Because they are a synthetic moment in my life. I have done some reading of their works and have seen each of them separately and all of them together. They are one of my experiences, an experience I want to gather together and express by elevating myself above it, if possible, or by sinking under it, if necessary.

These are the poets of New York, my city. I have seen and talked with each of them. And one night, how much I loved them and how much I hated them was so splendidly clear to my mind that I knew I must fight this overwhelming spectacle in or out of me in order to live to the next day. What I understood by literature was in danger of collapsing — depriving me of sleep, depriving me of what I call my soul. So, for my soul's sake, I sat down and wrote an attack. This:

I can't go to sleep. The darkness that flaps at the end of each day like a great black fan cannot blow my eyelids down. I am a pair of open eyes forever.

I must keep back my joy as a man holds his breath lest my joy shatter me bursting out of me. From the brain that is my heart a thousand messages have flown away. I am in love and I can't live if an answer is not given me. Perhaps I think none of you, my friends, would care to answer me; perhaps I am not sure one of you could give an answer. Thus I answer myself, and my sorrow is my hatred that you cannot answer me, that you are irremediably, tremendously different from what I am.

I hate you. A stiff bony beggar walking like a wooden marionette with dropped head suffices to say my sorrow. I am a god seeking around the world what there is need to create. Or the world is a god and I go begging of him to help me become a god. I am an unfinished god in the unfinished divinity which is the world — just the same as you are unfinished gods. And this, our quality of being unfinished is eternity, immortality and ever-changing life to me. I break and burst open, and I unfold continually, or I remain in a posture of perfect receptiveness. My action is beautiful, that of a flower: 1st, closed bud of fifteen petals, held by the fretting ready-to-break hand of the sepals; 2nd, each sepal falls and each petal unfolds to give a chance to each other petal; 3rd, petals laid out in three planes forming an absolute openness, openness to things of all direction, openness for giving and for taking. My action is more than that (perhaps there is no such flower as that). I am the incarnator, going quicker through radical changes than nature with her routine of seasons. I am the clenched fist of the worker and the lazy pale hands of the count dawdling over the curved arm of the chair. What makes people damned toward one another and damned upon the belly of the earth that accepts them one and all with gigantic patience and patient discrimination? What damns them is

142

the fact that a man can be but himself and no more — and when he's nothing he thinks it suffices since he is yet himself.

In the new mornings, my heart breaks as the sepals of the flowers break. My friends, Kreymborg, Bodenheim, Saphier, Williams, and Ridge, I hate you.

The two of you who sneer I hate, and the two of you who curse, and the five of you who do nothing. Sneer — what chained impotence is this? Of whom are you prisoners? Who is your boss that, unable to command him, you would pinch and bite and scratch with your sneers? Curse — you do not know the simple curse of a straight upward arm that bears a pointing finger like a gun bayonet. You have ceased to believe in plain statements because, you say, the men-of-nothing, the fakers, have corrupted them. Does an artist invent a new art *because* of his imitators? The simple statements were created by poets; only the poets know their use. The simple words are still, and exclusively, the poets'!

When the poets ceased using terms like God, divine, etc., out of the belief that they would be given a commercial value, the inverse terms were brought out by them: Satan, infernal, useless, beauty versus mob, beauty versus goodness. This retaliation against the public, when earnest and unconscious, has been the sign of the defeat of the poets; when conscious (if ever it was so) it was a sign of weariness or the lowliest of expedients. Thus you, too, defeated ones and sons of the defeated ones, talk of non-utilitarianism of art, as everybody in this century did who wrote down his own defeat (de Gourmont, Papini, Pound, Croce). This talk of non-utilitarianism, turn it one way or the other, is the same thing logically that every bourgeois does when he lives without reason and scope. The same thing every damned bourgeois does when he smiles with *condescensio* at what he calls "the artistic temperament."

Of all human activities, the only useful one is art. I'll maintain this axiom no matter where its corollaries will carry *you;* I'll maintain it even if it force you to conclusions such as these: the only action is apathy, the only practical the utterly unpractical. For what does the expression "to create" mean? It means "to hell with the mob, who will always misunderstand!" Yes, but then let us speak what we have to speak, in our language no matter how the mob has warped, stumped, and minced that language. You pure artists, you non-utilitarians, you half-and-half, you socialists, you souls of serenity, let us see supreme serenity, the last indifference, the highest pride, that of the man who, even if alone in the world, talks *the world's language.* Let us see you brave the danger which brings insanity and damnation to an artist, the danger of being taken for the megaphone of all the filthy symbols of death and the rest which wear such shining names as god, life, beauty, liberty, democracy, and peace, along the ash-can-guarded streets of the mob. That is art, its fight, its bitterness, its curse and its uselessness. If you want art to be absurd, what greater absurdity than to stand against millions.

Look out, I'm not blaming you for the lack of philosophical content in your work. There are signs of it, Kreymborg, Ridge, and Williams: that so-called philosophical content — stretches of cold-handed reasoning to prove that which is red hot, stretches of desert for the sake of the oasis here and there. I must indeed admit that my own work is full of that barrenness and that none of you has committed a crime of half the size of those one comes across — swamps — in the Lawyer Masters* barren great valley. Philosophy when it is great is poetry, when small . . . a trick, a technique, a work, a fallacious way of proving a fallacy. But I speak of the emotional content of your works, that which generally goes under the name of "form." The names that "form" has assumed through the ages (Romanticism, Naturalism, Impressionism, Realism, Symbolism) indicate different attempts at truth. And each of these names was, in its time, the definition of truth. Symbolism to me has meant Mallarmé creating a radically different language and therewith stating everything differently. Or Rimbaud, finding his "liberty in salvation." I speak of your form, that half-and-half-thing, that thing which cannot break loose from the cage of metrical rhythms and which clumsily strives toward the spontaneity of talk, that thing that is as broken, as queer, as grotesque, as half-killed as your wills are queer, grotesque, broken, and half-killed My will and your will: that is the fight and the attack in this article. I do not understand, and never

---

Editor's Note: Edgar Lee Masters.

will understand, what you, my friends, mean by new expressions, new images, originality.

You are old, truth has become a difficult thing to know and you call your swaggering-staggering, your stumbling-swearing, your climbing-crawling-falling, your lazy swaying, your minute elusive squirming after truth, you call this technique or what-not. (I love you because you are still after the old lady and still hoping to get hold of her by the shoulders one day and make her turn around, and be marvelously surprised to find her so young and so new.) I hate you because you suggest and like to suggest that what made you first write is no longer there, that your youth's will is gone, that you do what you do disinterestedly, for the sake of expressing some queer shape of yourself, which must of necessity be either your own shape or some shape you would like to attain — that is your unkillable will.

You want to be photographing machines, and it pleases you when your "negative" results are different from those of the other fellows. Your wills are half-killed and you walk around like men with their heads dangling from their trunks, held only by some bloody threads. You're useless, and you know it, and your sneer is your own bitterness. You do not want to give anything to the young, you cannot give anything to the young. For where are the books of your own daily deaths? The fight you started in the beginning has you exhausted. And because you are not fighting, I, who have written too many bad poems and have made too many mistakes already (but who, as every young man should, hear a new literature awaking with him), I damn you with the denomination of poets of old forms, past poets. Unless you are young, too, I must do that, for I, I want to be what the world misses.

You make me mad! You say that what is gall in my throat you have already swallowed and have not yet croaked thereof! I hate you — let me spit it out — because you're not boys, because you are not just over twenty (and I say that, who cannot be always twenty); he's dead when he's no more twenty, he's one of the too-many-names in the archives, he's a forgotten exclamation in the immense, quick-judging and damning head of God; he's a man passing in the street just once and never again . . . Looking at Papini's portrait, a simple girl I know said that he looked sixteen, twenty, and sixty. I said he was born in the Genesis and he has lived and spoken in the Apocalypse. One passes from a day to the next day through death. Death marks the age. Papini died in the last death, the death of himself and his world together, and his *Un Uomo Finito* is the report of such death. But where are your *Un Uomo Finitos?* Where are your references, how have you earned, how will you earn, the credit of readers and fellow-men, readers and fellow-men such as I? You are not sane, and still you are not as mad as I.

But there comes the moon to weep inside my window. This great lady's humility makes me humble too. I mute my insurrective trombone and I am contrite. You are as mad as gods must be. I have seen Kreymborg hold a chisel so fearfully, carefully, with his skinny hands and engrave a line that was as tremendously pregnant as a 305 shell. I have seen him behind one of his poems, an arrow before it's let go. I have seen him constrain himself with the strength of the ray-concentrator Sun, and I understood that in the face of God, in order that there be all the lines that the little flowers and the husky crags have, each line must be a synthesis.

With his mobility, Williams reaches almost every part of the truth at the same time — the synthesis of it being a mere exclamation, a magic single word.

The dear sufferer, Lola Ridge, has spoken of a wind in such a way that I saw the hand of God bringing clean stillness to man — and I was ashamed, I, the restlessness that has no direction.

In a portrait by Saphier, I saw that my hands were, and would always be, too rough to hold a bit of life (oh, anything, a little bit!) in adoration. I say to my arms that gesticulate, please, please, rest for a moment and let your posture be a synthetic one. I say to my face, here, look at the river, it's all laid out; when the sun falls in it there are many little ripples revealed, whirlpools that the sunlight beats the tempo to, many quiet spaces where the sun silently pours his gift of melted gold, many little tongues licking the shore that the sun sets a-singing. Be like that, quiet. Be like that, all spread out. See Bodenheim, how he is spread out. See Soffici, he went to war and brought it back in his face and his heart. Because in his open arms, like a Christ's, all the war entered; while I, I would have lowered my head and fought against the war, I would have seen nothing, I would have smashed my head and lost.

See Kreymborg; because he has been sitting so quiet the child in him didn't get scared and hasn't left him. It's still playing in him, that sad and crazy child, seeing all that the old man Kreymborg sees and not getting stupidly scared because the old man Kreymborg isn't running about knocking down furniture and trampling over flowers and lives as I do. Learn from them what it is that is too difficult for them to say because it is their lives, their faces, their names; learn that which is too difficult for me to ask, too sacrilegious to ask, foolish to ask — impossible for them to say in a better way than by merely being what they are.

But, please, I am disgusted with your little-review talk of technique and technicians. Easier than everything, commoner than everything, is to have a technique, to talk like Ezra Pound does in his "Subdivisions of the Poetical Department Store with Antiques for Sale Only to Those Who Know How the Oriental Pooh-Pooh-Chink Wore His Slippers." The fakers need a technique, they who go lying for a cent and lying more for a cent and a half.

If you are poets, as they say, I don't want to be a poet. I say you discovered yourselves and you're disgusted with the find and you are hiding behind a thick-woven, ragged curtain of image-words, stunts, tricks, of verse that lacks even the one-two-three-dip of rhymes which would at least make them decisively comic. If some aboriginal knowledge, the poetic one, ever escapes through the little inky beaks of your pens you are ashamed. Your black pens are ravens croaking over the stinking corpses of your wills — the stench of which can't help but filtrate in between the cracks and the chinks of your cracked and wrinkled poems. Like all the rest, you have forgotten your youth. You have been defeated by the world. If you say that you never fought, that will only place you as cowards. If you say nothing, then I'll shout into your ears that the world expects a formal surrender from you.

Let pass a man who believes alike in Christ's dead love as in Nietzsche's live hatred, in Wagner's grandeur as in Dostoievsky's simplicity, in Rimbaud's unearthly symbols as in Villon's lousiness, in Laforgue's beggarliness as in Blake's voluptuous mysticism. Let pass a man who wants all creeds to be his, you who would have no creed, and still less have anybody adopt a creed. I say "let pass," but I'm ready — and I rather like it — to knock you down and step over your bodies. Step over your prostrate bodies, for I'm a running thing, a hurried man. But if what I see is there, you are the last white fringes of a tide that is ebbing back into the abyss that is the world's womb. You will roll down into the abyss, you pebbles, you twigs, you starfishes and shells and sand and salt perfume — it will be better for you, jellyfishes, you would dry on the shore. You are no more men to me, in this beautiful year of 1919! And I, I am an enormous commonplace rolling over your delicate miniatures. I'm an enormous lady with large feet, such large feet that she can't help but step on your little flowers. I am the same enormous lady crying as sincerely as she can over the beautiful flowers that her feet destroyed.

> Let me look for my heart:
> In the loam, in the black earth of my country. My heart is buried deep in the heart of my country and it cannot complain.

> I have received a foolish, quite foolish, dispatch from my heart (yet who knows where it is?) It said:
> Quench my fire or I shall set fire to the world.

The End of Love

Where I worked as a beast of burden was at Gus's in Broad Street, where during the lunch-hour the whole of Wall Street came with its bank-clerks, employees; all amounting to more than eight hundred lunches. Working there I managed to collect about twenty dollars so as to buy a gold watch, a present for my wife. But I spent it instead with Mitter-lechner and a couple of whores. My wife was working in the country then and I wrote her what I had done, mentioning that it was, after all, her mission to keep me on the straight and narrow path. She replied that she had no interest in missions and didn't want to hear about my adventures. If she wanted the gold watch I had promised her, well, she could just go and buy it for herself.

There was also a C & L Restaurant where I waited on table with much wisdom and forethought. Here I rose to the heights of counterman. I fell in love with one waitress there, rather pretty, with very soft hands who took care of my tips for me. The waitresses showered me with lovely names, such as "sweetness," "handsome," "love," "precious." Once a man I was waiting on spoke gently to me. He told me, mildly, humbly, that he was a pederast. But enough of the places where I have worked! I curse them all! I never had a single hour of joyous labor, not one hour, unless I was drunk, as frequently happened. I dragged this weary body of mine, eternally tired, eternally ill, with a certain obstin-acy from place to place. I had to live, but I had all of America against me, all this never-ending urge to work. I called aloud wildly and endlessly for help, but no answer ever came. I sang my feeble songs like a lark lost in the immense sky of life. I was broken, weary; the few moments of comfort and peace came when I left a job with a few cents in my pocket — enough to last me a couple of days.

Saturday evenings I would join my wife in the country where she worked, and I would wash myself all over first and then put on talcum powder so that I was all fresh and perfumed when I saw her. Sunday I would sleep in Mr. Green's cottage, my wife's boss. Fine, beautiful days I spent there with my wife in the sun — for she was still pretty then. We seemed never to tire of each other in those days, but still it was the beginning of the end. I remember that neither of us knew the meaning of the English word "shallow" then, and we kept on repeating it to each other, hoping that one of us would divulge the meaning. Finally we confessed to each other that we didn't know what it meant.

Then when my wife was being operated on (anti-birth), I met Dorothy S., a painter. I fell in love with her because she was kind to me. (That was the way all my love-affairs began.) When I went to see my wife I had the letter in my pocket in which Dorothy S. told me "I love you." I went to her that evening and as I finally kissed her, her eyelids beat like dying butterflies. I decided to let them die, those dying butterflies . . . .

I never saw her again, but I met Caroline D. I do not know from what skies she fell into my arms. But I know that her former sweetheart once spent half the night under her window, knowing I was upstairs with her. (He was the man she married and subsequently divorced after . . . after . . . .) This is the way it began: a message was brought to my room asking me to telephone Caroline D. at her bank. I did so, rather surlily, and at the other end of the phone Caroline kept repeating: "You talk quite like a celebrity . . . you act like a celebrity . . . I want to meet you somewhere. . . ."

She was not beautiful, but she had a face full of mystery and the preface to mystery. She was tall and mighty, with full round breasts and powerful shoulders. (I never could forgive her for being stronger than I.) She had bulging chestnut eyes which seemed evil but were not. She was meek, in spite of her spiritual and physical strength, in spite of her eyes which seemed thoroughly evil, stubbornly bad. She dressed with great gorgeousness when she knew I was coming to see her, and she would tell me that I was almost Jesus or else a plain charlatan. She was very new to love and her *gaffes* were frequent and preposterous. *Turris Eburnea,* I don't know that I ever loved her. *Turris Eburnea,* she was terribly white.

One day my wife came back from the country unexpectedly and she visited my room while I was not there. I had hidden Caroline's letters under the bed, and my wife rummaged around in my absence and found the box in which they were concealed. Next morning she telephoned each of us: she telephoned me and asked me to come and see her, and she made a similar request of Caroline. When we both reached the place where she worked and were seated in the room with her, she suddenly jumped up and expressed her intention of calling the police. Caroline asked that I leave them alone together and after agreeing that I would get out and stay out while they consulted about me, I burst into the room again, shouting: "No, this is not fair, not fair at all!"

My wife was in the midst of the most hellish tirade I have ever listened to, and in fury I gave her a push that sent her flying. All this row so alarmed the poor little telephone operator stationed near the entrance that she sent for assistance, and when Caroline manged to make an ignominious escape (I following her), we met a group of people on the stairs, fighting their way up and shouting:

"Where is that woman? Where is that woman?"

I too joined the chorus of voices as I made my way down the stairs, crying too:

"Where is that woman? Where is she?"

But the negro porter was not fooled and he pursued me and caught me up at the subway station, but as soon as he laid hands on me the ticket-collector shouted at him to let me go.

She was a woman of great and small wrath, my wife. There was a certain power in her, for she drove me to insanity at times. She could never beg for pardon, and that signified a great weakness in her.

I said: I should make a prayer
with the sound of her footsteps
when she comes to my desolate room
bringing luxurious sweets.

I shall make a prayer
with the rhythm that is in her features,
with her voice for a music.

But, unexpectedly,
the prayer ran thus:

Deliver me
from the stubborness of this woman.
She is like a Sardinian ass,
a Sardinian ass, so small!

Deliver me
from the animalistic love
of this woman,
an enormous leech
at my breast.

She was a woman of great and small wrath,
She was a preposterous barbarian.
An obsolete moralist.
An obstreperous scolder.

Over my bed she crushed
the little children of my yesterdays:
over my bed she slew
the tiny birds of my tomorrows.
Over my bed she strewed
the little hypocritical toads
of her whims.

So I said:
I shall make a curse to God

with the anger in her voice.
I shall make blasphemy
with the ugliness of her face.
I shall make a malediction
with her unkind words.

And to think that we had once passed more than twelve
hours together without tiring of one another! Yes, sometimes we
had spent half the night sitting on a park-bench, talking and looking at each other. But now our love was gone. We trampled it
down with our feet until it was quiet, all gone, all finished. It was
the absolute destruction, the end of love.

After the affair with Caroline was over, my wife had wept
and wept until I was reduced to going to live with her again, but
now even this was past and we were as quiet as death. My wife no
longer grovelled at my feet with the eternal question, "Do you
love me?" And I no longer shouted the answer, eternal also,
"No!" What had been destroyed could not be mended. We were
surrounded by the calmness of death.

At first we had opposed our whole strength against this feeling of dying, but it was to no avail. Death was ours and only
death. We sat together by a small creek in the Bronx, and we suddenly knew how near to us it was, forming almost a part of our-
selves. Melancholy had obliterated us entirely, and how meekly
the little rivulet reflected and returned our melancholy! Here we
brought all our rage of love, our abject misery, hoping that the
sum of these gifts would be truly death. Little rivulet, you watched
our end and went on murmuring as you passed us by. I had known
the birth of love and now I knew its death.

Then I discovered that I had been made cuckold too. I had
sent Louis Grudin to the little town in Connecticut where my wife
was passing the summer, working, and when he came back he
told me he had met a Russian violinist with my wife. It seemed
to Lou that she seemed under a strain while talking of this violinist or to him.

When she returned, I spoke of Lou's visit to her and she

mentioned a few people she had introduced to him. But she did not mention the Russian violinist. That was the cue to the situation for me. I was sleeping with her in her room and I began shouting at her, giving full speech to my suspicion.

"Who is this Russian violinist Lou talked to me about?" I cried.

She was silent for a while and in that space of time I saw the entire truth which she had succeeded in hiding from me. I laughed aloud and, roaring with laughter, jumped out of bed and ran downstairs to my own room. Presently she too made her appearance in my room, and controlling myself I told her, pedantically and gravely, that she must consider me as a priest and that she should confess everything without attempting to exonerate herself.

"Do not, for once," I said, "try to put the fault for everything on me."

So she confessed the truth to me, but so uglily, with such meanness, with petty tears, with such a cowardly fear of me that I feared for her soul. Not only had she given herself to the Russian, but to another man as well — the hero of an ancient love-affair, a Spanish boy. I remembered with amazement the infernal hours she had spent calling me names, calling Caroline a whore, a snake, a vile woman.

Finally, Harriet Monroe came to New York and told me that if I wanted to come to Chicago she would help me to find a job there.

Chicago

W_{hen} Waldo Frank saw the
handwriting of my future employer he said spontaneously, "What
a horrible man!" And he was right. He had the face of a sour
Presbyterian minister, which he was. His name was Pasquale and
he was a shady character, an ugly brute. He was the editor of
The Citizen besides being a minister, and I never could imagine
what kind of sermons he preached to his congregation. They
must have been terrible if they resembled in any way their author's
soul. He had green eyes, with the iris misted (perhaps by cataract), which terrified one. He peppered his spaghetti, making it
quite uneatable, and once he told me that he had at one time seen
an Italian being hanged. He said he had laughed himself sick
at this event, which must have seemed to any other human being
a thing as lugubrious as a skull.

My work consisted of writing notes concerning the criminals
of Chicago and soliciting advertisements and subscriptions. He
was in league with bootleggers, and I once wrote an article for
him against the Italian gangster element in America. It almost
cost me my life, although I didn't know it. And this horrible man
was the father of a strapping girl who needed altogether different
things than Presbyterian sermons. I used to talk to her about religion, telling her that God is a sentimental symbol. Religion was
good for little old ladies, I told her; for tired people, for fools. I
said I loved Christ but that Christ is the denial of any Christian
sect, of all Christian religions. Christ might well be called a god
but he had preferred to be called a man, knowing instinctively
that the word "man" is larger and greater than the word "god."

Religion, I said, teaches the world to do without love, to do without sin, for religion forgives all sins. Mythology is beautiful, religion cramped and ugly. Why should men stoop to religion, I asked her, when religion is such an obscure, unsecure, truly unholy thing? I told her of the priests who had instructed me as a child; there was one who used to make a hell of a noise singing mass. He was always in a hurry: in a hurry in the confessional, in a hurry to sing mass, in a hurry to teach us, in a hurry to preach his sermon. Hurry, hurry. He was fat and arrogant and he was continuously chasing something or other. I fancied he chased his god around the dark corners of the church. (There was another priest who had been the teacher of the third elementary grade. He was a furious human being and I saw him once tear a bit of one of the pupil's ears off in his rage. And yet if one went to see him in his house, he was the sweetest ever. He would offer you wine and sweets, yet he was not a pederast. I say he was not a pederast because so many of the priests in my country are.)

My trip to Chicago was the first long trip I had taken in a train and I travelled like a lord in a lower berth. Waldo Frank and my wife accompanied me to the station and when I saw him later in Chicago, he said to me: "The little woman knew what was coming to her." I left my wife with the promise to send for her as soon as things looked clear, but this I never did. (My wife asked for and probably got a divorce. Her hypocrisy is obvious from one single fact: she wrote to me later that during the three years of our separation I had never sent her so much as a penny. What a hypocrite! As if she did not know that I never had so much as a penny to send. But all the same, some thanks are due her for having kept me, or almost kept me, for three years in New York. The rent of the West End Avenue room was always paid by her.)

Pasquale fired me soon, but very gently, without violence of any kind. And my second job in Chicago was in the office of *Poetry,* with that great mother of poets, Harriet Monroe. All her spinster years had accumulated in her great heart until now it overflowed and it was a real maternal love she gave. We often quarrelled long and loud about what should be accepted or rejected and when she furtively printed something I didn't like, there were howls in the office. I was associate-editor those few months there, but I was an undesirable worker and Harriet Monroe was dissatisfied with me. I must admit that I deserved her reproaches for I was a lazy good-for-nothing sort of cub. I slept long and determinedly, rested and looked lazily, not at the lake, but at the throngs of people who walked past. I told her her review was an absurdity — the mere idea of having to print every month a certain number of pages dedicated to poetry! (But from this absurdity came geniuses like Carl Sandburg, and that imbecile of a Masters who, as Alfred Kreymborg rightly said, treated universal matter with insularity.) I told her that her review was completely lacking in a sense of humor! I accused her of dragging about this heavy wagon of a review, this lifeless burden that was grey not only in color but in spirit. I called her a she-professor of English, but if I insulted her ferociously, madly, it was because at that time I insulted everything, and every man and woman.

(When Harriet Monroe came to see me in Italy years later, Signora Emma, the inn-keeper, described her in this way: "The cleanest little woman I've ever seen." Compared to you, Harriet, I was never anything but a poor poet, a tattered, bare-footed beggar. I will remember you always as the mother of all poets, the good and the bad, the saviour of all poets, who often saved my life just in time with a check.) The lady I am trying to describe was neither a great lady nor an insignificant woman, but she had a little of both in her. I have heard her with her voice trembling with indignation, and I have heard her laugh gaily like a child. (I know so well this strange type of little woman, and while shaking out the sack of one's words, one word must always be kept back to explain at her death the fact of her life.) Harriet Monroe, I thank you for the bread you gave me, I thank you for the maternal love you bestowed on me; you became my mother, and for this miracle I thank you. For the amnesia which you covered with the cloak of your memory, I thank you; for having come to Italy to find me in a little inn, I thank you; but still, though you printed my name, you were not a great editor. Tireless little woman, you are now dead. Those little fingers which held so many pages before your grey eyes are now empty and lying helpless in the grave.

One day I was given leave to go to Niagara, provided I be

back the same day from Tonawanda to Buffalo. I can find no
words with which to speak of this great waterfall. It is too great,
too tremendous, this inhuman, this soul-less Niagara. It is somehow the final acknowledgment of the greatness of the great
U. S. A. Niagara was to me an immensity that had, by miracle,
found a way of speaking. Like a miracle, too, here was water
that had acquired the hardness of stone, marvelous solidity. It
was equally beautiful in all its parts and I felt its name should be
perfection. So beautiful it was, like a hundred white stallions
galloping on, that I felt ashamed even to look at or lay hands on
such beauty.

In those last days in New York I had suffered paroxysms of
thought. I thought as hard as the Egyptian sphinx must have before it was made ridiculous by a broken nose. My thoughts were
dark, enclosed in mental darkness, because I hardly ever found
the words to express them. And I felt then this terrific fire that
is within me, a fire that constantly tries to escape me. But here in
Chicago I found no feverishness (except for the smell of feverishness when the wind blew the wrong way and brought the stench
of the stockyards to the town). They told me that Chicago was
one of the largest cities in the world. I knew nothing about that,
but I knew there was often green between the houses. Even the
little girls are milder and softer here than in New York.

The great forehead of the city is the facade facing the
Illinois Central. This great brow redeems much ugliness, much
of the drabness of the landscape, much filth and powdery horse-
dung. One of the signs that Chicago is happy is the awful dirt
it leaves in its streets, and it does not give a damn whether the
streets be many or few. I liked the funny little bridges on the
river of this hoodlum city, I liked its softness. New York screamed
or shouted at me, but Chicago stammered, it was still so very
young.

I had a job in Lincoln Park once, cutting off the diseased
branches from otherwise healthy trees and shooting arsenic and
lead poisoning over everything to kill the pretty little colored
caterpillars. There was all the poetry I needed in this job. I
smelled the great perfumed branches as they fell to the ground
in the heat of the long summer days. I love trees however they are,

strong or diseased, green or naked, standing quiet or shaking like trembling hands in the gale. I am a tree lover, but not as stupid as the one who wrote:

Poems are made by fools like me
But only God can make a tree . . .

(I agree as to the fools like me.) I have sometimes hugged a tree, hugged the trees of Lincoln Park. Sometimes I have held a tree in my arms and called it my darling and my beautiful, and it was dear to me, very dear to me. But in the long run, its unresponsiveness made me sick.

For its girls also, Chicago should be praised. They have mellow eyes — like Italian eyes — and they are large-hipped, saying that they will be future mothers. Their speech is slow and deep, their voices contralto rather than soprano, while the voices of New York girls were as sharp as knives in my heart. I was too poor or too shy to know much about it, but I believe they were generous too, these Chicago girls, about giving their bodies away. (Louis Grudin once told me that I loved only ugly women. This is true, perhaps because, I have said it before, that if an ugly woman's face changes it cannot be for the worse but only towards the beautiful. Ugly women have contemplation in their faces.)

Chicago girls paint themselves less awfully than in New York, and they are healthier to see. Chicago flings to the four walls of the skies a windy bet that she will survive seasons and seasons before sickening like New York. (But in the temple of learning, in the public library of Chicago there is this notice:

ADJUST YOUR CLOTHES BEFORE LEAVING.

Can you beat that? No, you surely can't.)

As Italy is called queen of the air because of her hundreds of planes, so America is queen of the air because of her skyscrapers. What America flaunts is what she knows best — a fairytale of the skies. She is the tallest bride of all the years, and she was married to her people in November, 1918, when she screamed her screams of horror and fear and topsy-turvy joy. She was married to her people, and millions of bits of paper served for rice.

I have seen New York rising from the water like a brand-new Venus, and to think that merely an economic factor gave rise to such beauty; namely, the high cost of ground, so that sky-scrapers had to be built. Riverside Drive has water at its hem while Chicago washes her dirty feet in the Michigan sea, and her feet are forever dirty.

But memories weep or mourn, all memories do. I had left the home and her. I could have painted the walls half blue and half pink and could have drawn a heavy-headed sunflower in the middle. I could have drawn my nightmares on the walls of my bedroom and laughed at them, having exalted them to art. I could have strung wreaths of oak leaves and maple leaves all around, and I could have strewn the floor with sand and pebbles and my bedroom with ashes. I could have bought silk handkerchiefs and hung them from the windows — different ones every day. I could have planted beans, parsley and morning-glories in a box full of dirt out on the fire-escape where it's forbidden to "place any encumbrance." And I could have written a tremendously happy treatise to show why the wops break one and and every law of the United States. But they don't — and it wouldn't have sufficed — and reform is reform and I chose revolution. I quit.

I quit. I am a vagabond again. I am a roomer. In a furnished-room house. One of the homes of the homeless, of the orphans, the whores, the pimps, the poor spinsters, the poor bachelors, the typical American Home: the Furnished Room. The New World is tired of the Family. The New World damns European shackles of the Family and has a new institution — a transitory institution in the transitory New World — the Furnished Room welcomes with miserable arms the hopeless rebels of the earth. I am the typical American, see? Unacknowledged. Nobody knows me and, as compensation, everybody knows me — so I talk crudely and democratically to everyone I like, for I love no one in especial.

The rich, the middle-class! Don't let them fool you about that — their houses are imitations, unreal and ugly — and there are hotels. Hotels and furnished rooms. And concubines, pimps, middlemen, and purveyors to these, the Lunch-room and the Restaurant. If you can eat in a restaurant all your life then you can sleep in a furnished room or a hotel all your life. Isn't my misery blinding me? — oh, Christ, I am crying — if I don't see well it's because there are tears before my eyes. I tell you, I have known too many who know nothing about the old negro song and nothing about New England and the pies that are made there and which are the tradition of the country — and many who do not know how tremendously and maybe successfully sacrilegious skyscrapers are. These are the homeless and I am one of them. They don't eat like men, they don't sleep like men, they don't see any colors. (Why have you taken the colors away from your cities? They will soon become blind. Aren't colors the sustenance of our eyesight, do they not determine, define our eyesight? You, the chemists, the doctors, the engineers, of America, you have made this country grey. Why do you handle grey things only, why does everything turn grey in your hands? Do you want us all to lose our eyesight? Why do you want to take the joy out of oranges and peaches — kill fruits?)

You'd want me to make a better, more specific complaint, wouldn't you? But this is my own and a million Greeks (oh, have you seen the beautiful Greeks that work in kitchens and restaurants, and have you heard them? They are still singing the songs of the mountains!). And this is the complaint of a million Italians (have you seen them going home from work, loaded down with two jackets and a sweater and with immense mittens to fight the cold, the skin of their necks like bark?); they say *"L'America, donne senza colore e frutta senza sapore"* — America, women without color and fruits without taste. And maybe they are right. Don't you see the millions of girls, almost all the poor little working girls, rouged and powdered, looking like halloween masks or funny dead faces?

I will say it better sometime — I think there is some use for such a complaint — but now I have no time, I'm going, I'm going along, I am going along, I am going along. Furnished rooms — they got me again. They took me back. There is always a brothel for a prostitute and always a sick lust in some one for her, no matter how old and sick she is, and so it was with me — the furnished room took me back. I make a petition for them who are in my same plight — the roomers, the hotel customers, the movie patrons. I cry tears that are diamonds and drops of silver and sapphires when the moonlight smites them. Now I am again a vagabond, spilling words from a hole in my pocket, knowing only other vagabonds, like me and urging them to wander around. I am a vagabond, and I shriek amongst my wrecks of memories and my failures like a crazy child among old toys. I have come to a country where there are no houses, I haven't seen any. Maybe down south, out west, or up north, but not where I have been. When we vagabonds are tired, we meet and sing old, very old songs that no one understands except us, and we call one another "brother" and "artist" — and we often weep together. We weep when we realize that there cannot be brothers without there being a family or artists without there being a home . . . . when we realize that we are liars too.

> That morning the dawn arose from the sodden grey city
>   pavements,
> And it was a sick grey breath.
> I had spent myself asking the night for sleep.
> Broken in pieces I was — only the evil spirit was whole
>   in me;
> There was a curse on my bitten bloody lips . . . .
> And then . . . .

> Oh, then the old accustomed, impudent ghost came in:
> He wore my bagged, ragged pants, and was unshaven;
> And his face was the one I had seen in the mirror
> Too many times.

The last job I had in Chicago consisted of carrying, from one end of the city to the other, sacks of corks. At times the sacks were bigger than I was and with the excuses that they were only corks, I was loaded like a mule. I owed this job to a Christian Scientist, my boss being a Christian Scientist as well. The girls in the street used to laugh at me because I tottered under the loads and dragged my feet — but is there anything a woman will not laugh at? At times, the weight was too much for me and it was almost impossible for me to get up the stairs to the elevated trains.

Annie Glick

I spread wide nets in the sea of my memory, but few fish are caught in them, all too few. Among them there is a beautiful starfish, as beautiful as it is useless, and it bears some resemblance to you, oh, Annie Glick! (Words, words, words . . . . words which serve only to nail me to my cross, words which serve only to gag me, words which destroy one another and which leave me more lonely and wretched than I was before. It is so long that I have courted this infamous figure of death, and even she rejects me. She repulses me so fiercely that I know that no one and nothing can want me.) Annie, I never humbled myself so as to ask a single gift of that inexorable *grande dame* which is life. I was content to embroider a regal cloak of fantasy with which to cover my quaking bones.

Annie, open the door of my memories and into that dark little room will come the illumination of words. There is a closeness, a staleness, a musty stink in there, but light will disperse the ghosts and the smell. Annie, you were my greatest love. Your immense beautiful eyes saw everything except my love. Those big beautiful eyes, racially dark, racially profound, had been bathed and re-bathed by thousands of years of tears until they were all the more brilliant and tender and soft. They accompanied me through the tumultous life of those American years. You were a Jewish girl, and I have already said how I respect your race. The Jews are usually small, nearly all small and ugly, so many amongst them are ugly and just see what fine names they have: Sun's Ray, Field of Roses, White as Snow, Moon's Ray, Precious Stone, Good Luck, which was your name. I think I know the reason for this irony: when the Jews left their ghetto and dispersed in the world it was necessary for them to be named, and it is due to the comic genius of certain bureaucrats that these ugly samples of humanity were given such high-sounding names. There is no other explanation for it. You, at any rate, Annie, had taken possession of all the beauty of your ancient ancestry.

If I have any faith in the female being, I owe this faith to you, first beautiful woman that I loved, vitally, humanly beautiful. (She was also rather the type of the little cheap stenographer and many people found this ridiculous but I found this alluring.) Your face was mysterious, but of a mystery not too profound or too difficult to solve. Annie, you had no pity for me. You scoffed at my misery and my poverty. You scoffed at my love for Rimbaud. Do you remember when I gave you the manuscript of my long poems on Marianne Moore you said that it expressed nothing but hate for that stupid woman? Annie, you were the furrow behind each of my thoughts, the peace between my too numerous wars, you were the use for all usable words: beautiful, ugly, holy, ferocious, marvelous, miserable. Your legs were imperial, but if I went so far as to put my hand on them you said: "No, no, I am not your wife."

I remember you telling me that you had loved me once for two hours. Out of a lifetime, only two hours. It was the evening we met and your two little hands were in mine, their softness no longer a quality but a state of the spirit. We began to speak about Elena, who had introduced us, and I said that I thought she was Lesbian; and then your two hands swooned without life within mine and I felt them turn cold although they did not turn cold at all. Then I looked into your face and I said: "But it's all finished now, isn't it?" You laughed hysterically. When you wiped your mouth after I kissed you, you exasperated me, for I was ill even then and you knew it and that frightened you. But on that fine day when you really loved me, you did not wipe my kisses away. The first time I kissed you I went home and wrote and wrote, because inspiration draws from the sleeping heart at times a great wail, at times a gentle word, at times a sigh, and then lets the heart slumber on.

You remember how often you came to my room and I pretended to be asleep when you came in, out of some strange sense of coquetry? You remember what joy you brought when you entered and with what love I looked at you although what you brought me then was not yet love, only a splendid promise. I called you "darling," and "dear," and "love," and "treasure," words that were new and strange to me, and in contradiction to the belief of Soffice that you cannot easily call a woman sweet names. You made these words brim to my lips and I gave them to you so simply, almost like giving you a present, Annie darling. Presents, presents, presents! You waited like a child for presents. (In those days I was still fashionable in Chicago and I was invited everywhere for dinner. One week I decided to accept every dinner invitation and so I saved a week's pay. With this money I bought you a coral necklace which delighted you.) But the thing I could never give you was the supreme gift, happiness. I always made you more unhappy than you were by nature.

You were the verandah of my life from which I looked out on all the world passing by. You were the stairs of my will, leading upward. Your breasts, pear-shaped, were beautiful and proud and strong. Your delicate little hands awoke desires which flashed to the fingertips of men. Once when you promised me a thousand kisses, I took you to the cinema instead. For all I know, I may have been then like a man whose trembling hands do not dare to pluck the flower for fear of bruising it. You were tenderness entire, you were a sinuous soft curve which would have carved the heart from the breast of a eunuch. I do not know what you are like today. I know that Russian beauties like you become flaccid with the years (for you were only a poor miserable woman after all). Dostoievsky wrote that women of your type cannot endure, and he was surely an authority on the subject.

How many days of hunger in Chicago did I kill with sleep! (Sleep of which I was later deprived during the many eras of my illness.) Sleep was then my greatest friend. I used to drown myself in sleep, terrible sleepless sleep, a sleep that was close to madness. The conception of this madness was given me by a book which I had read and which impressed me very much. When I read a book and found it beautiful I experienced a sort of appetite for madness, and this appetite was roused in me by Dostoievsky's *Crime and Punishment*. (At one time, too, after reading a chapter of Papini, I wept tears of fire and brought myself to the point of writing him a desperate letter, telling him wildly of my admiration for him. He was good enough to answer me and we exchanged letters for more than a year. Then I wrote him that his letters to me were vacuous and he replied in irritation that he could not take the time to worry over the destinies of all his disciples. I also wrote to Croce and he condescended to send me a postcard. I translated into English, and very badly, his breviary of aesthetics, a little book containing some splendid expressions of truth.)

The great thing which I had against *Crime and Punishment* was that Raskolnikov was not enough of an artist and therefore his crime was actually a crime and his punishment actually a punishment. Artists are different from anyone else because they create new differences, for words are always the same and alter only when the vision alters. Thus Wagner, that stammering encephalitic, began to walk straight when he composed *Parsifal,* his greatest work. It is the musicians who hear the footfall of every man on earth and hear the whisper of every falling leaf. They also hear sounds which do not exist at all, except in the life of their minds. Thus Wagner heard the remedy for his ailment, and, listening to the notes of it, was cured. It is only in death that eternal deafness can be.

Because you were the feminine entity every poet needs, Annie, I was held captive in your hands so long and you were captive in mine for so short a time. I disturbed your dreams and you disturbed every day this soul of mine already shattered by so many cold and loveless passions. Do you remember that for more than a year I tried to model your face in clay? Do you remember the excursion we took to the Chicago dunes and did not succeed in seeing the lake? It is a comic thing to go to the dunes without seeing the waters of the lake. Do you remember when you drew a pen-knife out and threatened to cut my veins? Do you remember when you said I was God's younger brother while I believed I was God himself? Annie, every hour of my life has a minute for you in it and this should make me a little more expert than I am in the art of living or the art of keeping alive at all. I capsized the bark of your purity and of your youth, entering furtively at night into your dreams, entering furtively by day into your reality.

It has taken centuries of gigantic sorrow —
sorrow of an old world-weary race —
to build the sorrow that is in your eyes,
you, magnificent girl.

> *You said: Love is a swallow.*
> *Why would you capture a swallow.*
> *Love is not servile like*
> *a canary.*

You, girl with the perfect elbows.
Like a young, well-leafed branch in the wind
You walked.

> *But you said: You are hungry and a*
> *beggar.*
> *Love is a princely*
> *affair.*

And I shook my rags.
I ascended towards you
on my bleeding knees
for you were very high and goddess.

> *I said: Dignity is a blind god*
> *stalking majestically*
> *in a dirty alley.*

You gave me sorrow for my daily bread.
You threw cheap words at me
and I found what scant nourishment was in them,
and bit into them like a rabid dog.

The Dill Pickle Club

This little club was the fair of freaks, the union of eccentrics, the forum of those who arrived at the wrong moment, were wrongly welcomed and came to the wrong place. The president of it was Jack Jones, the King of the Discontented and the Disconnected, and there he throned with his way of talking as funny as he was himself. He once gave me as much as seven dollars for reciting the part of Anatole in Schnitzler's *Wedding of Anatole*. (It seems to me I am with the dead, evoking as I do these spectres of the past. But I hope you are not dead, Jack Jones, because Chicago needs you. Chicago needs those two small rooms, one over the other, which were called "The Dill Pickle.")

He was the emperor of the intellectual flops, Jack Jones. He was a minister of lost souls, a shepherd of wailing spirits under the rain and wind of life's adversity. (By wailing I mean making an unpleasant noise which the ears harken to subtly and terribly.) They were all interested in you, men like Sherwood Anderson and Waldo Frank, these proud men; and even the police came to spy on this curious group which you had gathered together in your rooms. You were ugly, but your wife was uglier than you. Perhaps the police came because once, while rowing on the lake, you lost your wife overboard and someone stupidly said that you had killed her. She had short hair, almost like a man's and she was small and dirty and devoid of elegance, but Jack Jones, you loved her. Your hesitation before the realities of life is sometimes called socialism, sometimes communism, sometimes anarchism, but it is hesitation just the same, and during the brief moment of your hesitating you established this kingdom of failures, of the disinherited, of those who bore like beasts of burden the staggering weight of their opinions. There was open discussion of all the fields of American achievement in those two little, tiny rooms of yours.

Tucker Alley was the apotheosis of all the strange alleys of Chicago. In their gutters cats come to die and there is always a stray dog nosing in the refuse, but Jack Jones brought his love into the depths of this mysterious cramped street. These stricken alleyways had lost even the sense of sight in the filthy dark; dirty children played in the rubbish, nothing beautiful ever passed that way; except this fact which may be beautiful or not but which at any rate is true — one's back had to be bowed under a burden before one could pass through the little door that led to Tucker Alley. A burden of protest against man's foulness, or a burden of anguish or of illness or despair; but anyway a burden before one could enter the ranks of that high pure army that waged its battle in Jack Jones' two rooms. In his little domain grew only stunted trees, but the strong manure of his remedies was good. He clothed those who had nothing, fed those who were in want, gave to those who begged the few dollars he could in payment of the little speeches they made. What sort of business he actually did in his "Dill Pickle," I do not know. He was neither very rich nor very poor, this president of the disbanded whom he divided into groups, ate them, digested them, evacuated them, so that there was always room for more.

That first year in Chicago I was consumed, devoured by the disease of impatience. And to heighten my anguish now, Annie went to New York. My bed was like a grave and my songs died there. I lay in my bed, extraordinarily dreary, and one day Sherwood Anderson and his wonderful wife came to my room, bringing me fruit, a magnificent grapefruit. To receive a gift from such a man seemed to me an amazing thing, and I talked my head off to them. But all the time I talked I could see that they did not much believe in my queer state of being. They thought me melodramatic and a play-actor and altogether disreputable. It must have been difficult to accept all my foolishness at its face value, for I believed I was God, and for a brief time

I was for myself the Only God, the First God. I told Anderson that I could bear vulgarity and filth and stupidity no longer. Take the songs they sang in America, songs sung by serious business-men and young men actually entering into the mystery of life. One of them was:

"Nelly, the garbage man's daughter,
She lived quite near the swill.
And sweet was the smell of the garbage
But she was sweeter still."

I held a photograph in my hand all the time I talked. It was Annie's. Suddenly I burst into sobs (a thing that happened to me very frequently these days). This time I wept because I believed I had discovered a blemish in that very lovely face. I could remember none of her words, except those she wrote me. She wrote me nearly every day from New York and her letters were vapidities, more than stupid, inane. I answered them with violence and this made her angry, and so it became a vicious circle. When she was angry she allowed three or four days to pass without writing, and then I would leap out of bed and telegraph her in desperation. Then finally she wrote me that she had the right to sanity and the right to live. The right to live! So many people think they have it and they haven't it at all, because life is a delicate and beautiful thing, perishable as a piece of fine embroidery which poverty and carelessness can destroy over night.

I remembered how sweet her lips were the first time I kissed them and I went and I shall always go searching for one thing equal to the sweetness of that kiss. I remembered the sound of her voice, high and winged, on the point at any moment of becoming hysterical. I remembered how ugly she was when she wept, with her face swollen; and I told the memories of her that she was the bed of that poor drying river, of that great wide river, of that wild torrent that was Carnevali. I made this invocation to Death.

Let me
Close my eyes tight.
Still my arms,
Let me
Be.
Then,
Come!
Let me be utterly alone:
Do not let the awful understanding that comes with
The thought of Death
Bother me.
Your love was not strong enough to hold me.

Death takes things away:
I have them here in my hands,
The rags.

I do not understand the cosmic humor
That lets foolish impossibilities, like me, live.
I have made a mess of it,
But I am no debtor.

It's the yearning of a nervous man,
The yearning for peace,
The curiosity for a word:
FOREVER.

If she would only come quietly,
Like a lady —
The first lady and the last.

Just not to hear any longer
The noise swelling from the morning streets,
Nor the two desperate sparrows chirruping;
Just not to fear any longer
The landlady.

Jack Jones took pity on me that time I ran stumbling and desperate to him and then fell to the ground. He picked me up and said, "Poor boy!" He took me to Dr. Vacca, and although the heart may be a great psychiatrist it is certainly a poor psychologist, for it never understood the sources of my anxiety and torture nor how terribly I was the prey of neurotic obsessions which destroy the soul from within. (These neurologists seek to heal the soul and they know nothing about it; they do not know that to understand the human soul one must be a poet and scarcely any of them have any sense of the poetic.) I did not see Jack Jones again until two years later, when I was to return to Italy. He gave a farewell party in my honor (where I managed to collect a few dollars). When I was but a stray dog myself, he was still faithful to me, faithful as a husband who is unaware that his wife has grown ugly with illness and the years. He was my spiritual father more than any priest ever was, and like a priest using Latin words, he spoke a language all his own, part Irish, part American: For to Do, For to Make, For to Go. One paid one small quarter to enter his temple, for more than any priest he had a temple, small and shabby and without direction like all the greatest things.

The Crisis

I believed that the time had come for the pestilence of poets to be brought to an end — an end to the songs, the odes, the poems, all the old putrid bunk. Poets, like desperate sparrows, leaving their excrement everywhere. I was sick of the tender hearts which poets carry exposed in their hands, the bloody trophies of their war with life — carrying them over life's highways and byways with their bleeding mouths crying, "Help, help!" although they know very well that no one will ever listen to them. (For who the hell listens to the poets except other poets?) On one side lies the great world and on the other the little poet with his infinitesimal words; the king of form, the indefatigable dancer. The artist does not see that his domain is emptiness, his empire muteness, his regime disorder, his dance dislocation. Oh, the artists, these photographers of love, these movie-picture takers of adventure! Too many words have been said already, too many phrases written, too many songs sung aloud, too many dances danced. The artist speaks of God like a relative, he treats Him like a cousin, whether insulting or praising Him. And the artist is so in need of God, he needs so bitterly to have God hearken to his little words.

The other day I met a dancer. He had blue eyes and a lady's mouth and his voice was sickening soft. His name was Mr. Snake. When he lifted his arm, bent at the elbow, hand horizontal outward, I was afraid; and when of his legs he made a perfect twist, I laughed. In other words, I enjoyed his dancing and was very much interested in it.

"Mr. Snake, I think I want to learn how to dance."

"My dear man, dancing is art, every art — art."

"That doesn't make much of a difference to me."

"It makes all the difference in the world to me."

"Ah, you clever rascal!" said I, with a sneer of understanding. Shortly after, I went home. The sneer became embarrassed as I was walking on my way home. The sneer chilled as the stars laughed on top of my ungainly head. But at last it assumed its ultimate shape, becoming a grimace of fear as I saw moonlight break against a doorway and smooth the wind-swept sidewalk. I must learn dancing. It would be good for my legs, good for my arms, for my outward appearance, and I have often desired, I always desire that bright elegance which — I must learn how to dance.

I felt my knees, I looked down upon the shapeless bagging of my pants, saw my feet sprawling in my too large shoes and imagined with a quick pang my worn-out heels. I must learn how to dance. There I was, with my dangling arms, my heavy, uncontrolled and perhaps uncontrollable hands; my legs always bent a little forward, my belly pushed backward, my shoulders rounded forward. As I walked my head pecked the air like a helpless hen's. With the concentrated despair of twenty years of clumsiness suddenly revealed, I lifted a cursing hand. But the arm came up slowly and dislocatedly, without direction, refusing to be cast into a gesture. In the name of Mr. Snake, what was this? Where was I going — for, indeed, my body was not following! My head this way, my belly that, my knees that way! What was this?

I was in the shape of an ugliness, a drifting thing, a walking contradiction. I had been unconscious of a great ridiculous absurdity and it had, without my knowing, moulded me. Damn me! I thought I was going somewhere — along ecstatic streets crowned with glare of lamplight — and my body wasn't following. My *form* wasn't following, *I* wasn't following. I was only a shadow, that of Mr. Visionary who had so inspired me once, or any other shadow anyway. I was a warped effort on a road to the splendid somewhere which I had conceived one day . . . conceived beautifully one day, — oh, I remember that gesture, I remember the dance I had then begun.

God, I was a thwarted effort and my own damnation and my own end it was that twisted me down like that! I couldn't any more learn to dance. Oh, if I lift a finger now do I not know how far within me that motion begins! You couldn't change that far within. Mr. Snake, what can you do for me? Haven't I been aware of that which made me as I am now? I have, I know I hand. I can be saved. Mr. Snake . . . . ah, the hell with you, I don't need you! I'll learn, I'll learn, almighty stars, watching eyes upon this world, seers, judges, WATCH ME!

And I lifted myself up. I forced my body into a complete gesture of immobile contrition, knowing that if the gesture was true it would be the destruction of my former clumsiness, which was a weird root in the sodden depths of me. Perfectly immobile, in tears and frets, in deadly sweat, through every pore of my body, the years of filth that had clogged me oozed out of me. I don't know how I didn't die. Then it was that I felt ashamed of every word I had ever confessed to anyone else, then it was that the gross lie of what I had always called "my impetuous naive nature" assumed a form that frightened me beyond human words, then it was that I stood waiting, humble before the ash-can which open-mouthed watched me free myself. And the stars laughed insanely — unless it was my eyes were insane.

Then I moved. You know, there is some greatness in me, you know that I always saw it, the beacon shining very far — a little infinitely beyond every street's end, over the hump of this street that jumps into the abyss, accompanied to its perdition by the lampposts' procession. I always saw it, dim as lit fog, thinking it was probably nothing but lit fog. But now on top of a house a star shone, a hole revealing that the sky is a diamond palace covered with a blue cloth. Well, I had to hurry up, as I was at the end of my strength. I swung myself up, whirled through the air, writing a beautiful parabola over the skirt of night and

Cra - rck!

I fell on the side of a house and broke my bones in pieces. I hung in shreds from several laundry ropes until they came to get me. The last thing I saw on earth was the horrid mouth of a window which had been gaping that was fifty years.

In the crisis, I believed that I was walking the centuries

looking for my face, for the losing of my reality also meant the
losing of my face to me. I felt I belonged to the nineteenth
century more than to any other, perhaps entirely, insanely, to
the nineteenth century. The nineteenth century was made up of
masks: the masks of poetry, Paul Verlaine, Arthur Rimbaud,
Verhaeren, Carducci, Leopardi — all more or less crazy, all
more or less sick; and Baudelaire, altogether crazy. The masks
of music, with Schumann, Beethoven, the one crazy and a
suicide, the other deaf; and Donizetti, crazy too. I thought with
love of Van Gogh's suicide and the philosophy of Nietzsche.

I believed absolutely now that I was the Only God. But no
god was ever humbler than I, and no god ever made worse
blunders, and no god was ever as ugly as I was. No god had
ever satisfied me as this suddenly conceived god did, and no
god ever sprang as spontaneously to life, and no god wanted the
colors of the world so passionately as I. I believed no god had
ever been as good as I was, and by goodness I meant a very
large thing, something enormous, terrific, something so great
I did not know its name. Yet now that it has passed, it seems
futile, incredible. I was terrified by the totally new way the very
light from the window looked, such ethereal light, such flimsy
light, weak and shaking in the window. I thought I was dying,
or about to die, or even that I had accomplished death. Noises
took on another meaning, but the noise of my own voice was
the most terrible of all. I cried out as loud as possible my crazy
formula of godhead, repeating that I was for myself and for all
men the First God, the Only God, that I was a shipful of spices
come suddenly to port. But I was the one apostle of my own
religion: I respected the sun and the moon although, in my fierce
pride, I didn't need either of them very much. I had always
hated sophistication and now I wept and screamed for simplicity,
only simplicity was not to be taken for sheer idiocy. To be a
god, a true god, one must be filled with simple things: this was
the simplest way to reach the perfection of being god.

It happened while I was reading a book on Chinese history:
suddenly the knot of despair and dismay loosened in me and the
whole room reeled, and I stood up reeling, drunk. I was going
crazy and I knew it. Every vestige of reality had left me and

I was staggering and stumbling about, helpless in an uncertain world. I flew to Sherwood Anderson's and I asked him to give me something to eat, thinking that the mechanical action of eating would help bring me back to reality. I devoured the food he gave me but it was to no avail. With the excuse that his wife would be coming home soon and might be afraid of me in such a state, Sherwood Anderson fairly chased me out of the house. I reeled out into the snow, drunk with these awful symptoms of insanity, wandering through the streets that were forever unknown and forever known to me. My companions were the horrible Fear of Fears, the Fear that now, all of a sudden, I should no longer understand the meaning of anything; and the Misery of All Miseries: of knowing that the strength to distinguish one thing from another, and the will to distinguish even, is gone. I can still hear the awful noises I made as I went — the grumbling that I mistook for poetry, and the weeping that was the most hideous weeping in the world.

I knew now that it was only pride that had kept Sherwood Anderson nailed before me, listening to my tirades and my speeches, for he had surely always hated everything about me and his eyes said so clearly. And yet I had gone to him asking for the monstrous charity of understanding in the crisis. Out in the snow again I said out loud: now that corner is going to stop being a corner, that lamp-post cease being a lamp-post, that gutter no longer run with its burden of dirty water, because the beloved list of understandable things has been inadvertently destroyed, because in this immaculate sky-piece a screw has been loosened, a nut has gone daffy, has gone cuckoo, and the whole machine of reality has jumped the switch. I said: because I am or will be crazy presently, it is impossible for me ever to grasp reality again. And then something strange happened or did not happen: I felt that one of my eyes could not shut, that it would never be able to shut, and that it acted now quite separately from the other eye.

Prestige

It must have been about two in the morning when I got back to my room, and I stood looking at myself in the mirror, able to see nothing, to prove nothing. I spent the time until daylight shouting that I had found the formula of godhead, this is the formula: YES — NO and YES and NO. This is the formula of acceptance and denial, at the same time and at different times, and if simultaneous acceptance and denial could be achieved, then godhead would be at your door. It seemed to me that it was now all a matter of speed, to say these things fast enough and loud enough, but at the same time I knew it was not entirely a matter of speed. Above everything else, it was not deceit; it was no betrayal, it was not an apology for my weakness and my low-minded ways. I was not fooling myself. I was convinced that this was the reasoning that must be the one, the only one, for my particular metaphysical needs. Moreover, I believed it was a reasoning that could save everyone, for Tolstoy once said that no man is decisively one thing or another forever but that man is one thing at one time of his life and at another time he is another, and that it is blindness of the spirit not to see that man is never quite the same. This was a thought which helped me to shout louder and wilder the proclamation of my ready-made divinity, and I filled the house and the night with the repetitions of my formula for insanity: YES-NO, YES and NO, NO-YES.

Once during the night I left the room, thinking that death was dragging me through the door and down the hall. I screamed for help, yelling: "Help me, help me, I am dying!" I went out into the snow again, half-naked this time, but gods seldom catch cold. I sat down on my bed in my room again, so miserable, so desperate, believing so frantically that I was a god that I did not know I was an utter fool. No god before me had ever really been any good, I kept saying out loud; no god had ever really been not a fake, not one of them had ever been a really satisfying god. I scorned the idea of being a miracle maker; no real god ever made miracles, no real god needed this enforcement of his spirit. The great mistake Christ had made was that of saying "My kingdom is not of this earth" and then trying to prove, and proving, with miracles that his kingdom really was of this earth. As long as gods did not require miracles, it came to me that there were then surely many more gods than people had imagined — a whole new mythology or history of deism. Even the realists were gods of a sort.

At first I was appalled by the extraordinary simplicity of the thing. I had found the solution of life in the formula:

God is or God is not.
God neither is nor is not.
God absolutely is
or
God absolutely is not.

This was a sort of pantheism which I felt I had reached. I was the centre of the earth; the whole universe revolved around me. My four states of mind had to be and were now expressed in one single phrase: "Yes and no. Neither yes nor no. Yes or No." And then the wonder at its simplicity gave way to a sort of craftiness: after all, why should I consider death, why should I give a thought to death? The easiest thing in the world was to live and now I could live, survive forever because of this simple formula of godhead I had found.

> O altars of a little comfort, altars of a dyspeptic god gone
> crazy in America for lack of personality (hamburger
> steak, Irish stew, goulash, spaghetti, chop suey and
> curry!) O lunch-room counters!

O tripods of a little secure religion, tripods of a little secure
   beauty! O kitchen fires!
O bedraggled romances, O alcoholic ladies in crimson and
   green mists, O women so cheap and ingratiating, O
   sacrifices for you, ladies, of all the flesh and all the
   brains! O saloons!

My malediction on the cowards who are afraid of the word
   (the word is a kind sweet child, a kind sweet child!)
Malediction on the sacrifices of the dumb and deaf!

Hesitating everywhere, hesitating fearfully,
The few poets, they who weigh with delicate hands,
Walk in the unfrequented roads,
Maundering,
Crying and laughing
Against the rest.

The morning after the awful night I found my room filled
with women, and this seemed to me only another part of my
insanity. There were five or six women in my room and the
cackle, cackle, cackle was tremendous. Among them I recognized Mrs. O'Keefe, the landlady, big and protective; she seemed
to be directing the talk and the noise of the whole bunch. I
thought it strange that there were no men in my room, but this
was perhaps because they had already gone to work. I remember
they brought me ham and eggs to eat, and I ate them in the
room of another roomer. I heard them calling up Harriet Monroe
and after a short time she joined all the other women in the room.

The second night, Harriet Monroe spent sitting by my bed.
That little captain of the ragged, the mad army of poets, she sat
there all night and let me talk. I told her I had committed a
grave sin: that of loving success. I had nursed success, held it
close to my heart, watched it grow and develop, until the total
downfall came. In my life there had been nothing very triumphal
in either the ascent or the descent. Both were built on drab
foundations, both had a bottom of misery. It was my fault, for
I always went too passionately, too fiercely at people. Some I

scared and others I annoyed. There was that time at Bill Williams'
where I talked and talked and talked. I talked for a whole day
and in the evening I wanted to talk some more, but unfortunately
I was made to stop. There was no love, no homage in my words,
only an eagerness to be understood and therefore I blooming
well knocked their heads off.

I do not know how many dollars Harriet Monroe gave
me; I lost count of them long ago. But I know that for fifteen
days, part of which time was spent in the Psychopathic Ward of
a big hospital, I was God, the First, the Only God. I do not
remember having slept during these fifteen days, and probably
did not. A cyclone had struck me and whirled me from the earth
of common-places. There was little serenity in all this, but there
was no help for it. I must make apostles, I must gather disciples
about me. It was no partial craziness which possessed me but it
was a thing which now owned my whole soul. It had been coming
too long a time to pass me lightly. I had felt it coming towards
me with a remote and gradually increasing sound and strength,
this madness of mine. The extreme feebleness which is as well
a symptom of this illness, and which eventually succeeds in
robbing one of the power of movement, had been coming slowly
on me. This is an enormous illness, a primordial one: when one
is badly stricken, one crawls awkwardly about as the first men
must have done. According to Freud, it is easier to sing than
to speak, and so the first men must have done. There is something poetic about this illness: the eternal need to change one's
position is synonymous with the need to change expression, and
woe to him who uses the old positions as woe to the poet who
uses the old phraseology.

My faith became a kind of pragmatism now, simple to
excess, baffling yet beautiful and convincing; full of wonder, its
violence, its very violence being its indisputable truth. I could
even find the right words to describe it to others and in some
way I made apostles, talking endlessly, endlessly to the other
patients in Saint Luke's Hospital in the Psychopathic Ward.
Romance had been thrown on the rubbish heap, scientists created
nothing but ugly machines now, I said, and romance had gone
to the dogs. I am astonished at the amount of spiritual joy this

thought brought me. It seemed to me that my spirit and soul ached with the truth. I was joyous and aching all over with exalted spiritual anguish, and I was proud of this kind of pain. This godhead of mine was a release of many things to me; this god, however great a fake he was, was a great comfort, a great find, a valid discovery for the time that he endured.

Now I knew I was the master of death: he was the servant who would come when I called. I teased him, provoked him on purpose, challenged him. I called him vulgar and funny names, but I never once gave him the love he requested. I knew he was still far away, and I knew he would not hang around my bed for long watching me lying there. But once, just once, I certainly did feel his hands go over my body and leave me coldly sweating, rigidity in my muscles, despair in my heart, fear in my mouth, and a new craze in my eyes.

Convalescence

When I left the Psychopathic Ward I was taken to a sanatorium which was ruled over by the awful Dr. Newman. (At the end of my two-month sojourn there this monster told me he would put me in the bug-house if I ever fell into his hands again.) Hospitals have taken the better part of my life and of my soul. Hospitals are now the milestones which mark the different stages of my life; hospitals end by exhausting even the strongest of us. In hospitals, butcher-doctors dole out death, doctors who know nothing or nearly nothing; diagnosis and the methods of diagnosis must be false, since there are no diseases, there are only the ill.

My friends paid about fifty dollars a week for me in this sanatorium, and there I was showered with a lot of fine food. Visitors and money, every day visitors and money, the money a little more important than the visitors. Tennessee Mitchell came to see me, and her husband, Sherwood Anderson, but I could only think of the night he chased me from his house. Alfred Kreymborg and his lovely wife came, and Carl Sandburg, Robert McAlmon, Mitchell Dawson. Mitch was more than a visitor, this crazy man of letters, this big-hearted generous boy. I always imagined him as doing all kinds of phallic dances in solitude. This man was miserably a lawyer, poor kid. (His business was mostly with quarrelling Italians.) Eric Hjorth came there too, perhaps the most elusive of all the friends I had. His eyes were cold agate, like the fjords of his Scandinavia; they still shine in my memories for me. He said I was a great man, even in this period of my decadence, and I was grateful to him because I was in need of praise, like all poets, good or bad. He spent much money on me when he and my other friends paid these hospital fees.

But Annie Glick and Louis Grudin were the two beings who had mattered most to me, and it was of them that I thought with grief. (I have said a few words, utterly inadequate, about Lou. I have said more concerning Annie, and this was a mistake, for friendship is far more than love; it is a thing for the strong.) Louis was generously beautiful. His sensuality was fierce, but he himself was not aware of it. He was the strongest man physically that I had ever met, and his mind was as powerful as his body. He looked like a kindly prize-fighter. He was as violent in his tears as in his laughter. I loved him. I thought his poetry was great, and now I can only remember the following lines from a "Miniature of the Woolworth Building":

> There shall be peace,
> Pale glory in the mist
> When they will fashion their cities after you,
> White waterfall of granite
> From heaven.

And now, either for my sake or otherwise, Annie came back from New York. I do not know how it happened, but I knew that the time had passed for her to come, that she had come too late. It was no longer true for me that extremes meet; extremes were now the same thing. Hate and love, life and death, these were the same. She wept every time she came to see me, and if the first few times I dried her tears respectfully and with awe, after a while I got fed up with her crying and a bit later I got exasperated. These tears, which for women are a simple release, became ridiculous in the end. My tears, on the contrary, were terrible. But I did not weep for Annie or for love. In fact, Annie seemed a little ridiculous to me now and I made a little song which pleased me much at the time:

> Annie would not marry Jack
> She would not marry any-
> body not salamme-lack
> not even Lord Dunsany.

Once out of the sanatorium, I felt renewed, restored. I had never been so happy as now. It wasn't I that was new but the whole world around me. The springtime was all a-stir, all mobilized, all in a frenzy of dance and rhythm, all new and clean. I had on a fine overcoat that was a gift from Sherwood Anderson and this gave me a romantic look. He also gave me a cane which helped me to stand and walk and with which I played the role of elegance. All was cool, fresh, fine. Everything around me seemed important, vital, forceful, strong. I floated on the air of the wind-blown afternoons. I danced over city and country, glad, fearfully glad. I scarcely felt lonely any more and then only enough to temper my gladness; I was proud that I understood all this joy, this movement that was even more marvelous than joy, all this new, brand-new, coolness and freshness of life. I went off my head with joy one day because a small little girl I passed in the street called me "sweetheart." I was happy all day long. I danced, actually danced, and I painted pictures in my room, and I began to be a sculptor again, using plasticine.

Annie came to my room almost daily and even loved me a little bit. But in that night which followed the long splendid day of my convalescence, that sombre jungle in which the wild animals of my faculties roamed savagely, Annie became the Diana, the implacable huntress of my reason and my faculties. I knew that whenever two things approached and touched in this world the result was a kiss, that the infinitely delicate horizon touches the earth, kissing it; that there is no sound or poetry except when two things meet and embrace. But this contact of my illness with your health was a little of a ghastly kiss and you felt this, and it was this that made your face swell with weeping and become ugly. (He who nourishes himself on memories is already partly dead, and a man half dead has less right to life than a man wholly dead.) I, who could not walk erect any more, had become partly your clown and the garments you fashioned for me, Annie, were those of a harlequin. Annie, I scarcely know now if you were ugly or beautiful. Your face has been taken from my memory and I can only see you crying and crying; you cried because you could not love me.

(She is a sweet. It's the man who is ferocious and savage,

a poor sad man. They didn't give him any motherly care at all.
But she's a sweet. He wants to drag her ferociously into his cave
— you must excuse him. He wants to make a statue of death
and there is no other model. There was no other model when
the open sun had burnt out or scorched or melted all the other
girls.

But she went around of a morning, and having found a
simplified little flower she sat down by it and she's smiling still,
sitting down by the flower. Flowers and chips of sunlight and
grey pebbles shame the furious will-to-do of the man, so he hides
his head in the day and at night only he lifts a frowning face
to the stars. Poor boy, he loved the stars and they deceived him,
and as he loves them still he frowns at them in the night and
shrieks "Flirts!" He shrieks, but his heart is as lonely as a leaf-
less tree standing companionless over the shroud of the dunes.

Now the time has come for the last fight. He has the good
chance of seeing a darkness in the eyes of her and from that
darkness images of death arose before the hungry hands of the
man. That's the only reason he is still after her. Once she stood
shamefully naked before the cave of the man and sang:

> I shall laugh until
> your heart be
> a dark accompaniment
> to the shrill and thin music of my teeth.
> Then I'll go,
> then I'll go
> away.
> I'm shaking this bouquet,
> I'm shaking — don't you see? — this bouquet
> to make you come out of there.
> Then you can have the bouquet,
> spoiled for your sake
> and I'll go gather
> other and more flowers.
> I'll make a kid of you,
> you'll follow me.
> Follow, follow,

in the cortege
of the Fairy Queen
whom children follow.

But the time for Fairy Queens was shut in the graves of
books, so the man smiled pleasantly. And he smiled well. Because
he knew no Fairy Queen to have ever had legs as beautiful as the
old whore Death. He was proud of his love, his unrequited love,
and he was waiting for this love. His old love would come and lie
down by him and say not a word, his old love would be a rock
to echo his last word — that is what he thought.

He thought so, and he waited, his last word gripped within
the fist of his dry heart, smiling.)

There came too to my room a sort of object who described
himself as the brother-in-law of a toothless and stammering poet,
Maxwell Bodenheim. He had a stupid face with a protruding
lower lip which almost compensated for the rest. He installed
himself in my room and there was no wanting him to stay or not
— he simply remained. He objected to having to sleep on a quilt
on the floor as he wanted instead to sleep in bed with me, a thing
I never permitted him to do. He went out and looked for work,
found a job and stayed there like an old friend, he who was in
reality all too new. He disturbed me very much, but little did he
care, and even had he known that he disturbed me he would have
stayed on just the same. He dulled my nights; he was so absurd
that I almost liked him. He was an obscure soul who tried to ex
press himself in little stupid poems. He was surely the Lord of
Stupidity, but he was not altogether an oaf; had he been entirely
an oaf it would have been better, for then I would willingly have
turned him out.

He was almost haunting with his cretin remarks and his
childish ways, always seeking something which cannot possibly
be found, pausing now and then to look back the way he has
come with astounded wondering eyes. He had one of those faces
which you see better once you have turned the other way. He
approached one with an affectionate manner which ended by
captivating you. He even possessed a certain devious intelligence
which seemed to enable him to grasp things which were so

superior that he was totally incapable of understanding them. So true it is that the human intelligence is both frail and plastic, adjusting itself to all conceivable things. It is like gun-shot which, failing to kill an elephant, may happen to kill a bird. His name was Cosachebrilla (Thing that Shines) but he never shone at all. He was a Jew, of course, like his brother-in-law, the poet, whom I have called elsewhere a stinking mass with sleepy eyes. I don't know how the landlady did not perceive that he slept in my room, but she didn't.

Finally, his sister, Minnie Bodenheim came and she became a good friend to me, as kind a friend as if she had not slapped my face once when I insulted her husband in a speech. Minnie told me that my eyes had once looked like Valentino's, but this was only half a compliment because, as she said it, this meant they were no longer so. I took her to see Grasso, the Sicilian actor, and she tried hard to understand what he said. And now, perhaps in this very theatre, I was seized by a terrible nervous anxiety — the second stage of my illness — a cursed and horrible fear that something was about to happen which never happened: a terror of expectation, a continuous, an unflagging assault of anxiety. Here, in the first gallery, I felt my blood and body itching with the desire, not so much the desire as the necessity, to leap over the edge.

Grasso was in his period of decadence too, a tired and supine man who dragged himself with effort across the stage. He stammered hoarsely and feebly instead of proclaiming his lines, and I seemed to find in him some apotheosis of myself and my decline. He was approaching the end; this man who had been a lively and vibrating actor was no longer able to rouse the enthusiasm of American ladies who were accustomed to worse, and much worse, than this.

Eric Hjorth, who spoke of his mother as "my little Swedish mother," came to my room and sometimes slept with me. But "slept" is not the word, for I kept him awake all night so that he should accompany me down the scabrous ways of my insomnia. In this illness, either one sleeps or wakes for long unbroken periods, and I used to go shouting and raving at night along Lake Shore Drive. I used to cry aloud my mad barbarous songs, and sobbed against the trees, great tears falling from my eyes. If to weep is easy for a woman, it is a very difficult thing for a man. Man drags the cry of anguish from his breast, this equivalent to a woman's sob. It is torn from his depths, it seems to be torn out of his guts, and does more harm than good. Whoever heard me sob would have taken me for a madman, and it was indeed a madness.

Eric, whether you are alive or dead, I ask your forgiveness. I did nothing but disturb you and caused you incredible pain. In the furnished rooms we sought together, you looked for running water and I for open air, and so we never agreed. But your memory is sweet just the same. When we went into the country and I picked wild flowers I once asked you to carry them for me and you said you would not know what to do with all those weeds. But those weeds were beautiful to me, and the beautiful part of our friendship was that we were not alike.

Debacle and Damnation

Then the hours and days of misery came back to me and took full possession of me again. Where there had been friendship, a deluge of friends before, I now found only supercilious disdain. I had been sick too long. I should have known better. Everywhere I went now I met contempt. Before I had been invited even to the Cooper-Carlton by the Ben Bacharachs. (An intelligent bunch, these Bacharachs, who were ready to begin a philosophical discussion at any time. Walter Bacharach always sat smoking a fine big cigar, the finest cigar to be found in the American world.) But now the access to houses which remained open to anybody was denied to me. I was called "Carnevali" where before I had been simply Em. I had fallen, but I fell from high. This made it all the more painful, although more dignified too.

Once it was forbidden me to sit down at table with the other guests by the lady of the house; she who in other days had granted me favors of a forbidden kind. Here I met Mayo Wadler, a fine violinist, and during the evening she shouted loud enough for the whole roomful of people to hear that I was indecent with my continuous trembling. Oh, misery, misery, their misery as much as mine! The misery of petty things, the misery of big things, the misery in one's own soul and the misery all around one. But why this change, why? Simply because people got tired of hearing my name, tired of looking at me, tired of knowing how I had fallen from a terrific height and got smashed to awful, shameful, ignominious smithereens.

I was all over the place. I was abused by the Chicago hostesses for being too good, now I was accused of being too mild and meek. And now there was no more money to be had. I was forced to go around asking for a quarter from everyone I knew and from some I did not know. Sam Putnam was my chief benefactor and I revere his name. Finally, a great doctor told me that I should get out of cities, and my friends got more money together and sent me first of all to the Indiana dunes.

Here began the last great beautiful days of my life! Oh, my true loves, those unforgettable days, those incredible spring and summer months! The first night on the dunes was a prelude to what was to come: I found a burnt-down shanty, shrouded in what seemed to be an old sail, and there I went to sleep. I slept utterly alone and unafraid. This night and the nights to come were bitterly cold and I froze but I rejoiced. I trembled, trembled with my illness and with the cold, but I was happy. I could have taken into my arms the beauty of stars and sky and the beautiful rich black heaven.

As soon as I awoke in the morning, I rushed into the lake. Sometimes I would swim so far out into the lake that a great fear would overcome me, the fear of never reaching shore again. The fear of drowning would make me scream out for help although I knew there was no one to come to my rescue. I thought of the dunes as the sand-breasts of an unseen god and I would fall on them and kiss them many times. There was a suffused smile in the morning dunes and the waters of the lake answered back. The dunes were my white paradise of sand and back in the ravine was the mosquitoes green hell.

One day I stole a rope from some fishermen, and then I collected driftwood and made a raft. With the long stolen rope, I fastened my raft to shore. I drank sassafras tea, I climbed trees, I let my beard grow until I looked like Jesus Christ. I sang in the water and out, I sang in the daytime and I sang at night and exercized in order to get tired enough to sleep. The days were terrifically hot and the nights unbearably cold. At night the dunes were like ice-cream to my flesh, and during the day they were blasts from a roasting furnace. Once, as I was sitting on a stump, a wasp bit me ferociously. I took a special pleasure and wonder and interest in this smarting pain.

My life was thus divided: I got up at sunrise and went straight into the water. Then I came back and cooked my inevitable oatmeal and sometimes some flapjack, made in a haphazard way but pretty good at that. Then I would fall asleep swathed in sunlight, in a mild enough seeming sunlight, but at noon I would wake with a violent headache. (Beware, you who trust the light of day and fall asleep in the sun.) Then I would cook another meal for myself and spend almost all the rest of the day in the water, unless the lake was rough, which misplaced all the day's plans. Once a week I went to Chesterton to get the usual check from Mitchell Dawson. Between the sand dunes and Chesterton was a sort of little town. There I stopped to buy my food supply, and this weekly trip always exhausted me.

The dunes were delicate ladies, dressed in transparent pink muslin dresses at sunset and dawn, and I loved them so that they sapped my strength. Behind them was the green of the luxuriant vegetation; sand-cherries, quite edible, and wild grapes, not quite so edible, and the smell of the pine trees that is so keen that it searches and pries into your body, caressing it in its own way. I got drunk with bathing in the lake, and I would swim out quite a space, pushing my raft before me. Then I would climb on it and stand singing, singing, singing. I had a choice program, beginning with the swan song from "Lohengrin" and including "Ave Maria." The lake water was my absinthe, but the dunes were tremendous, almost uncanny in their power; fierce always, terrible always, always too exciting to my poor sick body. The only nasty thing about the dunes was the patch of poison ivy that grew near them.

No one got up at sunrise in order to bathe the way I did in the lake. No one saw rapture in the sand the way I did. I knew the odor of every leaf, the fragrance of every fruit. Great God, all was a tremendous perfume thrust back into one's nose. When I came back out of the water, I sang even more fiercely, I screamed with joy and drunkenness. By God, these dunes were mine, for I was no Sunday caller! I did not love them merely because I would soon leave them, but because it seemed to me they requited my love. I had become the real crazy man of the dunes. I walked naked as God made me all over the green of the dunes and the yellow of the sand. I was accused, that is the right word, of feeding on little fishes, of eating them raw. I was suspected of being the murderer of a man whose body was found, carbonized, in the dunes. But I was none of these things.

Then I went on to other places: to Milwaukee, who lifted a proud shoulder to Michigan Lake. She had no skyscrapers then, but she had a certain elegance, a certain prettiness. Weathers have always intrigued and mystified me and sometimes the taste of a certain day will bring back other days to me. I remember one dawn in the Minnesota woods — such sharp colors I can never forget: such violet, such blue, such deep red. The air and the colors were electric, threatening bad weather for the dawning day. In the loam of the Minnesota woods, under the already rotting leaves, in the fresh block bogs, I left a portion of my spirit and my youth. Sometimes a deer showed itself for a moment and then was gone again in the mystery of those woods. Prudish little beasts, living a life of tender fear. The loam, that perfumed rottenness, evoked tiny lakes of water under my feet as I walked, making that entrammeled voyage through the brush and the trees of the shore. Minnesota woods, untouched by man or woman — still untouched by the shame that goes with woman and the arrogance that goes with man — you tore the veils from my eyes until they were worthy to look at beauty. I found only one thing that was not beautiful in your woods: an orchid that looked like a swollen face.

There is a weather in Chicago that makes the lake waters green, sharp, almost unpleasant to the eye; and another weather that fills the sky with racing spaces of dark blue. These spaces of color are so clear, so pure that they have a virginal aspect, like a pure woman showing her breasts inadvertently. There are more than a hundred springtime weathers, and there is a summer weather when hot chocolate seems to have been poured onto the air. There is a weather of wet leaves after a storm, when little drops rain down if one touches a tree and the sun returns suddenly after a brief absence. There is a weather when the sky seems an omelette, and other weathers charged with the smell of flowers. Some are like the gas lit in a room.

For a while I lived in a shack in Ravinia, Illinois, with Mr. Jens Jensen, a worthy old man who bestowed on me great parts of his big heart. But I was so disorderly, so slovenly, so expensive (always telephoning to town), that he was forced to show me the door. There was no help for me, no cure, because of the major sin I had committed: that of loving success. Above all I was an envious man, madly jealous of all the writers who had got out more than one book. (I am jealous now, yes, jealous even of Shakespeare. I am frantically in need of praise, I am crazy about being considered a major poet, and the fact that there may be other poets greater than I am makes my heart sick.) I was slovenly in body and soul, downright lazy at times. I was like a dog barking at stones which he cannot pick up and throw.

For a while I fed on the remembrance of my success but now there was nothing left. After Jensen put me out, I went with thirty dollars to buy a tent and I went back to the dunes again. I who had been the god of blackness over the whiteness of the dunes was merely a sick man now. The sand seemed commonplace to me, life was a drab impossibility, not even physical exercize was worth a cent. I could no longer understand the humor of the cosmic prank that my existence was. I could not see the funny side of it any more. I could not see the point of dragging this infamous life along behind me as an idiot draws after him a crowd of jeering boys.

In Chicago there was a Greek who said one of the most majestic things I shall ever hear in this muted-down life, now that folklore has ceased being produced and folk-women wear hats. He owned a fruit store on North Avenue in which flowers also were sold. Because I saw carnations for thirty-five cents a dozen — as if they had been a commodity gone down at last — I entered. I had a cane and leaned on it. He said:

"What's the matter, sick?"

"Yes. Do I look it?"

"What's the matter, rheumatism?"

I said no and I explained, but he didn't get it, so rheumatism it had to be. He said:

"Young fellow like you, rheumatism! *To* my country, no rheumatism at all!"

I saw the sun and the moon mirrored on the face of Lake Michigan (as love was never mirrored on Annie's face), the lake with which I inebriated myself every morning when I was alone on the dunes, the lake of Carl Sandburg. . . . I had lain my broken body on the shore of Lake Superior, exhausted without having worked, spent without having given . . . Every night I went to bed saying:

"Tomorrow will be beautiful, for tomorrow comes out of the lake."

Sitting on a bench facing God's beautiful lake,
A poem to God beautiful.

Lake Michigan,
The love a poor sick body held
(Sifted by the sieve of a hundred nights of pain),
A poor sick body gave it all to you.

Your absinthe
Has intoxicated me.

Having risen out of your waters,
In front of my great eyes now
There is a mad blur of sunlight,
And the city spread out before me calling for a great curve:
"Come, enter, conquistador!"

The line of your horizon, pure and long, hitched to the
        infinite both ways,
Where the mist lies like Peace.
Swimming, I flirted with death,
Saw death running over the shadow-laced ripples;
And turned around as you threw water in my eyes
And laughed at death, as death's brother, the devil, would.

You slammed open the doors of the sky
And there stood the tremendous sun.

Lake, gilded in the morning,
I have come out of you,
A fresh-water Neptune;

And the water rang little bells
Trickling down
Along my flesh.

Lake, garden of the colors,
Sweet-breathing mouth of Chicago,
Words die in the fingers of a sick man,
As children dying on a poor father.
Take my promise, lake.

THE RETURN

I.   *To Dorothy Dudley Harvey*

After eight days of the monotony
Of sea and sky appeared
City-on-the-rock, proud and beautiful —
Gibraltar.

Then, after two days of Mediterranean,
Monstrous water-lilies of the sea
Budding forth on the ocean —
The Neapolitan islands.

Then the Neapolitan coast
Besprinkled, as with flowers, with little white houses;
And Mount Vesuvio forgetting its head
In a confusion of cloud and smoke;
Pusilleco, place of trysts.

Here begins my Italy —
Where memories spring like geysers
Crying at me where I place my feet;
Italy that receives with benignity
This shipwreck — my sick body,
And this feeble candle-light — my soul.

II.

I come from America, the land that gathers
The rebels, the miserable, the very poor;
The land of puerile and magnificent deeds:
The naive skyscrapers, votive candles
At the head of supine Manhattan.

I remember Manhattan Island crowned with docks.

I come from America where everything
Is bigger but less majestic;
Where there is no wine.
I arrived in the land of wine —
Wine for the soul.
Italy is a little family;
America is an orphan,
Independent and arrogant,
Crazy and sublime,
Without tradition to guide her,
Rushing headlong in a mad run which she calls progress.
Tremendously laborious America,
Builder of the mechanical cities.
But in the hurry people forget to love;
But in the hurry one drops and loses kindness.

And hunger is the patrimony of the emigrant;
Hunger, desolate and squalid —
For the fatherland,
For bread and for women, both dear.
America, you gather the hungry people
And give them new hungers for the old ones.

Where the skyscrapers grow, O America,
You have yelled your name to the four winds;
An ungracious, unkind yell —
That of a sour youth.

You are pitiless for the feeble,
The weak, whereas my country is
A sister of charity.

You are young and hurried; what threatens you
That you rush so, America?

You are young and your people,
Pitiless like the young, have hard eyes.
Here eyes are mellowed by the experience
Of two thousand years.
We are old and mellow —
We, the hungry.

How often in the streets of Manhattan
Have I thrown my hatred!
How often in those streets
Have I begged the Universe
To stop that crazy going and coming,
Or to drag me along too in that
Oblivion of hurry.

I have feared for you
The revenge of Love, O America!
How cheap is the sorrow of man!
People eat it with their bread;
It costs little in America —
It doesn't count.

III.

Genova with her flights of green trees
On her ascending squares;
Genova that goes to the hills
Like a great staircase.

Modern Bologna in the late evening
Seems a bureaucratic bazaar —
With her little shops and her promenading
Of semi-elegant youth.

Old Bologna, with her ancient red palaces
Defying the present. The infinite rows of the porches
Seem the work of an enormous mole.

Remember the lake of Chicago? —
The green absinthe of the lake of Chicago? —
How everything has grown small since I went away —
Since I am away!
And how early the city goes to sleep!
Remember Broadway in the night,
Bejewelled?

The Prefettura Palace is like
A squatting hydropical woman.
All offered me a bunch of memories,
Fresh and cool like edelweiss.

Bazzano, in a green and brown bowl,
Surrounded by hills as soft to the eyes
As a young woman's breast to the touch;
Bazzano delighted
With the songs of youngsters in the night,
With her church bells eternally in motion,
With her medieval castle on the highest spot of the town,
Challenging the storms that do not come,
Watching.

What and what for do you watch, O Tower?
Austria and the Pope have gone their miserable way;
And no danger threatens your fields,
Golden with the white grapes in autumn,
Silver with the new wheat in the spring
Where the snow comes only as a caress.

IV.

I have come back and have found you
All new and friendly, O Fatherland!
I have come back with a great burden,
With the experience of America in my head —
My head which now no longer beats the stars.

O Italy, O great shoe, do not
Kick me away again!

After The Return

W_{hoever} comes to Bazzano, whether triumphantly in an auto, or slowly on his own legs, or meekly on a horse, is struck by the fact that this is one of the commonest little country towns of Italy. In order to endure it for long, one should climb often to the highest part where the belfry and castle are. From there one can see the most splendid panorama ever. One can see Bologna, enormously beautified by distance, and Modena, and farther away, Verona, when the day is clear and no mist lies on the horizon.

Bazzano is partly bourgeois, that is true, but that fault is tempered by the beauty of its Lombardy poplars and its climbing streets, and of the songs sung by its young men at night. At night there is no quieter place in the whole universe. In America I felt there was no single place where the night was not troubled by the sound of trains and cars, but here only the wind sings among the acacia. When it is hot, very hot, there is a certain restlessness in the trees as though the wind were suffering. This bespeaks storms to come or relates the story of storms that have already passed. In winter the trees are ghostly, trying hard to remember the springtime and not succeeding.

Broken, poor, wretched, I came straight to this little village which offered me the hospitality of its hospital. I came back from America and was taken at once by the secretary of the commune to this place. Here I took up a residence of years in this palace of pus and blood, in the bedlam of the cries of the ill, nailed to a bed I scarcely ever left and then unwillingly. Not knowing what my illness was or how to cure it, the doctors gave me scopolamine — the "Truth Drug," as they call it in America. It is given to criminals in order to make them confess everything, but I found it made one confess things that one knew nothing of. It produces an immediate parching of the throat, then a complete stupor, and finally draws the victim down, down, down into the abyss of sleep. But for an interval it halts the terrible shaking of every limb.

This constant trembling is the most absurd, the most awful joke. Encephalitis, oh, glorious ailment, when I saw three dozen encephalitis patients I was terrified! There were some faltering past with gaping mouths (a gaping mouth is, according to Wells, a sign of mental weakness; according to Chesterton an infallible sign of encephalitis); others with ophthalmic eyes stared glazed and fixed at a certain point, always lateral or perpendicular but always set in the same way. (This is a symptom I have escaped luckily.) There were some who stammered and some who drooled, and the greatest of them all was an old priest called Bavoni (Drooler). But all of them trembled, all of them shook as if with uproarious laughter.

(Now I remember other priests, priests of my youth: there was a priest who instructed us in religion in one of the boarding-schools. He had an enormous nose which seemed to cut his words in half like a knife. There were two notorious degenerates, one of them a Bazzanese, who were expelled from the diocese for taking liberties with young people. This vice comes partly from the difficulty a priest has to get a woman, partly from the influence of the seminaries. There was another priest, the director of my first boarding-school: oh, how wise and sweet he was! How his beautiful hands held ours and how gentle was his smile! I never knew him to punish anybody. He was a priest, however, and that means that under his suavity lurked something dirty.)

There was one man in the hospital whose only symptom was to yawn constantly. This doesn't sound like much, but just think what a thing it is to have to raise your hand to your mouth, to have to feel your jaw dropping open all day long. And the drib-bling! Think of the incessant and monotonous effort of lifting a handkerchief to your lips all the time! There was another who kept hopping about, bending his right leg in such a way that he seemed continuously on the point of jumping into the air. And there was one who could not speak — and another who made a pirouette every few steps, and another who lifted his buttocks up in the palms of his hands, hitched them up vehemently before each step as he walked. And still another who hesitated a half hour before taking a step and then broke into a run. All of these cases terrified me at first — there was one man with a face exactly like an ape's who told me right off that he didn't believe in Darwin's theory; I was frightened at first and then I wanted to roar aloud with laughter, to scream with laughter, to laugh so majestically, so enormously that my laughter would conceal all these grotesques of humanity from the sight of the world. And then came another period when I believed that the encephaliti were the supremest beings of our race.

For instance, there was one boy, Aldo, who during his stay in the hospital had appendicitis, pneumonia, pleurisy, encephalitis, arthritis — seven or eight ailments, in fact. When I talked to him about my father, who still lived in Bologna, Aldo wept tears of pity for me and for the soul of that black-faced, black-hearted man. (Since then my father has died. I don't know how he died, but still he died, God damn his soul. He was not worthy of remaining in this world and if one of my letters to him has hastened his death, I am overjoyed. He wrote me that he did not like either Socialism or Fascism — his motto was "let the ship drift with the tide.") Aldo wept when I read my father's letters aloud to him, poor child, poor martyr. The thing is that in a hospital one begins life anew, we all become children and start over again. (There was one old, old man who cried like a child because he didn't want an enema.)

There was an Austrian, poor fellow, who hated me like death. One day I spat in his face. He was an enormous strong giant of a man who could have carried a ton under one arm as easily as a bag of straw, and he had struck me at four different times. Another time I shook my fist in his face and a yellowish smile crossed his features — a smile that expressed more hatred than I have ever seen in the world. Once when he was in the latrine, this accursed Austrian who hobbled about with one crutch, I took the crutch away and then called after him to follow me. I wanted to see if I could perform the miracle of making him walk alone.

There was another patient who, because he insisted on kissing the nurse, was tied to the bed where he piteously begged:

"I won't do it again! I promise not to do it again!"

Then Eric Hjorth came to see me! How well I remember the day he came! As I was under the effect of the drug, I kept talking to him in Italian and this angered him as he could not understand me. He had ordered a good dinner at the inn for us, but I could not go, too drugged, too lost in lethargy and sleep.

Bazzano

I once said that in Bazzano the snow came only as a caress. This is a lie, unless it is a matter of a caress being five feet in height. The snow came here fierce and unforgiving. The black and white wood-cuts of the landscape were more definite than ever. The soil, it seemed, had been hungry for snow. This little town deserves to be put on the map: for it is the typical Italian little town, hardly more than a village, with even its own town idiot who always fell asleep while the barber shaved him. (Vigilant mothers warned their female offspring against him.) Bazzano had its own songs, songs heard nowhere except in Bazzano. There was one about the barber which the boys sang in the streets at night:

> Moretto, Moretto, he has in his hair
> The natural wave that comes from nature,
> The waves of the sea.

In some of these songs there was a nostalgic beauty:

> The day that never was for him
> Can cause the drinker no pain;
> From the world he flees,
> And missing love he misses too
> The squalor of the day that never was.

And in others a certain viciousness:

When he touched her little teats
She ran straight to her mother
Who is an old whore
And who taught her to make love young.
He, rin tin tin,
Ho, rin tin tin,
Tin La.
Love is like a roulette wheel,
Always turning, always spinning.

When one begins to notice who dies and who doesn't, this is a sign that one has begun to live long in a place. (It may also be a sign that one is growing old.) There was Folla, that poor lover of a violin he hadn't touched for years, that miserable enthusiast of Beethoven of whom no one knew anything in this vile little town. He walked so slowly down the street that death easily overtook him. Then came Cristo. Cristo went around the streets of Bazzano with a newspaper that he carried twisted into a kind of club behind his back and which he never read. He was quarrelsome, bad; he would fly into rages when the boys followed him and called him, not names, but noises. The noise he hated worst to be called was something like this: Sh . . . sh . . . sh . . . sh. . . .

Then there was Arrigo Arcangely. He used to stand on the main road and yell stupid incoherent phrases at the passing automobiles. (He always saluted me and bowed to me extravagantly whenever I went out. He seemed to like me.) He was famous for the incomprehensible jargon he would shout at people. He hanged himself. He got tired of waiting for death.

And now I am back in Bazzano: one more of the thousand little country towns one may find all over Italy. With its castle — which one of these country towns hasn't a castle to boast of? And its fields right by the town. Fields that are generators of crickets and frogs that sing all night a supernumerary lullaby. The monsters of the towns are all in its streets. Chicherula is an old man with a military cap, who guides a small cart with nothing but the filthiest, most useless rubbish on it. Another one is Bouton: he stalks about the town naked-breasted striking himself on the chest and blowing through his mouth and nostrils a sort of whistling sound, somewhat like a locomotive. He balances a stick on his head and threatens all with a beating who do not stand him a drink; but he is more harmless than a stingless mosquito. Another is thoroughly alcoholized, who sleeps in the square night and day. Another is a swollen faced undergrown little animal, who works as a waiter in one of the too many wineshops of the town. Oh, yes, too many. This town that doesn't count more than six thousand inhabitants, has at least twelve wineshops.

And on Sunday much rustic chivalry goes on.

Near Bazzano the mountains are a majestic chorus. They are a black assembly. They surround Bazzano, holding it in a great-mother embrace.

And in the country surrounding Bazzano young ladies go for long walks with young men. And often these young ladies back from the fields find after a time themselves possessors of a large belly — a mystery that solves itself into a baby in nine months — all because of some long walk in the country with some young man or other.

In this town I suffered for three years in its hospital. Seeing and watching the dead and the dying; calling death a cheap whorish thing; calling death a boisterous and incongruous threat; calling death an insignificant every day affair; calling death a rough handed virago with none of the delicacy of death in one's own home. And watching the struggle against death put up by dying men. Once there was an old man with cancer in the stomach. It took him a week to die, but he died every moment of that week. He lost ground against death every day that was born. If he tried to sit up in bed he would faint. Then he was delirious, asking for a sack full of milk. So that he made his son laugh. But he didn't laugh; he was busy dying. It was death that put a fog in his brain. How it played with him, death did; how it twisted him and choked him and claimed, claimed, claimed him for its own. Finally he died; but death wasn't through with him; it was death that sent a swarm of flies over the cover under which he lay.

Death is horrid in a hospital, and life is worse still. Both are two mangy wolves pursuing a human prey. For life too hunts and pursues one, fighting with death, most undignifiedly. Life is forced to take an attitude of self-defence. A man died once whose last words were swearwords: "God is a hangman!" I dared not disagree with him. Oh! how many swearwords blossomed in that hospital, like ugly flowers, like bemired flowers, flowers bearing the mud of farmers' shoes.

Men with corrupted blood being glad that the next man had blood even more corrupted. Men with nephritis being glad for the tuberculosis of the next man. Men cruel and stupid who were once bright and tolerant.

How many different ways of lamenting have I not heard. No respect for any hour they had: they wailed, grunted, squalled, wept, cursed, squawked, squeaked, roared, at any and all hours. And how many different contortions of poor mouths, how many different grimaces of deleterious pain! There were, and there are still, two nurses and five sisters in the hospital. The two nurses still tend me. One is a big strapping young fellow who is more than a nurse to me now, having become one of my best friends. He is the most original man I met in the way of expressing himself. True, if sometimes rough, humor comes out of his mouth. We call that being genial in Italy. In each of the little towns within a radius of ten miles of Bazzano, he has a sweetheart. He is a married man. The other nurse I know too well to do more than mention him here.

I am an awkward, gawky creature, otherwise the song of hatred towards the hospital would reach God; it would disturb and bother Him; it would demand the abolition of sickness; and then of hospitals; and the glory and the triumph of health; and the abolition of doctors. Let them go and sweep streets who feed on the rubbish left by death.

These dead men marked with their deaths little periods in my Bazzano life. (Strangely enough, when one is young one scarcely notices the wretched dead, protected from their assault by the thoughtlessness, or the insanity, or the restless impatience of youth.) In the hospital I lived as in a dream among the living, the shaking. Only during sleep were we quiet and did we cease to tremble. This illness must have inspired the saying, "As long as you aren't dead, you're fine." During an instant of comparative quiet and repose, the slightest shock or movement even can start afresh the incessant, the relentless trembling. It is the falsest and at the same time the truest of all illnesses — it consists of nothing, practically nothing, but it is made of a multiplication of nothing until in the end it becomes an enormity. There were several idiots among us: one of them was my closest friend, a scientist, an old man. I could confide in him and talk to him freely. I made him understand that he could use what little money I had and he answered, with tears, that I had a great and generous heart. But when I gave him the money, he gave almost all of it away to other patients.

The head nurse was an adorable little woman and her white veil fluttered behind her like the wings of a butterfly. She seemed to me like one of the madonnas which my country hides in every nook and cranny, each madonna so different in its execution that they have become goddesses which the people worship, so making a polytheistic religion of Christianity. This nun-nurse took possession of our entire universe and did with us exactly as she pleased. She called us, these mad encephalitic dancers of death, her "treasures," her "darlings," her "loves." I would find myself murmuring to her: "Oh, dear, good, sacred, holy little sister of mine!"

Then Robert McAlmon came to Bazzano, with that strange ironical smile that was more like a grimace on his face. Seeing the filth of the place I was in, he paid a year for me in a private sanatorium, the Villa Rubazziana. There I began another life. This place was called the Rubazziana from the Italian *"rubare"* which means to rob. In fact, they take the shirt off a man's back as soon as they notice he has one on. It was red in the green of the pines, like a huge strawberry in the tall grass; not quite the color of a strawberry but rather that of a red cloth that has been washed too many times. A House of Health, they called it, but it was the House of Rotten Nerves. With the tendrils of these clipped, mangled, twisted nerves one could have made an embroidered handkerchief for God to blow His nose in. He deserves it.

On top of a hill, it surveyed the city: a high sentry. It was populated by at least fifty patients or guests, all of them very crazy, or else half crazy, or else half sane. When I arrived they put me in the best room of the place, and there came young Dr.

Kingpeels to speak of tremendous doses of arsenic, bromus, calcium, so that by reflection he made the place tremendous in my eyes. Kingpeels had small eyes that bespoke falsity, but he was not false, as I found out later on.

The room was so pretty, so beautiful, it had such lordly intimacies with my soul that my heart was slammed open and I said: this is just the place to get well in. I walked about the room for some hours, touching everything, looking everywhere, till I felt that the room belonged to me and then I was happy. (But they transferred me later into the ugliest room of the place. The spirit of triumphant entrance was thus abated and I was unhappy again.)

The first evening, having certain needs, I called the nurse and asked her to show me to the watercloset. A woman appeared, ugly and malignant. I asked her to look for my slippers in my suitcase. Having examined and contemplated my lingerie, she exclaimed:

"Where are your underclothes?"

"What are those things there if they're not underclothes?" I replied very angrily.

She was vindicating on me the moneyed aristocracy of the place. She tried to tell me, in the least possible amount of words, that I was a bum. I could have told her:

This man you see, horrible woman,
Is richer and more
aristocratic than perhaps all your guests.
My brain is aristocratic,
My nose and eyes and all the senses
are great aristocrats.
But if you knew this, woman,
you could no longer waddle about
like a proletarian goose.
You'd be too scared
to move a foot.

But I said nothing instead. The next morning I was awoken by a thousand and one birds singing together their hallelujah to the sky. It was as though a bomb had suddenly exploded and from its insides these birds had flown, singing, singing, singing. They were singing the glory of a very old good God who peacefully listened from the heights of a pure light-azure sky, scarcely grazed by a few pink-kissed clouds. They celebrated the billionth advent of the morning. (There was the music of the winds around the Villa Rubazziana as well as the music of the birds in the early morning.) Awoken by these singers, so many small birds, I imagined how it would be to move westward with the sun and find them girdling the belly of the old earth, celebrating this early mass of joy.

And the red sun over the tree trunks. It lay on them as light as the dust on the wings of a butterfly. It was ethereal, unreal almost. A brush made with the hair of the breeze had done this work. The blood of the essence of my own soul, it was. The trees were sublime with it, they could be called the trees of heaven since it was heaven's colors that lent them their personality.

The red gradually waned into a soft yellow and then I knew that the day had begun. I sat by the window and thought of my being in this new house, and the red on the tree trunks that was gradually waning into yellow, and the birds — and I swayed with the elegance of all this; I thought all this was extremely elegant.

And what I am doing in Bazzano? Living as miserably as possible with my sickness, but living, living thanks to a lord of generosity, to a princely giver, who expresses himself with such wonderful simplicity as this: "Yes, I will continue sending you money." A handsome man, this giver, to whom I am not able to write a delicate fine letter; perhaps because to write an adequate letter is too difficult seeing that he deserves princely words, so great a giver he is, so lordly generous he is, so princely a benefactor. A handsome stern face, his, a stern great man, he. He is a writer and one of the greatest writers America has had in all times. I am not ashamed of being a beggar; I am ashamed for not being able to tell him how fervently, how extraordinarily, how originally I love him. And my damnable letters contain always requests for books, for more money. Yes, I am a beggar

and he could make me feel so; but he doesn't. So, that all in all
I am an unashamed beggar, unashamed for better or for worse.
It frightens me to think of him, and his books torment me as he
does torment the characters of his books. He has the weight, the
presence and the grace of an Assyrian sculpture. Women must
certainly find him extraordinary but I doubt whether he finds any
woman to be extraordinary. I owe him homage and praise forever, and homage and praise he shall have from me even though
my heart run dry and my hand be no longer able to write. I shall
have left my voice; and if I grow dumb and deaf I shall have left
my eyes.

Train of Characters
Through the Villa Rubazziana

The director, who was also the owner of the place, had a red beard and was cunning and sly. He looked as though he was fooling you half the time. Professor Blacks, his name, and a disciple of Babinsky. He didn't look at all like a scientist since he didn't even wear glasses. But to open up the brains of psychopathics and neuropathics with the small and big keys of science was a cinch for him. He smiled on all sick people as though he believed they were faking their illnesses.

He led the caravan of the cross-myelitics, of the ataxics, the spinal-syphilitics, the polymelitics, who went wavering, trembling, waddling, swaying, cock-stepping, goose-stepping, sorrowfully-stepping after him. He knew the secret, the watchward, and the slogan. He led the caravans of the ladies whose husbands do not satisfy, the caravan of the encephalitics, sleeping as they walked, doubled over. This disciple of Babinsky handled power with ease, and triumphantly; but the story ran that he was as crazy as the craziest of his patients.

The young doctors adored him and had unbounded esteem for his vast knowledge, esteem that in the long run became servility. Women must have been crazy about him, because his red beard was really nice, almost beautiful. With the secret, the watchword, and the slogan, he led the caravan that goes towards death and was able to smile all along. When his patients died they had three doctors around them. He made them die easy.

He smiled like a good old Satan and the Rubazziana lay, like an island in a river, in the shadow of that smile. His responsibilities did not seem to bother him much, and his patients, healed or unhealed, made together a great chorus of praises that was to be heard wherever there were rotten nerves to mend, to sew, or to knock together. He smiled and his face was a mellow-red sun, and the light of that sun was made for true or fake happiness for his patients: for when he smiled, they all smiled back.

The first acquaintance was Arches. A young Fascist from Faenza, he had been accused of murdering a man during a Fascist punitive expedition. He was, however, innocent, but he hadn't left the scene of battle without receiving in his breast and arm I don't know how many ounces of gunshot. Women thought him very handsome, and his face was indeed sweet and gentle, but it was also rather insignificant. He used to say that he had one sweetheart, ever-ready, for each finger and toe. We passed the time listening to his love affairs.

He was waiting his trial and was meanwhile continually guarded by two carabineri whose uniforms added to the pic-turesqueness of the Villa. He was also the official gazette of the place and he spent much of his time talking with his carabineri. He spoke three-quarters of the time about women, one eighth of the time about hunting, and the other eighth about bees whom he knew from their birth to their death, just like a father who has outlived his sons.

Arches' face was gentle as a good woman's word told whisperingly to a very sick man. (Devotion and friendship were to him tacitly acknowledged duties.) His smile had several gradations: it was good, then nasty, then ironical. This last form lasted the longest and was the most habitual one. His smile was sometimes an irradiation of his face, a light and a halo. His body was small but it contained exactly his soul which was not at all big. But he was good company, making funny faces and singing comically to amuse people. His tragedy — hidden — was his insignificance. He had passed along the field of life stealing the worst grapes for lack of intelligence and little discernment. But he considered his booty very precious and praised himself about it.

To the whole Villa he was a pleasure and a joy. Young ladies flocked after him like chick-chickens after their probable mother. When he went away, several young ladies wept the desperate tears of regret. Arches' secret — what was it? To be quiet and to wait like a flower not totally bloomed. His secret was to adorn his banality with the picturesque colors that came from his Romagna: it was a love affair with a gramophone record (Schubert's Serenade); it was that his lascivious eyes were not quite his own; they were two skunks trying to sneak away (not that he was sneaky). If Fascists had been better men, that is truly great conquerors of the soul of Italy, Arches would have been an almost legendary hero. As it was, he was a mere invalid.

This fragment is in the form of an old-fashioned minuet:

Fedora is an American lady who came to see me with her sister at the Villa Rubazziana. Clarinets like a poplar's leaves thrilling, twinking and twinkling; O, clarinets whose chords are the very chords of my heart, play me a song of praise to God for the intelligence of this lady! Trombones, play me a music that will be like great big men, giants, in praise of this small, supple, and dearest lady! Saxophone, play the blues of Mister Me who have been left alone by the two most glorious sisters the whole world over; saxophone, play me the most vulgar melodies for she is of this earth and of this vulgus and she loves them both. She knew that the greater spiritualities are to be found in the loam and the dirt, and that the hand of an Italian farmer was major in the scale of aristocratic spirituality rather than the delicate viciously languorous hand of an Italian Count.

(She was the most aristocratic lady and she told me that she was too old to love me, and the devil if I know what a guy could say to that! Agree that she was too old, or say that she was not too old at all, or that she was still very young, nay, younger than myself? She said to me: "Talk to me as I talk to my child," and this humiliated me and did not help me to talk any better — in fact it embarrassed me. When she wept, I called her "Poor Fedora!"; and she cried: "Don't call me poor!")

I was able to go to town once a week to the theatre and we saw Petrolini, the Roman actor, together and she was enthusiastic. When from the height of a window an actor in a nightcap threw a piss-pot's contents upon the head of a serenader, she laughed and said that such things were not allowed in America. Her laugh was cool and fresh as a spring appearing suddenly in the crags of a mountainside: a laugh that one might wish to eat, like ice cream. After she had left me she wrote to me from Switzerland that the Alps have a way of standing up similar to Petrolini. Better glorification than that. . . . .

(You were really quite beautiful once, although the years have put a tragic mask on your face, as I told you, but you would not admit it, of course. You came twice to Bazzano, and the second time you refused to give yourself to me because you feared the illness. You wept, and this nauseated me. Are you aware that during the fifteen years which my illness has endured I have never once shed a tear? Sobs, yes, screams, yes; but I have forgotten how to weep.)

This little lady, whose slim body carries her head like the stem the flower, has hidden powers. She speaks with little shrieks that are very pretty, but behind her voice stands a sphinx of beauty and wisdom. My lady of across the sea, my distant love, the lady that lasts in my heart after all the other love affairs have miserably died. She is the blossoming of my thought, the bed where I rest and the earth that I tread: she is the universal joy and cosmic laughter.

Her small body contains delights; her small body is an amphora of joys. She too in New York, where the whirlwind of grime and dust tries to wrap her around, asks, as I did, for a little sylvan beauty. I love her in the morning because the sun that arises has a large wondering face, and the same wonder is in her eyes. I love her at noon when the sun is a knocker in the gong of the sky, for she belongs with sky and sun, so lightful and harmonious and powerful her spirit is. And I love her in the night when the too-romantic sky-rider weeps small silver tears because she too is pale and her tears are silver for my mind and gold for my heart.

(I remember your wild eyes and your little moans when you were in voluptuous ecstacy, but it was a vicious circle, it was a wretched little mystery, that of your personality and hence that of our love. You needed excitement and I was only a depressing load, you needed a stimulus and I was only a sedative; under this depression and lethargy this soul of mine kept shouting the story of my ghastly sickness. You did not seem to understand that the encephalitic does everything badly, even talk: that he cannot describe his intricacies except by words like these: I am confused, I am not well, I am dazed; while you expected madrigals from me, light verse, or delicately sad things which would not distress you too much. If I could have expressed what I felt, it would have been a wild, ferocious, terrible utterance.)

In my hollow cavernous heart she shines like an idol and to forget her would be to forget too many things that are the furniture of half of my past. I remember carrying big, huge bunches of lilacs to that sweetly and clean-smelling house of X Street in America. And I remember I was in love with her and with another sister of hers. I lived, those days, in a fog of ecstacy, drowsily and warmly wrapped around in that fog. I became her sister's lover then, but in my heart I had an adoration for her. She did not love me, ever; so that she will be surprised to hear of this now. She will be surprised and angry perhaps and she will call this writing absolutely false. But I know that what little truth my closed fist of sick man may let escape is in this writing.

(Do you remember that time in Washington Square, New York, when you told me you thought you loved me, while I was in love with your sister? She had been kind to me, and I was looking so eagerly then for a smiling word that I would have fallen in love with the first woman who gave it to me. Your sister was ugly, but I didn't care as long as she was kind. I believe you, I don't believe you, so continued the refrain of our stupidity. Poor little Fedora, mistress during one short indulgent night, mostly indulgent towards the lies I told you; if you feared the contamination of my illness, this fear of yours was understandable for the gift of it would have been to you a sorry gift indeed.)

Now we are far one from the other and maybe I shall never see her again. And upon my love I shall put a seal and throw the packet in a hidden corner of my heart. There to grow or die, to blossom or shrivel, to increase or dwindle away, to remain or to go. If they are roses they will bloom.

Continuation of Characters
Through the Villa Rubbazziana

Her face was almost distorted by a kind of sacrificial sorrow and she answered:

"I know what you want . . . ."

"Oh! Do you? A kiss, then, that's what I want."

The strange sorrow continued as she answered:

"When? Tomorrow?"

"No, now!"

She threw her arms about my neck, abruptly and hurriedly. Then she gave me a sweet kiss, murmuring the while, *"Oh! Monsieur Carnevali! Je vous aime!"*

The next day at my asking she said that she did not love me, that she was too young, that she sympathized with me and felt great affection towards me, but that the day before it had been a matter of *égarement.*

But one evening the light went out accidentally while she was in my room. I promised that I would not harm her, so she remained. (I could not even dream of possessing her.) So under the shelter of the darkness, she said:

"I often dream open-eyed. I dreamed then that I was back home in Cairo (her native town) and that suddenly the doorbell rang and a felt a swift keen emotion without knowing why. Then the servant came and said, 'Mr. Carnevali is there.' I jumped up flurried and excited and I went to the door, *et voilà, vous étiez là!* This has been one of my wild dreams."

She told me that it had been the first time she had kissed a man. And when I cupped my hands to touch her sweet soft teats, she said, *"Basta!* I don't want. . . ."

This had been an unfortunate and frivolous love affair. She

began allowing me an ever smaller portion of kisses and then, having been away two weeks, she came back and she did not want to kiss me anymore, in spite of the fact that I gave her a perfumed cake of soap and asked for a kiss in exchange. The sorrow I felt was small, proportionate to the smallness of the love affair. She left me only clean memories. It was not soul-rending and tempestuous and full of rage as most love affairs with me are. It was quiet and quite sweet. I rested in it as on a bed of roses, thornless ones, of course.

I called her sweet angel and my treasure but I was only trying to bluff my timidity.

Yet, even though I was quiet, my love was fierce enough to frighten her. She shrank from it and denied it. She said I must first get well, then talk to her of love and, possibly, marriage. She was such a little woman! Such a darling, so small and so ugly! I have always loved ugly women: to hell with all the novels of the world which talk only of beauties! I have always loved ugly women because it is the privilege of ugly women to become beautiful at times, on the most important moments of life: whereas a beautiful woman has all to lose by change, and such changes are bound to happen. Emotion, which distorts a beautiful face, sets an ugly one to a lovely rhythm. I mean of course ordinary ugliness and not deformity. There is an ugliness that can never redeem itself. There is also monstrous ugliness that repels. I mean the ugliness which is caused by irregularity of feature, that lacks the splendour of beauty. I have known once a beautiful girl who was also a noble-hearted, good-hearted individual. But I am sure that most beautiful women are nasty and cruel and affected and over-proud and mean and tiresome and boresome and stupid in such a way as only women can be.

I mean perhaps that ugly women have most always something beautiful that stands out more, given the surrounding ugliness. And then I think that intelligence distorts a face. All intelligent women of our days, or almost all, are not good looking. Weininger says that that is due to intelligent women being masculine. But I am getting all entangled in this pseudo-philosophical dissertation.

Dr. Kingpeels used to come every night to play poker with

me and Arches. On this occasion I let myself be provoked into certain confessions, and when they had gone I was steeped in strange fears. What would they do to me, now that I had confessed this and that? Would they expel me from the Rubazziana? These fears were as stupid as a paranoiac's. They were fixed ideas; I call them thus for want of a better name. I shall explain: When my nerves are quieted by the scopolamine the association of ideas runs regularly and fast. I have, so to speak, about a hundred different thoughts within the space of a minute (I think it is the expression of such a process that Joyce's art is made of). When, instead, I am hypernervous my thoughts get stuck in the mud of fixedness and the association of ideas stops completely. And it is this fixedness that is painful, almost physically so.

One nice day, Kingpeels and professor Komebacks brought with them Dr. Suckles. This young man was beautiful and sympathetic. He had a romantic face and I told him so. Romance was all over his face as simply as butter on bread. Once he made a diagnosis of Kingpeels:

"He is full of nervous ticks. I would lock him up in a room, in the dark, for a week. He'd get rid of them, all right, all right. He crosses his legs in farmer's style when speaking even with the highest medical authorities. He is idiotic," said Suckles. I objected, "He is also very good." "Yes," he answered, "if very good means also very idiotic," replied he. "He is lazy. When a sick man bothers him with his complaints, he is ready to send him to hell. He would like only easy sick men, such as you, Carnevali. With his face that calls for slaps, his nonchalant swaying, his absurd way of walking, he is a perfect fool. And lazy? You tell 'em! He is inevitably buried in the Villa and won't get out of it. So lazy he is that he can't put in two hours study in the day. I encouraged him by way of telling him to study with me, that I was glad to have him study with me. Nothing doing! He can't study; he cannot even think of emancipating himself by way of study. He is the ghost of the Villa: stupidly everywhere and at every time."

There was at the time in the smaller villa (where the very sick were) an old lady whose name was Mrs. Thighs, who was the boresomest bore ever. If she somehow got hold of you, you were in for the most boring, miles-winded talk in the world. Her name was not merely Mrs. Thighs; the completed article was manifold (like one of those names of French writers of the eighteenth century). Here it is: Mrs. Emma, Garlic, Thighs and Toads. You could never mention the name of a celebrity, but that she assured you that she had met him or her, and that she or he was a guest at her five-o'clocks.

She actually knew five or six languages and the grammars thereof. She really had a wonderful memory. We laughed about her. She had an unbounded belief in my power as a writer and she used to praise me infinitely. She asked me once or twice why I didn't write to the king of England (for her it was a small matter to write to a king; she was continually writing to Mussolini). She was a poor, hapless woman. Her brother had succeeded in imprisoning her in the Villa, and he was very nasty about her. About this she wailed continually. She wore a wig that was like a great bird's nest fallen on her head upside down.

When she had met anybody, one should hear the praise she bestowed on the person she met! She used to stop all the relatives of the patients, and when they came a second time they inevitably asked about Mrs. Thighs. Some of these relatives cared more for her than for the patients themselves. After Arches had gone, she was the gazette of the place. They all acknowledged her high and steady intelligence and even Suckles describing her called her a great pot of intelligence and boresomeness.

She came to know of the story I intended to write about the Villa and at once implored me to spare her, not to be harsh on her. And I know I am being harsh: but I am here to relate what struck me in the different people I met and cannot be delicate when delicateness would be deception. Through her I met a little girl I fell in love with. I hear you say, proverbially gentle but in reality nasty, reader, that I fall in love *too* often. I don't know about that *too,* but I do fall in love often. Love ought to be a standing condition with young men, young men should be in love all the time. Well, I do fall in love often; what would you have me do about it? Refrain from writing about it? No, since I am deeply interested in my own love affairs. I repeat it, young men should be in love all the time; the emotion causing a convulsion of all their feelings, they become less dull and more interesting, yes, far more interesting.

So it was love's turn to come again. This time the young lady in question was rather ugly. (She, thus, fulfilled all my requirements, says my malicious reader.) She had a pyramidal neck and a snub nose and a voice pregnant with spittle; but she had beautiful expressive eyes and she had wonderful smooth hands and all her skin was smoother than a butterfly's wings. Her eyes revolutionized my soul from the very beginning. She had epileptic fits during which she had to prop herself against something or somebody if she did not wish to fall. Once I was near her with another young lady and she had the fit. She suddenly shifted from the young lady's support to mine and I held her in a sweet embrace. A few days afterward I kissed her for the first time. A love affair that was all ecstacies and frenzy thus began. I used to talk to her with hand on my heart, romantically. I went so far as to tell her that if she were to be *enceinte* by another man, I'd marry her just the same.

This little thing had a mother — alas! she had a mother. The mother was her shadow, her ghost. Her shadow: always behind her. Her ghost: she kept appearing as an apparition, always, everytime I asked her daughter for a kiss. She was, otherwise, a very kind woman, especially kind to me.

Once Dr. Kingpeels surprised us kissing. The next day he came into my room and I was in for a long reproaching talk:

"You must understand that she is sick, that any emotion might be fatal to her. Young men are a vice with her, her mother told me so. And I know that she has come to your room. . . . I shall speak to Dr. Blacks about it." And he did too.

Dr. Blacks thought the thing rather grave, but that did not force him to action since he was more indolent than scrupulous.

I loved you very much, really. You were the joy of my fingers when I touched your skin. (She was all silken, in the face, in the hands and in the arms.) Your deep eyes told an ancient amorous tale. And listening to that tale I was in bliss. (She too was small. I like small women because they are more easily besieged by love and its armaments. It is the right of a woman, that of being small. I came to love even her voice which was ugly indeed, full of saliva and trembling and stuttering a little. I came to love even her laugh which was exaggeratedly uproarious.)

My little silken girl! I loved your eyes because they were as two violets hidden in the grass of your ugliness. You were like a little mouse. With your snub nose defying seriousness, respectability and pedantry. So easy it was to hold you in my arms; so easy to kiss you; so easy to tell you beautiful words that bathed you as a shower of cherry-blossom petals.

I left my door open all night and the light burning in the hall, hoping that you'd come and you never came. You were too scared of your gentle-hearted mother whom I liked well too. When there was a company surrounding us you made a pretty grimace with your lips to mean a kiss. And I was thereupon boiling in the broth of an idiotic happiness. Ah! love is a vivifier, yes, but it is also an idiotizer. I was running after you and you kept me on runnng with such phrases as "I love you," whispered hurriedly. Our love was mostly whispers. I put a little self importance now in saying the words *I loved,* but then it was altogether an undignified affair. However, I loved her tempestuously. Imagine a forest: in it a thousand monkeys screaming together; that was the noise this love made in my heart. Undignified? Yes, but Goddam dignity. Alas! the end of love affairs, how sad and disintegrating a feeling! How all the inner paraphernalia is upset and tattering. Like a housewrecking: leaving a regret for not having done a hundred things one might have done. A regret for a phrase unsaid, a confession unmade, a declaration unuttered. One is left like a poor child playing amongst the stones of a wrecked house, trying hard to imagine that the stones are toys. One is left with one's bloody heart in one's hands, not knowing what to do with it and deciding to throw it away.

Nothrills, sick with a nervous breakdown, had become one of my best friends. Seeing that my passion was dangerous for me, he set about to abate my enthusiasm. That little girl was next to him at the table and they had the following dialogue.

"I see you get troubled when the waitress comes in," said she.

"No, why?"

"You like women, don't you?" And so saying she let fall a hand on his thigh. Such things multiplied. Nothrills had his place changed at the table. Nothrills was a good friend. With his hempen hair, his snub nose, he was almost ridiculous. He talked splendidly, like an old actor. He had ceaseless troubles with his family, his studies, his business. He used to sit by my bed and talk till three o'clock in the morning. He told and retold his troubles. His chief trouble was that he knew too well what his troubles were. He was a little man: rather ridiculous with his South of Italy accent. But he had certain powers. Although he had a mind, his body was small and his face absurd. The tumult of suffering he was going through at that time hindered his being as intelligent as he might otherwise have been. He was a cauldron of pains and words. Sometimes at night, alone in his little room, he used to groan and moan in a heartrending fashion. But the doctors seemed not to take him seriously. They made him stay in his room for fifteen days right after he had come to the Villa. I used to go and see him and he lent me some books. Sometimes he was quite desperate. His despair was acrid, almost stinking. So intimate was he with his despair, so easily he talked about it, that I think that was the reason why the doctors did not believe him, that was the reason why it was hard to believe him. His body was always itching. He was terribly afraid of noises. And he had a small quantity of energy that got spent very quickly. When I was full of scopolamine I was more energetic than he, that is, more enduring than he.

Let the following be like a storm:

Coast was the man who was affected with a kind of raging epilepsy; he shouted and screamed like a truck driver. He deceived me with that little stupid silken thing and did the dirtiest things imaginable to her. Coast was the man with the Radio: that damn nuisance, the radio; when you got something good on it, which happened rather rarely, the wireless began to wheeze and sneeze, to squawk and squeak and shriek, and took all the pleasure out of one's life. The only thing one could hear well was ragtime: English ragtime and not American. Oh yes! and she came to my room and kissed me using her lips in such a way as to remind me of a fledging opening its mouth when the mother comes with food. And the last time she came, she did not want to be kissed. Mrs. Thighs one day came from the city with a hat that looked like a belligerent cock, and Mr. Coast hailed her, singing *kirikiki!!!* And I left the door open at night hoping crazily that she would come, and when she would come I'd have her and then force her mother to consent to our marriage. And Mr. Suckles and Arches had a great quarrel in my room in which it was understood that Arches had called Suckles a double-faced man: Arches was running out of my room when I stepped down from my bed in my nightshirt and tried to placate him, but all was useless and Arches went out of my room in a great, immense rage. Suckles, when Arches had gone out, said of him that he could be nothing but stupid, being so friendly with his *carabineri;* and he was horribly ignorant of even the simplest notions. But then they made up pretty soon. There came a nondescript young lady who had several screws loose on the top floor. She talked and talked till your head split. She was put away in the little Villa where the more serious cases were, and she was never heard of more. And Nothrills danced with young ladies, but after his speech in my room the silken thing had so spoken against him that no young lady would dance with him more. And every time I came downstairs from my room (I had a phonograph with records, a present from Sig. Gallese, which I kept downstairs) I found one more disc missing. It was the damned chamber maids that broke them and then hid the pieces. Then came the Marquis Dumbs. He had the eyes of a toad and a thin-lipped mouth: bulging eyes and a crude mouth. He said he played his 25,000 lire nightly, and he said he was a descendant from Mutius Scevola, witness his ring that had a coat of arms on it and in which you could see an arm burning on top of a tripod. He was a cultured man and he knew no end about histories of all the nations, and a fine conversationalist he was. Then there came Count Yescin, a pederast, who came often to my room telling me of wicked adventures with women of all sorts, strange tales rather unbelievable in his mouth. I spotted

him right away, I said: that's a fairy, the very first time I saw
him. He had the face of an old spinster, that peculiar neither
young nor old face of the pederast, a wasted face, a face like a
cemetery where his vice was simply readable. He read poems,
written by himself, with certain gestures of his hands that were
melodramatic and incongruous. He brushed his hair back, having
before made a sweeping gesture with his hands. His prose was
beautiful indeed, and he said he was also a painter: orgies of color
were in his work. But I never thought of considering him like a
brother, a brother for art's sake, a brother in art. I somehow
connected his vice (though natural it is a vice) with his work
and such consideration was forbidding. The marquis often came
to ask me for a little money, so broke he was with his 25,000
or less lost the evening before. He ridiculed the gracious king of
Italy and told smutty stories about our crown prince. Then came
the brother of the silken thing, a very suave young man with
whom I soon became friends. Although he stayed but a few
days. He was as sweet as a sweet sixteen, rather a lazy personality, slow and cautious but altogether sympathetic. He told
me that I would surely get well (I hereby send to hell every one
who has told me that I soon would get well, the damned liars!)
but I was careful not to tell him anything about my love for his
sister. And after she was gone I kept the door open at night for
another woman who, of course, never came: she was a skinny
lady who went to the water closet often every night (and on the
way to the W.C. was my room) and when she was there she
made such funny noises. To keep the door open and to wait for
things that never happened had become a mania for me. And
there were the Misses Gonelow who were like this: one was very
beautiful, the face of a conquisatrice, with eyes as black as black
cats and wonderful glossy hair not cut *à la garçonne* (one must
say that, these days); the other was thin and long gone in consumption, quiet and sweet, quiet and sweet, calmly awaiting
death, the most lasting and best friend, the lover with cool lips,
carrying strength and loving weakness, death, the lover of the
deep caresses, the lover who gives the longest kiss.

And I am afraid that all this was more of a drizzle than a
storm.

However, these are the last drops:

And my nights were the same and my days were the same, and at night I heard the far away bell ring the hours . . . . ding . . . . ding . . . . Ding! while I lay seeking sleep in the crevices of the night.

And sometimes a hedgehog or some like animal squealed in the garden . . . . squeee . . . . squeeeee!

Then I made friends with Fireplaces. He was a tall Sicilian: his black hair was blue, and he was handsome. But, like a Sicilian, he had slow gestures (that may have been the sickness indeed), and was cold-blooded. He was like a drunken philosopher, a sleeply owl, a truck-stopping, because of his sickness, a garlic-stinking aristocrat, an encephalitic beauty, a dead cockerel, a poor fish, an irritated toad, a dumb conversationalist, a deaf violin player, a fixed-eyed flirt, a sleepy-eyed fencer, a funny-way-of-walking fellow, stiffly elegant, a foolish critic, an impotent colossus, a stupid he-man, a frivolous, heavy man, a butterfly on top of an elephant. This man fell in love with a tiny bit of a woman, half crazy, stupid and unattractive. One night while Dr. Taday (of whom I shall speak later) was in my room with the Big Whore (or her later also), he came in my room, dragging after him the little woman. Then, for one reason or another, the woman began to weep most pitifully, and he brought her away to her room where he spent his time maneuvering over her body, till Taday went out of my room to see them.

There came another lady: a beauty of a woman, although past her thirties. She was all flowers: her hair like black marigolds, her lips two red carnations, her face a white peony, her arms soft and smooth like a magnolia flower. She was a triumph of a woman. An imposing personality. A true lady, authoritative and haughty. A true woman, her eyes forever lit with a flame that made one think of happy lovers. As she wore a very décolleté dress, one could guess at the beauty of her breasts; the mystery thereof merged with the mystery of her eyes and mouth. She was big, great, I should say. She was a river winding slowly and voluptuously. She was a luscious cherry tree in bloom. But enough of these trite metaphors. She was beautiful, but she was stupid too. In fact, she was soon in love with my dear Sicilian friend.

Taday was a young doctor who came to the Rubazziana as a substitute night doctor, with no salary and a meal a day, rather a meal and a half since he took *café-au-lait* in the morning. He was the type of a conqueror, with a beautiful mouth that made women dream of him. He had hair that was stubbornly unkempt and his soul was like his hair, unkempt and a little savage. He did not care for menials and lost no time over them. Son himself of poor parents, he had been so good in his studies as to pass three classes in only a year. He was like a mine: outside nothing gave warning of the wealth of feelings and affection that were hidden way deep, covered up by a show of wildness. He was like a forest where fruits, big, great, fruits, were hidden in the foliage.

We had long discussions concerning one topic and another. I used to maintain that there were no laws in nature or anywhere else, and he the contrary. He also stood up for one single moral law, whereby I supported the view that there was a moral law for each individual (thus the falseness of all penal codes). In fact, I talked as a poet (is it too presumptuous to say so?) and he as a logical man. I damned logic and all binding theories, my philosophy was no philosophy at all and his was more orderly and arranged than I could put up with.

He was a conqueror: in fact, he had great hopes in which no lowness entered. He hoped to become a great colonial doctor, and he dreamed of marrying the rich lady who came to the house to take care of her dying husband (she did anything but that indeed), and whom Fireplaces fell in love with (the lady I have spoken of as being a cherry tree in bloom). He was a red-mouthed, handsome doctor, Taday. And he did not care for menials or small things at all. He trampled upon much that was nice and interesting, but he did not do so with heavy feet. He had, therefore, placed his hopes as high as possible or impossible. By the way, the woman was a countess. Taday would not believe that Fireplaces slept with her (slept nothing at all, rather stayed awake with (blessed be the old nonsensical expressions). And he did not believe it because the countess had been generous and lavish of very special favors to him. And then the countess presented the two of them with gold covered fountain pens. Taday would never believe that the fountain pen Fireplaces flaunted was a present from her.

The Rubazziana had become a brothel with a tangle of unplatonic love affairs. Perhaps the mummy married the idiot after all, or perhaps not. He went back to Sicily, Fireplaces, and I never heard more of him. He is, in me, stale memory, unpleasant reminiscence, a thing to think of when one is miserable and no good thought comes, an ugly bas relief, a sculpture made in mud, rotten spiritually, and the remembrance of a handsome face but witless and naked.

To The Memory of Ernest Walsh

T here came to see me at the Villa then Signor Gallese with Signorina Testadimoro.* They brought me to the theatre where we saw one of those actresses who imitates the Duse and where the first actor roars and jumps and shrieks to show his unsatiable anger. Where the actor plays the way all actors in Italy play, the same way of getting angry, the same, absolutely, inflexion of voice: a think that nauseates. After the theatre they brought me to a swell hotel and I passed the night. There he spoke while he was half-drunk. And he said many beautiful things.

There was a cow in a jade meadow beside a jade river . . . . so went the lullaby-fable of Signorina Testadimoro.

He said there was no death in either of us, and while so saying his face was glowing with a halo. He said that poets were the holy men, the principal worshippers at every religion, the prophets, the great scolders, the most indulgent towards the weeping world, the best judges, absolute judges. And while he spoke, my friend was a magistrate of splendors, giver of pardons, the most religious of the skeptical: but laughing at God for His divine paraphernalia. His divine self-importance (who will say that he has always had time for God?). A halo shone around his beautiful head. I understood but one thing: that this man must be always sacred to me.

And the river flowed slowly, slowly, slowly, sleepingly, sleepingly, sleepingly. And the cow was faaast asleep, faaaaaast asleep.

---

*Editor's Note: Ernest Walsh and Ethel Moorhead.

Yes, I understood one thing only: the marvelous holiness of this man in my eyes. Words, words, words to praise you, my dearest, where are all the words to praise you, my dearest? Your beauty that night had a poignancy that knocked at my heart for entrance (at my wooden heart for entrance). And I lay there, impotent to say a word. Oh, my friend, blessed be the wine that made you talk so to me. Blessed be your half-drunkenness. I will carry with me to my death the image of that hotel room and you talking to me, sitting by my bed. . . . .

I had something to tell you then and I do so now: I have remained under the wreckage of my soul, half-destroyed, panting and a-tremble. Hundreds of nights of misery have putrefied my bitterness and it now stinks in my nostrils. I am no longer sad, and what is sadder than not to be sad any more? I am no longer sad: my heart is worn and wrinkled and it gives forth no pretty-colored flames of sadness, languorous flames of sadness, but rank smoke and stench of regret, and crazy yearning.

You, my friend, know my tremendously, enormously ridiculous sickness. My complaints have at last become timid birds in the horrid presence of an ogre. Oh, the atrocious in--somnia, and after one has fallen asleep at last, the awakening with the sickness one had dreamed of not having.

And the cow and the river and the meadow were fast asleep, faast asleep.

And the impotence to do one's own work, and the impotence to think one's own thoughts, and the impotence to sleep one's own nights; and the impotence to tell one's own friend "I love you" in such a way as to make him believe it; and the impotence to sing, and the impotence to be intelligible when speaking of one's own sickness. Whom or what shall I accuse? Nothing to do but to shed the burning tears of despair and fear and dismay, to croak at last with all my youth squandered for nothing at all, for nothing at all!

This poor sick man, vowed to sickness like myself, ah, but he was no sick man that night! He uttered healthy thoughts that night. He spoke of art with depth and insight: depth because he took the cool water of his thoughts from a deep well, insight because he pierced the secret of art. A God-forsaken man, like myself . . . . not like myself because he was uncomplaining whereas I am swollen with complaints. He was pure and wise like a modern Socrates. His forehead was a tryst for dreams and thoughts. His white pure and taut forehead, where no worm of sophistication crept. His long hair seemed to consecrate an idea of goodness — his hair was good-natured with its long sweep and no curls. An eagle, he was, this dear friend, soaring over the cemetery where the dead artists of the world stank of their old age. He said:

"Where there is beauty is no death. There is no death in us either. Where there is beauty there is art. Art should concern the life of everyday. All should be exalted by it. It should be the eucharistic bread and the eucharistic wine. Have a holy communion with art, you who are blind, you who are deaf, you whose souls are numb with solitude and despair.

"All the trades should become beautiful. Love should move our hands, love should sanctify our work, and that love is also called art! The artists carry through the ages the flower of the civilization they lived in, they seek the eternal in the mortal. What is this talk of modern art, new art? Is art an object, a chair, a dish, a toy that it can be new or old? Shakespeare is still one of our best present-day writers. It is the present-day writer that is in Shakespeare that counts. There are as few men today that understand Shakespeare as in the time that Shakespeare wrote his masterpieces. Not one more, not one less.

"The artists are the salt of the earth. They are the recorders of civilizations. Where there are artists the flowers bloom and the fruits blossom. Sophistication is the old age of art that could not reach anybody. Simplicity is the ever-new sun and moon."

These things said or thought or knew my dear friend, Signor Gallese. And I loved him for it. And now he is dead, my dearest, my lovely, my great friend is dead. What is there to say after that; that encloses all the sorrow my heart can bear. He loved life and yet he died before I did. He died, while I go on making half-hearted love to life in every night of insomnia, I go on inventing tiny poems to life while he is dead, dead, dead. He was so full of joy, he was such a splendid youth, but why evoke his beauty now? Every evocation is remembrance and all remembrance is sorrow.

I remember when he came to the Villa Rubazziana, that generous, happy, and strong man! He brought me a wagon-load of cigarettes. He brought me eau-de-cologne and wetted my forehead with it. I imagine myself wiping his icy forehead and calling him aloud. I imagine myself able to make him speak, the dead — who knows? I loved him so well and so long that perhaps the miracle could be accomplished. . . .

Swift, clean, clear, luminous, moving beauty is in the poems and prose of the dead Ernest Walsh. Unlike so much of the dry absurd or abstract poetry which so many youngsters are setting loose upon the world, these poems are emotional in the purest way. A delicate heart and a mind tempered and keen as steel: these things he had and these things count.

As an editor he got out, with Miss Moorhead, the best English-speaking magazine. His condemnation of certain literary persons, and the prose bestowed by him on some others, was always as unstinted as rushing torrent waters. The hurricane which blew through his mind continually found expression in violently beautiful prose essays and poems, and his prose essays were made of the stuff of poetry. We could never stop quoting:

> My gay heart knows
> what an old chimney knows about a roof.

or

> Her nakedness put a distance between us —
> the distance a man feels
> between himself and the stars.

or

> Has the sea no grief
> that it speaks
> all grief but its own?

He surrendered himself to poetry, knowing that the muse would be always by him. . . . Beauty for him was veins running slow blood under white skin. He was indeed beautiful as his work is. Beauty was his daily Eucharist. He wanted to make of eating a beautiful thing, witness his cooking recipes which he naively called "à la Walsh." We imagine with a pang his working while his relentless sickness tormented him. But his poems up to the last ones written in strange English were tremendously healthy; healthy and cool and fresh in the mouth of the reader.

He attacked the things which displeased him and made the fight worth while. He struggled with the defects and short-comings of life and came out of the struggle triumphant. He came out beautiful and radiant, splendid as his beautiful fore-head. A pleasant, happy spirit, his; a strong, ready fighter. His relentless sickness, his suffering, he turned into poems, but with great shyness, a wonderful reticence. Miss Moorhead was his great friend. She was good for him in that she let him always produce, create. His poems are of the stuff of granite. I see them as avenues of stone houses, and above them a flying angel. His best poems are those hurled out of his heart. They sing by dint of their own velocity. Their speed is music. When so many poets are obscure (which, by the way, means dark) he is simple as sunlight, as simple as waters running clear over clean sands.

Right is Yvor Winters when he says his death has been the greatest literary tragedy of this half century. For me, how-ever, the tragedy was more intimate, less literary. We should be reverent before this dead man who, besides editing *This Quarter,* left a ripe harvest of poems and prose. I don't know how great a poet he was, this dearest of boys who died too soon; but to me he was a very great poet for I never derived such pleasure in reading poetry as I found in reading his work. He was a poet, gentlemen, and he went on his way, away from you all, on his way of loneliness and pain. Though dead, he is still going, going, going. He is the magistrate and the judge in the case against you all, gentlemen. Watch him go and keep still. He doesn't need your help at all, at all. He doesn't need your sympathy. A face suffused with poetry, he had, and his ways were those of a great poet; his letters were documents of majesty. He is engrossed in such sorrow as none of you know. Bow down, gentlemen, on your knees.

A History

February 25. That pretty little priest, the chaplain of our church, is the victim of a country-wide scandal: they accuse him of having done certain things with Piumi's wife. Now Piumi is a very fine, a very intelligent young man, enterprising and clever; he has built a radio set all by his own wits, and he is a very fine mechanician. The little chaplain has been denounced directly to the Archbishop of Bologna, by means of an anonymous letter, and he is in terrible despair. He is a tiny little priest and all the ladies think the world of him and they pet him and they love him. He is very fond of young boys (he was once the captain of the Boy Scouts); perhaps a bit too fond of young boys. He goes on long bicycle rides with some of them and once also went with the son of my landlord, Alfonso, who is a handsome young boy and a deadly bore.

The chaplain is a friend of Piumi, and the accusation seems foolish enough. The scandal is so widespread that when one asked of another: Do you believe it?, it was right away understood he meant the chaplain's case.

The chaplain scutles by like any Miss. He has a small voice and talks a deal too much. He doesn't talk, he cackles. With his black long skirt waving in the wind, he trots about like any Miss. He once read a story of mine and said that there was no trace of thought in it. I shall look out for further developments.

February 28. It is my conviction that all children have a touch and more than that a touch of madness. Their ways of shouting, singing, playing are often prettily and often horribly irrational. I heard today a little boy who found joy in singing this simple but edifying song:

Today is not tomorrow,
Tomorrow is not today;
and day after tomorrow is not
Tomorrow.

He must have repeated this song for at least fifty times, at any rate until I was disgusted.

They, however, do not ever sing, they scream. They do not walk, they skip. They do not eat, they swallow all sorts of rotten things. They do not use proper places for their corporal needs, they prefer doing it by a hedge or even in the middle of the road. They shout for joy and they scream for sorrow, without any consideration for Poor Me. Their world is not ours; it is infinitely bigger than ours, and infinitely more picturesque.

And yet, if madmen, they are still dear, dear madmen. I do not think there ever was in the world a child that could have been called ugly. All of them are pretty. And I am sure there never was in the world a child whose mind and heart was not pure. They are made of noble metal; they do not rust, no matter how badly exposed.

February 29. My room. A table covered entirely by a heap of magazines and books: they look like the seven dresses of La Tuda (a monster woman of Bazzano who wears seven dresses). They look like a man with a cape. They look like a careless bazaar on a market day.

A small night table is littered with drugs, an half apothecary shop.

A bureau whose drawers never close well (like a man whose slant teeth forbid his mouth to shut well) carries the two brushes I have and my phonograph records.

The mirror is cockeyed.

Another table where there are letters and papers and on

which the typewriter sits quietly.

The selz-water bottle contains a liquid that seems poisonous. Among the letters a red blotch, like a rock protruding out of the sea, my English dictionary. An ink bottle as empty as poverty.

The ferocious smell of denatured alcohol comes from the night table.

Upon a spot of permanent humidity stands the wash-basin, covered like a priest in high uniform, with the white hand-towel. A portmanteau where perch my clothes in order that they may get saturated with dust. Two trunks and three suit cases. O boy! I am a rich man, that I am!

A revolution of shirts and b.v.d.'s in the bureau's drawers.

The floor is diseased, broken and cracked and badly healed with splotches of grey cement.

Two electric lights. Didn't I say that I was rich?

In this room tanglefooted by my yesterdays, I sleep and live most of the time. A hurried man, forced by sickness to go slow.

My typing machine always awaits my hands. It and the phonograph give a mechanistic touch to the face of the room. A bottle of pop appears to be a Cretan statuette of a lady. On the bureau is also a row of neckties. On my table, conspicuous, *The American Mercury,* that scandal monger.

On the night table the bottle of scopolamine, my oil for walking and writing, my lubricating oil for my wretched joints. Maker of dreams, the scopolamine . . . . but I shall talk more about it.

March 1. They have discovered the author of the anonymous letter to the Archbishop of Bolgna. He is the brother of the late chaplain, a fool and a coward. He had employed a little schoolgirl to write the letter for him. Now he plays the crazy man. The reason: mere envy, it seems. From the self-styled crazy man they can obtain nothing but incoherent yells. But they are certain that he is the guilty party, and they threaten to shut him up in a lunatic asylum.

March 2. Cimbra, the goldsmith, has gone bankrupt. Rossi, the baker, had signed for her a guaranty for four thousand lire, and he is now in terrible despair. Rossi can't laugh anymore; he goes around the town like a rabid dog. Rossi swears to God and the saints that they won't catch him again. The mayor of the town is in the same plight, and so is Raffello, the seller of bologna and salami; they are the three major losers. They may as well put their heads together and weep on one another's shoulders, and into one another's waistcoat pockets. Mrs. Rossi swears that she will go to Cimbra's shop and take away all the gold she'll find there. But they told her she had better not do so.

"But" says Mrs. Rossi, "when I see her I shall tell her: take that pretty little skirt away from your legs and walk naked in the town; it is our money that bought it! Ruffle your well combed hair and put ashes on it; it is our money that lets you be so spick and span! Walk less majestically, you prim little whore! Stop inviting people to your house, it is not your house, not yours, you dirty slut! You big s...ter, you. You big p...er!, you." Thus goes the lament of Mrs. Rossi, and she goes on: "I counted upon going to the sea, to Rimini this Summer, but here is Rimini for us! We are already Riminized!"

It is the fourth time that Cimbra fails; she is used to it. What bewilders me is that Rossi could be lured into signing for such a sum; he should have known that she, having failed three times, could as well fail again.

March 3. The winds murmur of the last vestige of winter. They speak harshly still. The street sweeper has still cyanotic hands. The country is still peeled, to use Gilio's expression, peeled and depilated. The elms that carry the grapevines are still naked. Their two arms are praying and cursing: a curse to the winter and a prayer for spring. Spring is surely coming but its coming is fitful and desultory.

March 5. Celia, Cimbra's servant girl has had a baby without her having provided herself previously with a husband. Gilio's wife, as jealous as hell, was certain that the baby was Gilio's. She threatened to murder him in his sleep, to leave her home, to scream in the public square Gilio's infamy, to break up the family and take their only child away from his father. But Gilio managed to swear solemnly to her that he was guiltless, and so she was pacified. Gilio swore the same thing to me too. "That I may become blind and not see my own child anymore. That my child drop dead as I enter the house tonight and that I may bust on this very instant, if it's true that Celia's baby is my own."

March 6. There was a time, when I did not know English, that English as I saw it written had a very strange effect on me; it appeared to be like freight trains clanging along; the W gave it a most mechanical air. It seems the most modern of languages, the machine language. Now it has gained the look of an Italian dialect. But! notice that all languages have a similar look — the Russian too, judging from Russian names, which are all I know of Russian: Nastasya, Timofey, Afanasy, *etc. etc.*

I have noticed that Italian language is to the dialect what English written is to American spoken: for example, *Discórrere,* Italian, becomes Dscarer, as Hot becomes Haht. This is probably due to Italian dialects being a jungle of arts of the language. But I admit that it is the dialect that resembles the language and not the language that resembles the dialect.

March 10. Mrs. Rossi told me a tale that conclusively proves that Boccaccio and Brantome are immortal:

There was a woman, a Bazzanese, who had her lover in her bed and was with all probability enjoying him, when, as it so ofen happens in Boccaccio, the husband, who had been away on business, returned suddenly. She got up and out of bed before the husband had reached the bedroom, and suddenly started to scream: "Thief, thief, Catch him, catch him!" In the turmoil that followed, the lover got safely away. It was a risky proceeding, since the lover might have been taken for the thief, and, if so, it would have fared badly with him. But, as it was, it succeeded. That is, it succeeded for the moment, because the husband might later on have heard the story which is going very freely around all Bazzano.

March 15. If you tell a man that he is handsome, he will very probably answer that he isn't. Same thing if you tell him he is very strong, good, sweet, etc., etc. But if you tell him he is sincere he will, ninety nine times in a hundred, agree with you. As though sincerity were a lesser quality than the above mentioned ones, instead of being as it is, the most rare and difficult of all. This is probably due to the fact that sincerity depends more on the will than do the other qualities.

March 18. The mayor, that is the *podestà* (since Mussolini has decided to make Italy look Roman or medieval), there are no longer mayors but only *podestàs;* the *podestà,* I say, is a fat faced little gentleman who, besides being fat faced, is also a little fatheaded. He did absolutely nothing for the town or against it since he came into power. His major doings are these: he walks lazily about the town and then goes to Mrs. Rossi's shop to chatter for an hour or so, talks to the noodle-making boys, goes home to dinner, comes out again, takes another lazy little walk, then goes away in his automobile to a little village nearby where he runs an apothecary shop. Always with a pleasant smile and a little voice. He is the purest image of doing-nothingness. What for his being here? Mussolini says so, and the Madonna is satisfied. He is, however, like all fascists, a man of strong opinions, borrowed of course from the men who stand higher up above him. He is the first authority of the town, oh boy! He can send any man he wants to the boundary line, oh boy! He can have you shut up even for your singing the Marseillaise, even though it be the French National Song and have nothing to do with Italy's fortune and the higher destinies of the Fatherland.

He is one of the masks of Mussolini's great *bal masqué,* which begins with the *Balillas* (kind of boy-scouts) and ends up with the consuls. More power to him, at any rate, even though he doesn't know what to with the little power he has.

April 5. How noisy are Italians! It seems as though there were a theater, between the acts, downstairs. Four Italians can beat a score of Americans in loud talking. And as though talking aloud were not enough to be understood, they gesticulate ferociously. And the cause of it? Simply, generally, a simple question of opinion as to some difficult point of card playing, a peaceful, though belligerent in its form, discussion. They appear to want to tear the house down. More boisterous than a fascist revolution, more prepotent than Mussolini, roaring louder than Niagara, these Italian card players!

April 6. Happiness: I look out of the window and salute a passer-by and I know I am happy. I shall go down to the land-lady and ask her if she too is happy. "Mrs. Corinne, are you happy? Because I am happy, you know." She smiles, she says, "I am glad." Not such a happiness, boisterous and big, as the one that prompted Carducci to write his song of love. No, in this small room such happiness would break its wings against the walls, but a happiness such as will fit this small room, a happiness I can cuddle close in my arms, and possess entirely indisputably. A well-educated happiness. Sweet is to know somebody and greet him from my window. Sweet is to lie down and slumber away an hour, sweet is to wait for Spring to come, Spring that, now, has a taste of Winter in its wonderful mouth. Delicious air comes from the window and wraps my legs and my head. I lie, passive and quiescent. This, my happiness, is as delicate as a field flower. It shall soon break to pieces and fall off me, like a garment. My dear books are all around me; but I do not read; I do not want any literature to interfere. I look at them and I am glad, glad that they are there at all. I want to touch things with religion. I would go out and take a long walk, ever so long a walk; but I know that

I'd get tired and that would destroy my happiness — better stay here and sip this happiness, slowly and with care.

April 12. Listen here: this is a good one: This morning the scopolamine had no effect on me whatever. To the taste also, it was distilled water. I called my landlord and I told him so. He went to the drug store and had it made over again. He took it into his head to say that I had told him that perhaps they had played a trick on me. He comes back and tells me: "I told him you thought it was a jest, and he said you should feel ashamed to say such a thing to him, and that if you persisted in calling it a jest, he wouldn't give you the medicine anymore." And the good of it is that he repeated this thing to me, so I should feel impressed by it. I was so bewildered by his shamelessness, that I could utter no word.

April 15. There was once a man who noticed that to read certain lines of a certain book would cause him to have terribly beautiful dreams. So he reread and he reread these lines until, one bad night, the dreams ceased coming.

He read more lines of that certain book, and the dreams returned, but not so strongly beautiful as before. He read more and more lines, until that certain book was no longer sufficient. And then the man ate words, until he was infected by those black microbes, words. His belly became a store room of words and then a library of books, and then a palace built with those black microbes, words. The man began to vomit and he threw out all the words and kept puking words for so many and so many days. Then his nights became as black as nothingness, as empty as nothingness, starless, horrid. Only a little word, a monosyllable, was left for him to cry; and it was an English word such as love and death, such as big and great, nice and fine, a monosyllable. The beautiful dreams returned, with a beauty akin to the thousand and one nights, with a sort of beauty similar to that of Maxwell Parrish's pictures; for the man was no artist and did not know Picasso, and such beauty as Maxwell Parrish's sufficed to edify him.

One little English word gave him back his dreams, but in each dream there was a little of death. And more and more was there of death in his dreams, until the last dream came everlasting: from that the man never woke again. For no one dreams of death without having seen her and no one sees death but the sure-to-die.

April 25. Some people's conception of humor: my landlord's, for instance, is to shout my name very loud when he sees me. It always reaches me accompanied by an unpleasant shock. I detest him cordially when he does that, but I shall never tell him so. I am a man who tries hard to be pleasant and to please, except with my best friends whom I insult profusely and vastly. I scatter around me pleasant words. But in certain cases I am not able to be pleasant, and that is when I ought most to be so: for instance with Bob, by dear benefactor, I cannot because I consider pleasantness a too small gift for him to have from me, that may be the reason. Nay, that *is* the reason.

May 4. And then the guests began to pour in. There came first a young lady who kept saying that her feet were cold, and stayed at it. She was quite pretty and when for a moment we were alone I contemplated the possibility of my kissing her; but nothing came of it. Then her father came who had drunk already more than a few glasses of white wine. White wine is generally stronger than black and it goes to the head immediately. By black wine I mean what in America is called red wine.

He started to speak to me: "I will tell thee a story." "How," says his daughter, "do you *thou* him?" "Then," said the old man, "I shall tell us a story. I saw snow in Castelfranco." He was slobbering already and his eyes were exceedingly dirty. Three more daughters of the drunken fellow, and one son, came in. The son guffawed loudly at his father's pranks. A poor woman with all her children about her, and her husband, came in. The old man said aloud, "They are going right away," which made the son laugh to split his head.

"Oh, I am a very mysterious man," the old man began. "I met a train covered with snow in Castelfranco. It came from Turin. I would have gone on it but I had no money. Oh, I am quite a mysterious man. If I kick a hedge, money springs from it. If I go out at night, I am bound to come back with two thousand lire in my pocket." And so saying he gulped more wine. Then he started to dance with Gilio's mother (his sister) and it was pleasant to see the old woman scuttle and shake her B.T.M. like any little girl. They broke a glass from the cupboard. "Oh, I am a very mysterious man . . . , but that train loaded with snow. Listen to me, *sh, sh, sh,* everybody! I am going to tell a story: In two years hunting I caught fifteen sparrows. Once a farmer had a hare tied to a rope. I . . . shot . . . at . . . the hare and I hit . . . the . . . rope," and a few minutes after the old man was snoring in the midst of the company, nothing loth. . . .

May 20. Mrs. Rossi approaches being the best kind of Italian lady there is on the Italian map. Her talk is as large and as genial as it is unscrupulous; for to hear her talk of men's drawers, of fotters, of s—t and piss and f—k is no drawback at all. How different from those American ladies for whom *for Christ's sake* and *for God's sake* are blasphemous words! She is as clean and as fresh and as rosy as a flower under her immaculately white hair. Yes, she is hardly forty and her hair is all white, a marvel indeed. She has five children, each of them more beautiful than the other. Aldo, with his feminine beauty, with his little nose and small mouth: and Nino, quite virile though handsome, too; and Rina, a pretty little lady; and Néro, the buster; and Alfred, her last, like a small field flower. Mrs. Rossi's conversational qualities are the prettiest and most picturesque. Her talk is all a blossoming of original words. It is a joy to listen to her. She has an opinion about everyone in Bazzano, and her sincerity doesn't let her keep to herself that opinion. Her observations are as deep as a canyon. She is a whitehaired young woman, and she is a whitehaired mother, and she is a whitehaired old woman.

May 25. Carluccio, who fixes autos and bicycles, has an old father. This father shows his muzzle every now and then; he is a man that resembles a sleepy old dog. A remarkably peaceful old man, he goes off to sleep even in the middle of a conversation, just dozes off, like a stream of slow water. Sometimes he makes desperate efforts to talk and succeeds in being terribly idiotic. Once, speaking to a farmer, he came to the three words, *so to say*. Well, he kept repeating those three words with an additional *so to speak,* and he never got beyond that, poor sleepy old dog.

May 27. Gilio is a he-nurse at the hospital. He is genial and amusing. He laughs very little and his ways are as original as his words. He doesn't get along too well with his wife, for whom, in the time of her illness (consumption), he made untold sacrifices. She so angers him as to tear from him phrases such as this, "You should kiss the ground after I have passed!" But I am sure he loves her well enough in spite of the fact that that he deceives her everywhere. In fact Gilio has a sweetheart in every little town surrounding Bazzano; and sometimes he does not limit himself to one only. He has two or three in the same small town. He has the muscles of a prizefighter. I advised him that he should become one, but he can't decide. It is too long a step from the trade of nurse to that of a prizefighter, even though the nurses to must undergo such terrible physical strain. His long legs are not long enough for that step. Out of the hospital, all of the fun-making qualities of this dear man show up.

Strictly a loyal friend he is.

He is handsome, though his features, taking them one by one, are rather ugly. He has too small an upper lip, and his eyes too near to his nose, and the nose of an owl. There were days in the past, however, when he was dressed up that he looked like a prince (better than that prince of Wales, for instance). Now he is not so very elegant and not so very handsome, but he is doing well enough in that way. There is a little that is unfathomable in him. His smile is sometimes obscure, his face dark. He is so strictly respectful of anyone that he can't stand anybody lacking in respect towards him. His rage is mighty and he lets go such terrible swings and uppercuts that I am wondering his fist has not yet been forbidden. To insult him is no profitable job. He is as strong as the bas-relief of an Assyrian bull. I am a friend of his because he has lived with me so many terrible years of hospital life, and then because I choose that he be my friend (not that I apologize for this fact).

I have seen the brutal side of him. Once we had hired a horse for a small journey and the little sorry horse suddenly came to a halt and would not go ahead. Well, Gilio kicked him in the belly with all his might. I expected the animal to die on the spot, so deep was his groan. I never left Gilio in peace after that. He has the hard, often licentious, sense of humor that is a heritage and a tradition, country style (in scrambled eggs), that has a flavor of the countryside and the smell of the loam. A sense of humor that is often bitterly ironic and which sometimes has the softness of words whispered by lovers. All softness and sweetness, when genuinely come from the loam, the vulgus.

He is clean to the point of absurdity. He washes his genitals once a day and he is always disinfecting himself. It seems as though the hospital scares him a little. From my room, which is a hundred paces away from the hospital, he hears the bell ring that calls him to the bedside of some impatient patient. That too means that he fears the hospital a little. At the hospital, where he works as conscientiously as few others do, he is known as a grumbler. But the grumbling is altogether harmless and the sick men soon make the discovery. His low voice accounts for the name also. When he talks he seems to grumble. He belongs to one of the oldest families of Bazzano, known for their ways and habits. His mother is a very fine little old woman with very white teeth and a beautiful smile thereof. His wife too is nice, substantial, perhaps a bit too fat and patient. Were she not patient, there would be hell in his house. He says there is hell anyway, and we must believe him. Women fall for him, one and all. He has that sensuous look in his eyes that makes them fall. These Italian women discern in him the able-bodied man, the exuberant lover, the plain lover, the stallion. They being first of all afraid of any sophistication. I mean the women of the vulgus, the farmers' wives, the workers' wives, the dressmakers. As for the other and upper classes, Gilio pays no attention to them, hating as he does any woman who contents herself with words and looks, however sensuous and langourous the looks. Hates them because, as he says, there is nothing doing with them.

June 1. Marino, the barber, is not only a barber, but he is also an intelligent young man, blaming life, a stepmother to him. He reads much and makes a continuous effort at culture. But, if nothing else, his handwriting shows his hypo-education. But I know he suffers from this, and he is thereby redeemed. Who knows, perhaps fate has been meek to him, putting him in that trade? Who knows that if he were a rich man he probably would be one of those faceless youths that haunt even Bazzano? And who knows if he, despoiled of that nostalgia for culture, would not lose that interesting look in his face, that nostalgic look?

His pleasantness and kindness are the patrimony he needs for his face, and therefore they are not pleasantness and kindness. His happy smile also serves his trade. It is not much of a smile and not so happy. Here is the Pagliacci psychology once more.

Laugh, O, clown.
of your broken love,
laugh of the sorrow
that poisons your heart.

Hear it on the gramophone disc. His Master's Voice, sung by Caruso . . . . Price? . . . too much.

Meanwhile Marino is busy shaving and oiling and caressing ugly faces, and cutting lousy hair. Meanwhile he is being a barber. And there is nothing on the farthest horizon that bespeaks a change of any kind. He will be a barber all his life. Nostalgia is nostalgia, but facts are irremediably facts.

June 25. There are women whose ugliness I could almost say is pretty. Women who have faces that under any emotion become harmonious. That kind of ugliness I love in women.

There are women whose faces are so ugly as to be deformed and monstrous. And these are generally of little intelligence and Xanthippes all.

There are women who have beautiful voices; these are angels of Paradise however ugly they may otherwise be.

There are women who have beautiful mouths. I prefer a large mouth to a small one.

There are women in moving picture plays, who struggle violently with villains they do not care for; for me there is nothing more obscene than seeing any woman perform in that manner. There is something filthy in her uncovering her weakness and helplessness. Violence from one side and weakness on the other are to me obscene.

There are women who are pretty only at times; these I like.

There are women who are always ready to squeeze their lachrymal glands empty of liquid; these I detest.

There are women who love very much without much discrimination; they seem always to be in love with some other fellow — stupid enough tactics.

There are women whose only business is to nag relentlessly. It is their trade and their most important occupation. It is a duty that was cast upon them in the ages of ages. It is a disease to them. I shan't say what I feel about such women.

I know of no woman who was ever for a man grown old the stick-to-lean-upon of his old age. I know of no woman who was ever grateful.

Gratefulness is a heavy burden to bear and a woman's shoulders are too weak to carry it.

Of the million piano players there are in woman-hood there has hardly come forth one real artist.

I was always for the vote for women inasmuch as voting is a silly business anyway and no one will be improved by it. The vote is worth so little that they may as well have it.

June 27.

IT IS VERY LITTLE

To call you friend is a little thing
You for whom friendship is much, is all.

To call you dear is a very little thing
You who are dearest of all
I bring you simple daisies and buttercups,
But that is very little
For there is nothing simpler than your dear ways.

I bring you love but this is very little
Because I have squandered so much love in my life.

I can bring you nothing big, nothing great.
I'm a poor bereaved poet, I have only words to offer.

June 29. Why should I live today?

Because there is hope in the world that the next few days at least will not be so hot.

Today I was reading a book that a publishing house had just sent me when suddenly dropped from it a picture, a photograph. A most horrid young man of at least twenty-five. The nasty face of a moron, with a flat nose and a mouth that seems a cut across the face, without corners. Long hair, curly and crisp, and a necktie so small knotted that it tells me the photo cannot be older than two or three years. Behind, the thing has these queer words: "To him whom I love so much, I swear eternal faith to him." Aside from the lack of grammar the writing is neither too vulgar nor is it refined. He makes me think of a small man; but that may be an illusion of mine similar to the one I have felt when reading Sherlock Holmes (or a book about the gentleman thief, Arséne Lupin — (oh where, oh where is the gentleman?—), I had the impression that the detective had a long black beard and an overcoat always on him. Better still:

when I was reading Sherwood Anderson's work in the *Seven Arts,* before having seen him, I imagined him to be a very tall man with a very long and very black moustache; and when, being in Chicago, I finally had a chance to meet Sherwood Anderson, I mistook him for Llewellyn Jones, just because said gentleman was taller than anyone there.

I shouldn't have known that the book had been used by some other reader before me if I hadn't noticed that some of the pages had been carelessly cut.

He shall stay with me, this stranger, and he shall be my evil spirit, he shall be my bogey man. He comes from nowhere and he is nobody, but he is awfully ugly.

I supposed that the book was a girl's. It is everything but a book for girls (*The Adventures of Felicita,* by the Chevalier de Nerciat). It may be a book for such girls as would bestow favors upon such a lover as that: nothing short of a nymphomaniac.

He shall watch me live with his awful eyes. He will be an eternal reproach for whatever I do or say or think. His awful face shall watch me and me only. He cannot be my intimate friend, so he will be my intimate enemy. My evil spirit: the spirit of my evil words and my evil doings. The nastiness that is in me I shall see reflected on that terrible face. Poor bum, which he probably is, poor unsubtle, stupid bum.

July 1. Who knows if, when the wind is most strong, it is so because it is angry or if its being strong is merely one of its qualities?

Who knows if, when the jackass brays, he expresses tremendous sorrow or if his braying means only a quality of his?

Who knows if, when the peacock screams, he feels as badly as he sounds or if he is in a perfectly normal undisturbed condition?

But perhaps the lion, when he roars, feels tremendous and powerful and ferocious.

And the fishes who keep being silent; do they mean it?"

The trouble is that we can judge of such things only from a human point of view.

July 3. Casti's rhymes seem facile to the utmost. But that is too noticeable and one begins to be suspicious. It is Cavalier Marino's rhymes which come down and stream along with the quality of running water. One does not notice his rhyming and that is perhaps true facility.

July 5. Why do I go on living today?

Because I woke up happy for no reason at all, and I am still happy for no reason at all.

Andreoli is the nastiest man in Bazzano. He has been sharking during the war and he is now a rich man. He goes around saying: "Once they put meat in the boiler once every three months, now they put the boiler up with meat in it three times a week. It is high time that they should be educated and taught to be humble, these damn farmers and workers."

There is something almost pleasant however in some of his speeches: once a man came to his shop to buy some rice. He stopped before the sack of rice of the best quality and said he wanted a kilo of rice of that kind.

Then, while Andreoli was packing the goods, he said he'd pay afterwards. Andreoli unpacked the rice, threw it again into the sack, and said: "If I who am I eat the second quality rice, you who cannot pay right away eat the rice of the best quality? Nothing doing. You'll take the second quality or nothing at all."

His wife goes around flaunting earrings as big as medium-sized apples; her hands are all covered with rings and she speaks, making grimaces, of her "purse" which is "always full;" and she speaks of his son with as many grimaces while her son is a rascal who plays poker and spends money on a lot of foolish girls.

Utterly out of place, these sharks, and still they stick and not even omnipotent Mussolini can get rid of them.

July 15. Pieretto Degli Espoti is another he-nurse at the hospital. He likes full wine bottles, full medicine bottles, full pocketbooks, abundant meals, little sleep and hard work. Pep, that's his watchword. The sick men may well be contented with him; there is nothing he wouldn't do for a sick man, even to pulling the excrement out of his anus. A dying man is sacred to him. A very sick man is his God. He knows the joy of squandering a whole enormous bottle of Lysoform to disinfect the room after a man has died there. It is with sheer joy that he spills the Lysoform.

In his youth he used to go around as a nurse to sick gentlemen, and his going around had two scopes: first, to be of service to his masters; then, love-making. Meanwhile, as he sent nothing home, his poor wife had to slave her weary self, work like a jackass, to send his children ahead, for better or for worse. Then he came back to Bazzano and set to work at the hospital. This he suddenly left to go to Tripoli; more tribulation for his poor wife, same story all over again, who had by now the help of Pieretto's eldest son, Lelio, who worked for three lire a week (something like sixty American cents, *al par*). Pieretto came back without a cent but provided with a strong resolution to do well. And he did well, too. He took good care of his children and did not deceive his wife.

Any more than was strictly necessary. Strange to say, with all his original ways he hasn't much of a vote when he's in company; he must laugh at other people's jokes and at best listen. Perhaps it is because of his political ideas. But, no, it isn't. It is that they think he hasn't much to say and let him say nothing at all. Politically he is, and this must go completely to his credit, the same as he was ten, five and fifteen years ago. I add *almost* to his credit because such continuity must be laziness of mind. His aspect is that of a merchant of cows and oxen. There is no more refined look to him, in spite of his job having a certain dignity of its own. Of course, this dignity is all exterior, because his business concerns mostly pisspots, and brooms, and pus and putrefaction. Full and round, Pieretto seems rather to roll than walk. The pit-a-patter of his steps one hears as soon as one enters the hospital. He trots about, performs.

But perhaps the reason why Pieretto sounds minor-toned when in company is this: he never screams, jumps, or roars; in fact he is quite dignified, and the rest revenge themselves on this dignity by keeping him under the yoke, by means of paying little attention to him, or ignoring him altogether. But I am sure Pieretto suffers, specially because he is unaware of his show of dignity. He does not laugh well, and this knowledge may be the key to his entire character. He drinks an awful lot and is scarcely ever drunk. One night, however, he was well and drunk. He staggered up the slope to his house and finally got to his door. There he fumbled with his key for ten minutes and finally, tired or disgusted, he let go such a fart as would have split a glass asunder if one would have dared to go near him in time to put that glass near his ass. Once he tried to stop drinking and smoking, but two days after he had begun his abstinence (after he had gone on the water wagon, to put it more Americanly), he began to have fainting symptoms and almost fell to the ground, his head going round and round. At last he saved himself by means of a glass of wine and a cigar which he enjoyed more than any wine or cigar he had taken in his whole life.

July 25. This man who looks queer and funny when he talks: that's myself.

This man who had the toad of adulation always on his lips: that's myself.

This man who laughs easily and too much: that's myself.

This man who often confesses himself but who takes offence when anybody believes in his confession: that's myself.

This man envious to puerility, envious to death: that's myself.

This man who cannot walk and doesn't know why: that's myself.

This man with not a few unspeakable habits: that's myself.

This man who fears women: that's myself.

This man who must have something horrid about him since women do not love him: that's myself.

This eternal beggar: that's myself.

This man who is not strong enough to hate anybody: that's myself.

This desperate poet who cannot write of his despair: that's myself.

If he hates anything he hates literature, out of his own smallness only: that's myself.

He goes around making gifts of his little money and then telling everybody about it, thus destroying completely the beauty of his action: that's myself.

Weak but sincere (in spite of La Rochefoucauld): that's myself.

A fire escape in travail (as Mr. Bynner put it): that's myself.

A bomb unexploded and unexplodable: that's myself.

He believes in nothing and flaunts his disbelief by saying that God is his personal enemy: that's myself.

What should I live for today? A little of life is due me because I have done some charitable actions today. Out of modesty I will not say what actions.

August 1. There is a man in Bazzano whom Mrs. Rossi calls "the man of the caverns," and he looked it when he was still going around the town in underwear (that is, without a jacket or a shirt) with a pitch black beard and all rags. Now he stays at home, consumptive. He spits blood all over the floor. He has three children that scratch about the house like chick-chickens. The wife is an idiot who says laughingly that the doctor in the city has said both the man's lungs are infected with the disease. When they'll be good and ready, the authorities will send the man to a hospital for chronics. Meanwhile, the man infects the whole quarter which is as teeming with children as any other quarter in Bazzano. To whom shall I send my blasphemous words? Whom shall I curse?

August 5. There is a gentle indirect manner of being lascivious, and that's the Catholic sister's way. When Gilio went with two sisters to Le Burdrre, where the convent is, one of the sisters was the hospital's Mother Superior. Gilio found a girl and began talking to her, which was at once (too at once) noticed by the Mother Superior and blamed accordingly. But there was a little laugh in her voice as she scolded Gilio. Then in the car, coming back, Gilio began talking girls to the chauffeur and the Mother made a sign to the sister with her to stop talking and listen to what Gilio said. The tiny plot was frustrated, however, because Gilio soon noticed what was the matter and stopped talking. Why should I live today? Because I have two new pairs of socks and I am glad I have.

August 10. They have been telling me that to live a long time in a small country village one's soul grows small and cramped. It would be so if there weren't a beautiful sky (when it is beautiful), if there weren't a moon to shine on sweethearts, if there weren't a sun like a fist beating on the gong of the sky. If there weren't the long days of rain and clouds. At any rate, here the fields are near and the mountains are near, bedecked with chestnut trees; the festoons of the vines and the grape-trees that lean affectionately on the elm tree. NO, a cramped soul thrives better in the mysterious streets of the city; a cramped soul finds more images of crampedness in the towers that seek the sun, in the canyons to the bottom of which the sun hardly ever reaches. Farmers are a different matter; they tear their sustenance from the breast of mother earth: for the earth does not yield anything to them willingly. They are concerned with the fare of dunghills, and they look up to the sky otherwise than to see whether it's going to rain or not. And they look greedily on the ground. They contaminate the soil with financial problems. They are mercenary and therefore unbeautiful. And that is why they dress so badly. When they wear something new, after two days the suit looks as though its owner had slept many nights with that suit on. Beauty gives herself spontaneously. You cannot pay for it. The false elegance, the bureaucratic aspects of modern cities, they all speak of smallness, but here the poplars are great and ancient and they flaunt their elegance that is worth a thousand times more than a city elegance. And the continual klaxons and trumpets of automobiles challenge a city's soul that is already tired and exhausted with noises. Amusements, yes, to go and hear an actor that screams and jumps on the stage in a frenzy, or to see the last cinematographic idiocy from the United States (for one must know that the latter is idiotic and that the former is the way of all Italian actors, one or two excluded).

The city breeds small men and poorlooking women. Its wombs are the dirty streets. The city, greedy, eats the country slowly but relentlessly. Little by little the trees fall, the fields are polluted, the hot breath of the city takes the place of the murmuring breeze of the country. The octupus of the city stiffles and kills. Too much literature comes from the city and too little from the country. Literature is a thing of darkness and crowdiness, a speculation on human passions, a rotten flower on the dunghill of men's souls. Literature therefore is a thing for the city. Thoreau believed in the place where he was living and by his belief he made books where the essence of the place in which he lived shines and glitters. A great courage was his and with courage he won. I also believe in the place where I am living. I will have courage too.

August 20. I am grateful to a friend of mine for his offering me a cigarette. There was much spontaneity in the gesture that I recall with great pleasure. (It's two o'clock at night.) Yes, it was a pretty and yet powerful gesture of which he was certainly not aware. He turned his arms thus and thus. . . . Delightful, delightful!

Why should I go on living today?

Because a little letter from a dear friend is reason enough why I should be living. Little reason because the letter is little, pretty reason because the letter is pretty. Deep reason as deep as my affection for the man who wrote it. And above all sufficient reason.

Last Memories

One night, between Friday and Saturday, the awful crime took place. It announced itself by means of a little shock and then a series of little shocks which did not frighten anybody. But then, tired of playing about with insipid little quiverings, it decided to give a good big shudder. And then the giant was upon us: — earthquake!

The thorough helplessness before this terrible thing is what gets my goat. The futile, frantic rebellion against its presence was almost the most fearful thing about it. I was like a baby on a rock in mid-ocean, in a wild, tossing ocean, choked by the spray from the enormous waves that smashed against the rock. Imagine a town that has slept its five hundred years of quiet, suddenly flung into an impossible situation by this crazy business: the quaking of the earth! It was a dirty business of fear, cries, cowardice, escape — escaping from where to where? A madness of running, blind with terror, mangling everything crazily beneath one's feet as one ran. I knew all the categories of fear and in the end I believed this: the name of the worst fear is "earthquake fear." It gave me a violent pain in the belly and brain which lasted for months after the last shock had passed. It was a giant, but it had delicate little fingers: look at the bits of plaster that it picked off the walls and ceiling and threw onto the floor!

LET ME FIND MY HEART

It is perhaps in a little blue hole, entwined with an octopus, that I shall find my young friend, my friend of a season, one far away, one of an almost forgotten season of sun and sea on the riviera of the setting sun.

258

I slept one night with him and he endowed me with the sweetest names, but there was nothing pederastic about it, for he was young and strong and loved women very much, and I did too. (Then I was very handsome, but now is the period when there is no beauty for me. Now I am almost bald-headed, but I like to believe I am still handsome because the voice of one woman has told me I still am.) We spent a night of fleas and bed-bugs together, itching, tossing, scratching. (Like that old bore of American literature, Ezra Pound, who itches with a literary eczema. The more he itches the more he scratches, and the more he scratches the more he itches: a vicious circle devoid of beauty. He is a nocturnal barker who keeps so many people awake who are in need of sleep.)

During the day, Gioomin and I used to go along the sea-shore in the shallow water which abruptly deepened, looking for porous stones in which the worms to fish with were hidden. Once he took me far, far out in a little row-boat and I was frightened, afraid that one vigorous pull on the oar might capsize the boat. That day the weather was spoiling and it seemed to me that the deep blue of the water concealed a veiled but final threat.

I wish I could speak about him with enthusiasm, but to voice enthusiasm I should at least be able to rise from this bed which sucks my energy and life and leaves me empty and desolate, flaccid as a jelly-fish on a rock. I wish I could give vent to a howl of joy thinking of those wonderful moments which have set now like the sun setting in the sea forever. He was the Neptune of that beautiful Tyrrhenian Sea. He was the strongest on the beach and he displayed his muscles under his brown skin with a pride that approached ferocity. I look upon him as on a fine picture in a shining golden frame.

Varazze was his town, his own, and its mountains and sea were green. The land there was like the elbow of an arm extending into the water and cradling the quiet and the tumult, as a mother's arm cradles the head of her little girl. He was everything I had wanted to be, Gioomin: strong as the rocks which the sea needs centuries to undermine, brown as the stone of the reefs, a fearless diver, laughing out loud. The world is for him and for the strong, while I am only a weak fist lifted against God, or like two sickly hands joined in prayer, but always a wretched, ill-shapen thing.

Oh, Lady Death, take me, is now the common refrain of all my songs! Take me with you and I will be docile as a child and I will follow obediently in your footsteps without terror, knowing you are the divine mistress and the divine gift of God. I will not so much as slay a worm who comes to greet me and crosses my path, oh, Lady Death! I will be good and kind to all those who are going the same way. I will not talk too loud and too much the way I always did in life. I will merely stammer a few words in your ear. . . . .